Advance praise for *Another Hyderabad in Deccan*

This fascinating anthology uncovers history that has escaped the grip of institutional archives. The authors offer an archaeology of varied artistic and craft practices as an alternative vision of Hyderabad and the Deccan, post-independence.

There is not just one Hyderabad. The authors unveil the Deccani multiplicity by drawing on minority histories to resist the dominance of a singular narrative. The recognition of deep involvement of communities in shaping the many-layered facets of cities serves as an important methodological invitation to all researchers. This 'contextual conversation' offers an exchange between dominant and subaltern historical accounts.

The book thus provides the groundwork for a rediscovery of cities by focusing on the interactive and intersected material and artistic practices – a must-read for all students of crafts, arts, heritage and cities.

Professor Wiebe E. Bijker
Maastricht University, The Netherlands

In this thought-provoking volume, a new generation of scholars asks new questions using innovative sources and methodologies to explore the visual and material culture of the Deccan's storied past. A much too storied past. Peeling back layers of colonial narrative and received wisdoms, the nine chapters compel us to consider unacknowledged and understudied Deccani multiplicities, going beyond the archive to bring forth the voices, intentionalities and movements of marginalized artisans and communities, from vernacular Islamic architecture, to Dravida temple painters, to influential twenty-first-century weavers – a model for knowledge producers everywhere seeking alternative ways to envision the historical past.

Sarah Fee, PhD
Senior Curator, Global Fashion & Textiles
Royal Ontario Museum, Toronto
Associate Professor (status only), Dept. of Art History
University of Toronto

Another Hyderabad in Deccan

Another Hyderabad in Deccan

Material Culture and Artistic Practice in South Asia

Edited by

Baishali Ghosh and Rajarshi Sengupta

BLOOMSBURY
NEW DELHI • LONDON • OXFORD • NEW YORK • SYDNEY

BLOOMSBURY INDIA
Bloomsbury Publishing India Pvt. Ltd
Second Floor, LSC Building No. 4, DDA Complex, Pocket C – 6 & 7,
Vasant Kunj, New Delhi, 110070

Bloomsbury, Bloomsbury Academic India, and the Diana logo are trademarks of Bloomsbury Publishing Plc.

First published in India 2025
This edition published 2025

Bloomsbury Academic India
An imprint of Bloomsbury Publishing Plc.

ISBN: HB: 978-93-61312-03-8; eBook: 978-93-61312-47-2
2 4 6 8 10 9 7 5 3 1

Typeset by Integra Software Services Pvt. Ltd.
Printed and bound in India by Replika Press Pvt. Ltd

Bloomsbury Publishing Plc makes every effort to ensure that the paper used in the manufacture of our books is a natural, recyclable product made from wood grown in well-managed forests. Our manufacturing processes conform to the environmental regulations of the country of origin.

To find out more about our authors and books, visit www.bloomsbury.com and sign up for our newsletters.

To

Our Students

Contents

Figures

Acknowledgements

We want our students to know that this book is indebted to them. Their questions, curiosity and discussions beyond the classrooms and courses in Art History and Visual Studies at the University of Hyderabad, specifically during the fieldwork and their exploration of various artistic facets in Hyderabad, have encouraged us to develop this anthology over the years.

We thank the University of Hyderabad for the Chancellor's Award 2019, which paved the way for making this book.

Since the inception of the academic programme of Art History and Visual Studies in 2010, the Department of Fine Arts has been at the crossroads of many scholars – particularly Parvez Kabir, Asok Kumar Das, Virginia Whiles, Gary Michael Tartakov and Yousuf Saeed – who shared their ideas on research methodology, concepts and personal experiences that are quietly crawled in making this anthology. We thank Annapurna Garimella, Aloka Parasher-Sen, Santhosh Sakhinala, Vaishnavi Ramanathan, Shanti Swaroopini and Arunima Shankar for their extramural discussions which contributed to our learning. We are also grateful to Koonal Duggal and Anju Christine for their time in reading the earlier versions of this manuscript and offering comments. Our colleagues, especially Suneel Mamadapur and LNV Srinivas, have extended their generous assistance to stand by us.

We thank the contributors for their engagement while working on a range of critical comments on their chapters and making this anthology collective. Our thanks are also due to Bijay Nath for his help in dealing with the digital glitches.

This book would not have been possible without the timely support of R. Chandra Sekhar from Bloomsbury. We are grateful to the publishing house – Bloomsbury, its team and the anonymous reviewers for their efforts to enrich our beloved project.

Baishali Ghosh and Rajarshi Sengupta
Hyderabad and Kanpur

Introduction

Baishali Ghosh and Rajarshi Sengupta

This anthology of nine essays reflects upon the unconfessed visual repository of a city—Hyderabad-Deccan as a way of survival. The nine essays unravel the embodied network of artisanal practices in the city, Hyderabad, which is the palimpsest of cultivated and collected material culture and is yet to be fully explored. The anthology puts the essays in conversation with memories of the people, photographic records, scribbles, maps, assimilating histories, biographies, habitual practices and experiential knowledge. The quintessential component of the nine essays is their commitment to historicity and city—Hyderabad, and the Deccan region as a repository of visual, archival and ethnographic content.

The essays in this book broach diverse topics, including the architectural *silsilā* or legacy of a Qutb Shahi Dargāh in relation to the contemporary buildings of today's sprawling Hyderabad in Deccan; the recognition and representation of Deccani *eidgāh*s, an understudied vernacular Islamic architectural form of South Asia; a now dusty health museum which was once set up by the Nizams; Buddhist objects of a state museum; the career trajectory of a 'traditional craftsman' in a government organization in India; the journey of a car driver becoming a master dyer in the Dastakar Andhra organization; a network of migrant temple painters in Hyderabad; and the lives of the family photo albums of subaltern settlements in Hyderabad. The essays stand at the crossroads of the authors' thorough archival research, journal entries from their fieldwork and memories of the people at various junctures of their explorations, with the visual and sonic records, drawings, notes, maps, graffiti and ephemeral materials that a site and day produce every day. Together, they contribute to re-mapping Hyderabad and the Deccan region by tracing material histories, muted biographies, artisanal practices and embodied knowledge.

The robust and rich institutional archives are often inaccessible to the beginners in art historical research in India because of complex procedure and lack of research support in art historical studies. Though the ideas of archive and scholarly knowledge are intertwined, their close relationship to power structures cannot be denied. Achille Mbembe writes, 'The archive, therefore, is fundamentally a matter of discrimination and of selection, which, in the end, results in the granting of a privileged status to certain written documents, and the refusal of that same status to others, thereby judged "unarchivable." The archive is, therefore, not a piece of data, but a status' (Mbembe 2002: 19–26). Jordanna Bailkin argues that decolonization as an archival event is a social process; it calls for tracing the lives that are difficult to locate in the colonial archival process and access (Bailkin 2015: 885–91). Huda Tayob draws our attention to the need of probing 'the histories both against and along archival grain … to emerge around, above and beyond the inherited materials histories of the sites … ' (Tayob 2021). This applied to the authors of this volume too, who had to struggle to voice their 'research'. Knowing that any archival record tries to complete a partial and fragmented representation, the authors had to dwell on their research by exploring the knowledge production of orality, text and artistic practices. The authors of this book are 'agents of social changes': their 'progress' in research is not unaffected by the socio-economic standings of the institutions and their own means of livelihood.

We, the editors, therefore propose that Hyderabad ought to be recognized as an archive of tangible and intangible historical materials that are juxtaposed with the authors' subject position and experiences. In many ways, the essays in this anthology make critical interventions and contribute new approaches to the existing art historical studies on Hyderabad. The themes in this anthology revolve around the representation of artefacts, architecture, artisanal practice and institutions, which are analysed to unfold the translations, scholarly debates and inquisitorial materials. This anthology does not intend to offer a definitive paradigm, but it introduces the entwined pragmatic artistic practices, critical thoughts and collective art historical studies.

This anthology prioritizes accounts that have escaped the grip of institutional archives. To fill this vacuum, we elected to foreground archaeology of the varied artistic practices of this region as an alternative way to envision the historical past of Hyderabad in post-independence India. Each author has dealt with the dusty, shadowy grey and unacknowledged areas of visual and material culture: their historicity and contemporaneity. We bring these nine essays into conversation with much of the rich scholarship that establishes the region's social, cultural, architectural and artisanal practices and aims to contribute to the understudied aspects of the histories and material culture in Hyderabad-Deccan. We attempt to trace the authors' primary questions and the processes of enquiry. We adopted the empirical, performative and interactive methodologies to disseminate the dialectical relationship between experience and its expression, which we call the 'anthropology of experience' by borrowing the term from the book – *The Anthropology of Experience* of Victor W. Turner and Edward M. Burner (1986). In the book Victor Turner argues:

> an anthropology of experience finds in certain recurrent forms of social experience – social dramas among them – sources of aesthetic form, … derive from the subjunctive, liminal, reflexive, exploratory heart of social drama, where the structures of group experience are replicated, dismembered, re-membered,

> refashioned, and mutely or vocally made meaningful – even when, as is so often the case in declining cultures, 'the meaning is that there is no meaning'.
>
> (Turner 1986: 43)

Thus, Hyderabad-Deccan emerges as a testing ground for new research experience. The range of topics and questions in this anthology might appear asymmetrical, but in this they are similar to the built environment of Hyderabad which comes with its own complexities and contradictions. The essays in this volume traverse across ideas, imageries and the many unusual nooks and crannies of Hyderabad, which have hitherto often remained mere footnotes in the ceremonial scholarship. By unearthing these accounts, this anthology aims to provide a solid ground for further discussion and to spur debates on the connected histories.

Crossroads of Cultural Inheritance: Hyderabad and the Deccan

Hyderabad inherited the dry and bouldered land of the Deccan plateau; thus, it belongs to the genealogy of the environmental and cultural history of the Deccan. It thrived in this region on multiplicity and lacked a 'single, perennial political core'—a fact that subsequently garnered less attention of scholars interested in studying its socio-cultural dynamics during the twentieth century (Eaton 2005: 1).

The Deccan plateau that is surrounded by the Malabar Coast on the west, the Vindhya Mountain range on the north and the Coromandel Coast on the east and escarpment of moist deciduous forest on the south connects Hyderabad with the societies of the coastal regions and rocky terrain. Thus, Hyderabad has always been porous, leading to the assimilation and inhabitation of regional languages such as Telugu, Kannada, Marathi, Tamil, Malayalam and Urdu as well as Persian and Arabic. The communities and their social practices in the Deccan have given a unique identity to this land as well as provided insights to make sense of its layered histories. The perception of a historical site is not frozen in time but depends on the creative recovery or reuse of the site. A characteristic feature of the southern landscape is its megaliths, which were built as burial or memorial sites starting from the Iron Age (Morrison 2016: 629). One such megalith that stood unexplored by the scholars for long in the Hyderabad Central University (now known as the University of Hyderabad) campus (TNN 2015; Nanisetti 2019; Tiwari 2021) is an endangered remnant of the 'South Neolithic' (Allchin 1963). Once it was dated, the correlation between time and the site changed. Realizing the history of this site was initiated with the acquisition of this land, which was once part of Kancha-Gachibowli village, to set up the university in 1974 (Rao 1990: 53–4); it compels us to push the timeline of this site to the third century BCE. Does that mean the time span between constructing the megalith and establishment of the university campus is sedentary? Around 2 km northwest from this archaeological site lies a seasonal lake beside a hillock popularly known as 'check dam', which is a residual signpost of trails of the water bodies such as Patancheru Cheruvu, Nanakramguda Kunta, Nalagandla Cheruvu, Manikonda Jagir Kunta, Gopi Cheruvu in Lingampally, Nalla Cheruvu in Tellapur and dismantled settlements around these water bodies. Absence of recorded accounts of such both geological and human organism compels us to think beyond the existing historiographical and archaeological frameworks (Parasher Sen 2020: 276). Furthermore, disappearance of such water bodies and Deccani rocks with the sprawling urbanization in present Hyderabad has challenged the paradigm of common and shared resources in the communities and their means of survival (Ramachandraiah and Prasad 2004). However, by the water, an assemblage of rocks is considered sacred by the locals. Periodically, the rocks are painted with altering stripes of white and red to attest its importance as a site of veneration. If the megalithic site was rejuvenated by the archaeologists, this sacred rock site has been kept alive by the continual veneration by believers. Thus, the University of Hyderabad in post-independence India has many challenges to address the institutional encompassment of the archaeology of knowledge in a Foucauldian sense. This example foregrounds our approach to explore Hyderabad as a notion: recognition of the deep involvement of communities and young researchers in unearthing the many layered facets of Deccani histories as a simultaneous development of institutional narratives.

The institutional accounts of this region suffered a long history of negligence which perhaps started with misidentification. The colonial scholar-administrators presented an exclusionary version of the South Asian past to justify British rule; this version complied with the contemporary understandings of 'history' (Flatt 2019: 10). For example, the rivalry between the Deccan Sultanates and the Vijayanagara Empire was contextualized by foregrounding religious differences in the late-nineteenth- and early-twentieth-century archaeological accounts; this shaped the scholarship in the field for subsequent decades (Bhandarkar 1895; Gribble 1896; Sewell 1900; Michell 1995). Needless to say, the seventh Nizam Mir Osman Ali Khan's reluctance to dissolve the Hyderabad state's princely identity and join the newly independent India was seen as the historical continuation of Islamic rulers to reinstate the priority of religion. Established in 1914, the archaeological department of the Nizam's dominion carried out expeditions in Ellora, Ajanta, Bidar and Bijapur among other places and published detailed documentation (Yazdani 1917, 1930, 1944). Whereas the Buddhist, Hindu and Jain caves almost instantly received scholarly attention both nationally and internationally, the early modern monuments largely remained understudied. A prolific historian Ghulam Yazdani, who served as the head of the archaeological department between 1914 and 1943, not only laid the groundwork for Deccan studies but led a generation of historians who further contributed to the field.[1] Ironically, much like his beloved Deccan, Yazdani's contribution remained underappreciated. Even though some early attempts, including a publication by the archaeological department, were made to retrieve the architectural parts of the Golconda fortress—the seat of the Qutb Shahi kingdom (1518–1687)—a comprehensive account of this historic site is yet absent.[2] With its commanding physical presence on the plateau, the fortress stands as a reminder of the abundance of socio-cultural and historical facets of the Deccani livelihood which remains unearthed.

A recent drive to envision the ephemeral histories of the Deccan foregrounds a key question: how to reconstruct practices which thrived in the past without leaving substantial traces (Juneja 2012: xxi). This methodological approach reflects the concerns for safeguarding ephemeral practices delineated by the 2003 UNESCO Intangible Cultural Heritage Convention and the scholarship assessing the historicity of cultural practices (Ruggles and Silverman 2009: 1; Perks and Thomson 2015). Pre-colonial Deccani gardens emerged as a prospective yet challenging area to investigate this question while enriching the interplay between tangibility and ephemerality (Ali and Flatt 2012). Gardens are somewhere between representations and embodiment; they are not only constructed spaces but also repositories of sensory experiences. Despite being carefully designed, many garden spaces in the Deccan have changed over time due to human interactions and lack of conservation efforts (Ali and Flatt 2012: 2). The retrieval of affects, emotions and sensory responses from the material remnants is central to constructing early modern histories and subjectivities (Houghteling 2018: 124–47; Rizvi 2018: 1–20). A proclivity in these studies towards bridging craft making, oral narratives and social practices with inanimate cultural objects and monuments has expanded the scope of historical enquiry.[3] The turn to the potentials of sensory perceptions demonstrates that memorizing past experiences in the present can effectively inform knowledge about a past which has left little tangible signs for contemporary researchers (Taussig 1993; Seremetakis 1994). The stress on intangibility, orality and bodily perceptions widened the perimeters of investigating suppressed and neglected facets of the Deccani past.

Diversified cultural and linguistic practices and trading activities gave rise to Deccani cosmopolitanism, evidenced in the region at least since the early medieval era. Synonymous with the region, Dakhani—a regional language that has been spoken by the courtiers and Sufis as early as the mid-fourteenth century—borrowed from *Khadi Boli*, Urdu, Marathi and Telugu, among many other languages (Rafi 2018: 159). Initiated as 'a common path of least resistance' between the indigenous inhabitants of the Deccan and the immigrant rulers, courtiers, saints and traders, as T. N. Devare suggested, the composite vocabulary of Dakhani evolved into a repository of literary excellence (Devare 2018: 346). Similarly, many Urdu words such as *kursī* (chair) and *kaagaz* (paper) were assimilated into the Telugu lexicon. Linguistic assimilation ran parallel to the development of religious syncretism after the Bhakti movement and the spread of Sufi teachings in the fourteenth and fifteenth centuries (Shaheen and Shahid 2018: 98–9). Migrant Sufi saints from Central Asia, Iran, Arab countries and other parts of the subcontinent to the region enriched the development of a sacred saintly geography through a rich literary practice, including the translation of Arabic texts into Persian and scholarly commentaries (*hāshiyya*) on earlier religious texts (Green 2006: 50–4). Spanning across Kannada, Telugu and Marathi-speaking regions, the Deccan Sultanates largely contributed to the development of Dakhani—

primarily spoken by the Muslims—to find a middle ground between courtly Persian and regional vernaculars (Dayal 2017: 550). However, during and after the Mughal occupation in the Deccan, Dakhani obtained a subordinate position to the sophistication of Urdu. The dominance of Urdu over the 'aesthetically feminine' Dakhani resulted in the Nizams—rulers of the Hyderabad state appointed by the Mughals—adopting a more Persianized version of Urdu for the court, which also led the educated inhabitants of this region to subsequently neglect this regional mode of verbal expression (Kugle 2016: 221). The renewed interest in Dakhani in the twentieth century was prompted by the genre of humour—especially the stage adaptation of Babban Khan's literary creation *Adrak ke Panje*—which gradually led to the development of Hyderabadi films (Sharma 2018: 33). Variations of Dakhani are still widely spoken across the region by Muslims as well as other communities. Its stronghold in the popular realm suggests that the charm of this composite language was retained by the public despite the lack of courtly patronage.

The migration of people and exchange of social capital have offered cultural and ecological mutation in Deccan since Protohistory period, tracing back to the Neolithic folks followed by Chalcolithic communities in the Central Deccan (Subbarao 1958: 23). The topographical location of Deccan with the Ghats' forests and natural passes, and the monsoon-fed rivers connecting it with the coasts of the Arabian Sea and Bay of Bengal, allowed the exchange and expansion of various actors through the Deccan Traps. The Deccan, for example, strived to establish their presence in the Safavid and Ottoman kingdoms—in other words, beyond the geographical limits of South Asia (Wagoner and Weinstein 2017: 791). These provincial centres assimilated metropolitan cultural norms with already-existing regional practices. The exchange of royal robes, luxury textiles and exquisite metalware was at the centre stage of these cultural mediations. Sanjay Subrahmanyam notes that the agents of these transmissions were traders and ambassadors, such as Augustin Herryard and François Bernier, who communicated between local communities and Europeans, and also between different kingdoms and groups within southern India (Subrahmanyam 2017: 15). Foreign traders, often referred to as *paraṅgi* (in Telugu), had a prominent presence in the Deccan region (Reddy 1991: 17). The Animela inscription of 1531, at the Kamalapuram taluk in the present Kadapa district, noted that merchants and people from fifty-six regions were present in that region during the mid-sixteenth century (Reddy 1991: 42).[4] Widely known as *Siddis* or *Habshīs*, the migrant traders, sailors, mercenaries and slaves from mostly East Africa and the successive generations maintained a significant presence in the Deccan. Their Bantu/Swahili language survived through the adaptation of regional languages such as Urdu, Telugu and Kannada in their music, performance and habitus of daily lives (Lodhi 2008: 301–4). In popular culture, the representation of the Africans in the Deccan has centred around slaves and slave-generals, such as Malik Amber (1548–1626), whereas Siddis served as job seekers, merchants, midwives, herbalists and military professionals (Yimene 2007: 323). It is proposed that the migration of semi-skilled and unskilled workers out of the Deccan has contributed to the spirit of cultural exchange in recent times (Mukherjee 2017: 92). The *Barkas,* or the descendants of the Hadrami military men and bodyguards from Yemen in southern Hyderabad, have increasingly migrated to the relatively smaller towns in the Gulf, resulting in the economic as well as 'social remittance' between the 'hostland' and 'homeland' (Mukherjee 2017: 96). *Marfa baaja*, a popular form of music, indispensable to marriages and celebrations even today in the old city, was shaped by the migrant Siddis and Hadramis (Amenda 2018: 299). The back-and-forth migration of people over centuries remains as an active agent of sociological and cultural changes in the Deccan.

The intercommunal encounters – conflictual and cooperational – penetrated through the courtly as well as the public culture, allowing many particularities of the regional forms of visual, bodily and performative practices to flourish (Prakash 2004). Breaking away from the dynastic frames of Deccani history and material culture has surfaced in the recent scholarship to consider the 'lives' of people, objects and practices that thrived in this land for centuries or left a perennial impact on the Deccani societies (Overton 2020: 5). Finbarr Barry Flood and Deborah Hutton's comprehensive analysis of the intercultural motifs in early modern South Asian and Deccani visual culture contextualize the emergence of a complex visual culture (Flood 2009: 62–5; Hutton 2012: 134). The Vijayanagara kingdom in southern India was considered a Hindu kingdom that prevented the spread of Islam to their territory. Since the 1990s, scholars have strongly argued against this earlier assumption (Michell 1999). Philip Wagoner presents a compelling argument about the transformation of the Hindu culture of Vijayanagara through its interaction with Islam by tracing the history of *kullayi* (a towering headgear) and *kabayi* (a long tunic) as Vijayanagara courtly attire (Wagoner 1996). Wagoner argues that the Hindu court culture of Vijayanagara was 'deeply transformed' by the interactions with Islamic cultures (Wagoner 1996: 852). Flood responds to Wagoner's argument about cross-cultural dressing in the Vijayanagara court and proposes that the cross-cultural encounters were restricted to the realm of not the courtly elites but also artisans, workers and soldiers (Flood 2009: 61–88). Naveen Kanalu's discussions around *Pirla Panduga*—a Deccani variant of Muharram (a festival of remembrance that commemorates the martyrdom of Hussayn, Prophet Muhammad's grandson) observed by both Hindu and Muslim weavers—support intercommunal artisanal encounters in this region (Kanalu 2016: 130–3). The practice of Muharram among the Hindu and Muslim weavers and other artisanal communities in the colonial Deccan surfaced as a result of sustained occupational bonds and trade connections (Kanalu 2016: 139). The annual Shi'a ritual of mourning found resonance within the grief of the migrant weavers of this region evolving into a syncretistic Deccani practice. Even though the cultural transformations discussed above have developed within their specific contexts, portable objects such as gifts and clothes and artisanal practice such as cloth making interweave these patterns of exchange.

In contrast to the transmittable objects, the immovable monuments in this region also display distinctive traits of exchanges. Whereas the unique location of this region was posed as the key to the development of 'hybrid' temple structures in the established scholarship, recent studies prioritize the conscious decisions made by the architects and builders (Kaligotla 2016: 3). In her close analysis of the seventh-century (circa) temple hamlet Pattadakal, Kaligotla argues that the amalgamation of *Nāgara* (North Indian) and *Drāviḍa* (South Indian) architectural elements in the temples was far from being accidental and rather reflects a conscious arrangement to set up a dialogue between architectural styles (Kaligotla 2016: 7–9). Since these temples were developed over time, artisans learned to accommodate the pre-existing structures and stylistic features into their design lexicon. Composite architectural forms were similarly a retrieval of the past legacy; specific memories associated with the past were revived through construction projects. An inscription (1074–5 CE) in old Kannada from the Chalukya king Somesvara II's reign was placed on the official doorway to the citadel of Adil Shahi Bijapur (1538–9 CE), possibly as a gesture of Ibrahim Adil Shah's commitment to the region's revered past and to consolidate his power (Eaton and

Wagoner 2014: 129–31). A selective and strategic refurbishing of the Aravattukhambada temple of Bankapur, again a Chalukyan temple complex, into a Jami Mosque marking Ali Adil Shah's victory over the tributary ruler Velappa Raya reflects the Adil Shahi interest to situate themselves in line with the Chalukyan rulers of the past (Eaton and Wagoner 2014: 139–45). The striking mosque did not feature domes or minarets—both of which are considered key features of an Islamic congregational prayer hall—to retain the prime characteristics of the Chalukyan temple, while destroying the figural sculptures from the interior of the *mandapa*. On the other hand, the early-seventeenth-century Maratha rulers, who served both the Deccan Sultanates and the Mughal Army, asserted architectural elements from the Nizam Shahis of Ahmednagar into their palaces and commemorative structures (Sohoni 2018: 36–7). According to Pushkar Sohoni, 'low springing lines for the arches' and 'squinched vaulting' observed in the memorial structures of Sindkhed Raja of Maharashtra are reminiscent of the Nizam Shahi architectural conventions (Sohoni 2018: 36). Alka Patel (2012) underscores the enmeshed relationship between domestic, religious and political performances and architectural preferences under the patronage of the merchant-bankers in the Nizam's State of Hyderabad (*c*. 1780–1948). The merchant-bankers employed the craftsmen and mason from Gujarat and Rajasthan specialized in distinct woodcraft and masonry walls in building the residence, Gosain *maṭhas*, and *dewals* (small temples). For example, the designs of flora and bird, exceptionally thick masonry wall, bent entrances with heavy door in the houses of the merchant-bankers in Paithan are the significant visual and preserving architectural fragments suggesting the protection of community wealth and property in the region suffered from Maratha-Mughal confrontation; these architectural features were blended with the peculiar Mughal-Bangla architectural forms at the residences of the merchant-bankers in Nizam's Hyderabad (Patel 2012: 148–51). Thus, the transmission of architectural knowledge and recontextualization of significant architectural fragments over the centuries in the Deccan dismiss the dichotomy between northern and southern temple architecture, Sultanate and Hindu monuments, and razing and reconstruction.

The visual culture around the portable regional craft has been investigated from multiple perspectives, positioning materials and artisans to the heart of the new narratives. Undoubtedly, the early modern Deccani courtly culture and art objects remained the most prominent among the wide range of material practices (Haidar and Sardar 2011; Haidar and Sardar 2015; Ramaswami and Singh 2015). Prioritizing material practice has presented innovative ways to question the chronological framework of categorizing Deccani craft and expanded the scope of interdisciplinary research. The scroll painting of Cheriyal that continues to be practised at least since the early modern era has developed as a collaborative practice of narrators and *naqqāsh* painters portraying regional versions of Hindu epics to community *puranas* (Mittal 2013). In Chandan Bose's study, the utilization of tamarind seeds, pigments, paper and cloth during the production of narrative scrolls was established parallel to nourishing and translating their generationally acquired knowledge into the scrolls; in Bose's consideration, that is 'writing their narratives' (Bose 2019). Craft as well as ethnography are posed as simultaneous physical, cognitive and linguistic activities, which call attention to not only the artisanal histories but the politics of ethnography and history writing. The craft of long and layered dyeing processes involved in making the painted and printed fabrics in the villages of the Coromandel coast in the eastern Deccan is a living archive of the water ecology, plant lives and materiality of the artisanal knowledge which counter the colonial record (Sengupta 2019). Drawing references from the commentaries of the Buddhist and Jain texts, Phyllis Granoff discusses how the craft of dyeing threads and cloths is enmeshed with the intellectual tradition, the sensory faculties and the objects responsive to given the complexity of colouring agents that produce patterns on cloth (2004: 155–7).

Another specialized craft which remained understudied until the 1990s is indigenous wootz steel or *ūkku* (in Telugu) making in Deccan (Srinivasan 1994: 49). Damascus blades in Persia are believed to be made with steel exported from Golconda, considering their high carbon content—a key feature of wootz steel. Archaeometallurgical finds suggest the existence of rice hulls in the refractory material for manufacturing this distinctive steel (Srinivasan 1994: 56); rice being a regional staple and rice husk being utilized in regional dyeing practice, it is unsurprising that the Deccani smiths understood its material benefits. While pushing back the roots and routes of regional knowledge to the Protohistoric period, R. E. M. Wheeler foregrounds the significance of 'Andhra Ware' and 'Rouletted Ware' with atypical surface treatment and clay bodies, indicating its production industries across Deccan and their circulation beyond Deccan (Wheeler et al. 1946; Wheeler 1984). Around the second century before and after the Common Era, the artisans' making of a unique style of sculptures with distinct clay and technique was a result of material trade and aesthetic exchanges between the Deccan and overseas (Ghosh 2019). Bendapudi Subbarao reports the highly developed stone blade industry in Hyderabad-Deccan (1955: 129). Praveena Gullapalli stresses on the iron smelting relationship to copper and gold works in the Iron Age (2009: 442–54). The stonecutting communities (such as vaddera) – whose expertise aided in flattening rocks to create land for making infrastructure such as roads, flyovers and buildings for developing IT and other industries in rocky Hyderabad (Messier 2018) – are also the connecting signpost of the Deccan's geological and cultural past with their knowledge of stone, water, iron and climatic relations with these materials. They were at the core in building the infrastructure and architecture like step wells (*bowli*), forts, temples, tombs, gateways, walls for the royals and commoners since the fifth century. Their geological knowledge of Deccan is an intangible repository of the complex histories of lands, locals, settlers, governments and ecology (Mohammad 2013; Messier 2018). A comprehensive understanding of materials, interrelations between forging, smelting and sculpting different materials such as metal, stone, clay and the artisans' engagement with them allows us to analyse the historical Deccani craft in various materials, including household items and weaponry, beyond the framework of iconography and trade networks. In other words, historical Deccani artefacts scattered in institutional and individual collections are needed to be reintegrated into their community, cultural and regional roots.

Situated in the heart of Deccan, the city of Hyderabad has historically evidenced a creative and collective manifestation of the multiple communities residing here. The suffix attached to the names of the various neighbourhoods often responded to the environmental and architectural peculiarities in Persian, Urdu, Telugu and Hindi (Azam 2018).[5] To interpret the unique cultural and linguistic identity of the city, which traces its origin back to the site of Chichalam (presently Chanchalguda), a paradigm built on the localized means of cultural practices must be prioritized (Sharma 2018: 21). Scholarship suggests that the initial plan of the city drew from overseas Persian as well as local Hindu cosmogrammatic structures (Eaton and Wagoner 2014: 220–2). Instead of tracing the origin of this city plan to Isfahan or Samarkand, recent scholarship stresses its close relationship to the historic city of Warangal in Telangana. Since its establishment as a Qutb Shahi city, Hyderabad had been ruled by Shi'a and Sunni courtiers, but its architectural programmatic shows ambiguity in relation to doctrinal instructions. Even though the iconic Charminar features four tower minarets, this component is mostly absent in the Qutb Shahi mosques in the city and beyond; instead, they feature parapets and ornate finials, which seem to be an amalgamation of Shi'a belief, technical and financial considerations, and a long-standing regional practice of making micro-architecture within built structures (Lambourn 2010: 142–6). The city lost its political prominence after the Mughal occupation, which resulted in the literati leaving the city for Aurangabad. Nizam-ul-Mulk's reestablishment of the city in the eighteenth century entailed providing refuge to migrant administrators, traders, cultivators and literati from northern India, Central Asia and the Middle East and nurturing the spirit of co-existence in the Deccan (Faruqui 2013: 32–9).

Unlike its earlier history, the state of Hyderabad (1724–1948) evidenced unprecedented territoriality at the peak of the Nationalist movement in the early-twentieth-century subcontinent. An absence of the negotiations – seen during the formative phase of Hyderabad – in the 1930s spurring violent communal tensions between ruling Muslims and majoritarian Hindus in this state led to its turbulent annexation of the newly formed independent India in 1948 (Faruqui 2013: 39; Purushotham 2015: 442–3). This resulted in a large-scale migration of Muslim artisans out of the state, especially to Pakistan and overseas.[6] The endeavour of the Andhra activists to produce a regional political community out of the Madras Presidency while strengthening the anti-colonial struggle in the early twentieth century sowed the seeds of the formation of states created along linguistic lines. With an uneasy incorporation of Telangana region in the Telugu majority state of Andhra Pradesh in 1956, the possibilities of future conflict within the Telugu communities were left open, which eventually acted as a catalyst to carve the state of Telangana out of Andhra in 2014, with Hyderabad as the acting capital of both states. Whereas the major political developments in the city and the Deccan for the last seventy years contributed to the consolidation of communal and linguistic identities, the spirit of interregional migration as seen in the earlier history of the city was evoked in the 1990s. In the western periphery of the city – close to where the University of Hyderabad campus stands today – a fairly recent attempt was made to attract professionals skilled in the field of technology from all over the country with the inauguration of the HITEC city. The knowledge corridor was established by the then chief minister of the state of Andhra Pradesh centred around the closed cylindrical multi-storeyed Cyber Towers built in 1998 (Das 2016: 58–60). The construction of new urban spaces in Hyderabad has been proclaimed by erecting towering structures in a city where the famous Charminar was one of the few such structures, as delineated in Omar Khalidi's comprehensive documentation of the architecture of Hyderabad, marking the changing stylistic preferences for building construction in the city since the Qutb Shahi period to the late twentieth century (Khalidi 2009); however, unlike the wide, inviting arched facades of the Qutb Shahi monument, the new icon of the burgeoning metropolis generates awe by its fortress-like form and limited public access. Through this course of events, one aspect of the regional culture remained almost constant: the subordinate position of Dakhani, earlier in relation to Persian and Urdu, and now Hindi.

Key Questions and Frameworks

The one concept that undergirds all the essays is 'migration' that involves movement, transfer, transit, shift, dislocation and relocation, departure and arrival. The migration of human and non-human actors in the cognitive, sensorial, material, geological and socio-cultural milieu calls for alternatives and review in the approaches of the existing scholarships on Hyderabad and Deccan. For example, the present Health Museum in Hyderabad was first moved to the Trophy Hall (presently known as the Jawahar Bal Bhawan) in 1952 and relocated to the Ajanta Pavilion in Hyderabad Public Gardens in 1966. The poor records and sparse reports on the Health Museum offer almost nothing that could help us speculate about what caused the consecutive shifts in the museum display since its inception. Today, each object in the Health Museum—the case study of the second chapter—is a remnant of the idealized and imagined modernity of the Nizams, marking the migration of India from 'pre' to 'post' independence. However, the present building of the Health Museum once held copies of Ajanta paintings. The chaitya arch of the facade of the Health Museum building bears insignia that reveals the purpose for which the building was once constructed. Simultaneously, the Buddhist objects on display in the State Museum, Hyderabad, which is at the centre of discussion in the first chapter, have turned vulnerable in the aftermath of the state bifurcation of Andhra Pradesh in 2014. The fate of the objects will possibly be decided based on their sites of excavation in the present-day Andhra Pradesh and Telangana. Thus, the objects are remarkably resilient to the state narratives. Their resettlement in the museum is entangled with the aesthetics of electoral political sovereignties. The museum objects and their movement are intrinsically connected with land, stories and orality, which James Clifford notes is the 'contact zone', where an 'organising structure as a *collection* becomes an ongoing historical, political and *moral* relationship – a power charged set of exchanges, of push and pull' (Clifford 1997: 188–219). Drawing upon Clifford, we suggest that the objects in the museum occupy a 'transit zone' in post-independence India. They are often situated in a state of transit and wait to move to the next destination; the movements of the objects are halted and they are hosted by the institutions or individuals for a certain period as part of the process of repatriation, repossession and relocation.

Both the objects and spaces stay between the beholder and the belonging, proprietors and stakeholders. In January 2021, scholars and researchers worldwide expressed concern about the fate of the archival material of the National Museum in New Delhi and the Indira Gandhi National Centre for the Arts (IGNCA), as their relocation seemed inevitable due to the newly announced Central Vista project. Since 2018, the artefacts of the Gurusaday Museum in Kolkata stand in the transit zone of the museum as the museum was shut down—due to the disappearance of funding and power tussles—are waiting to move to their next destination. Thus, the spatial discourse of the museum and transitory objects in post-independence India calls for revisiting the realignment of power, patronage and temporality. Nevertheless, the migration of mundane objects—such as the photos and photo albums and the belongings of ordinary people and migrant labourers probed in the fifth chapter—is always in transit, owing to the conditions of their livelihood.

The nomadic aspect of the objects—whether they are in a museum or a house—is a characteristic that is entangled with India's position as a decolonized and developing country. For example, the abolition of the zamindari system and princely states by the 1950s compelled many heirs of zamindars and royalty to transfer their personal belongings (land, architecture and objects) to museums, such as the Salar Jung Museum, the Mysuru Palace and Residential Museum, and the City Palace in Jaipur. A recent example is the Central Vista Redevelopment Project and its entanglement with the archive and museum's collection.[7] The Jaya He GVK New Museum (popularly known as the Mumbai Airport Museum) at Terminal 2 of the Chhatrapati Shivaji International Airport is another classic example. A third example is the under-construction project on art objects in the rotating exhibition and permanent exhibits at Terminal 2 of the Kempegowda International Airport in Bengaluru, which foregrounds how art objects are entangled with the narratives of 'decolonized' and 'developing' India.[8] The advanced technology is deployed and added to the infrastructure of the institution (here, museum) to indicate the upgraded economic status of India as a 'developing' country. Thus, technological advancement with an alignment of the economy alter the function and meaning of the objects wherever they are hosted, as it is deeply rooted in the economic condition of the patrons and their position.[9] However, studies on the lives of objects offer cross-cultural pollination in the making and caring of objects.[10] It is significant to understand that along with the objects, many tangible and intangible elements, such as sensorial experiences and emotions, are cross-pollinated. Whether in a museum or a commoner's house, objects are always in transit; in this sense the objects are migrants.

Migration not only enables movement but redefines the self and its relationship to others. The absence of a sense of history of the 'other' (here material, artistic practice and architecture) and ill-paired imageries are rooted and routed in the process of migration. This is reflected in some of the key questions presented by the authors in this anthology. For example: why is the *eidgāh* wall 'othered' in studies of South Asian Islamic architecture, and why did it receive so much attention by the colonial travellers; how the system of specialization in craft practice in the institution of decolonized India's 'other' is entwined with the skills of craft and artistic practices. Linda Nochlin argues that the making of 'others' is 'intrinsically embedded in the intersected multiple historical narratives other than European literature' (Nochlin 1989: 36–48). Thus, 'othering' is an act that is deployed to contrast, compare and etch out differences in artistic practices. Othering is employed to subvert the centre and alter the position of the 'margin' and 'pivot', thus challenging the idea of a work of art and its place of origin and offering us a paradigm to understand the circulation of artistic materials and creativity (Shalem 2012: 3–4). For example, Chapter 7 poses the question why the *eidgāh* on the premises of the royal tombs of the Qutb Shahi kin remained outside the frames of the photographers even though it was a much sought-after location for photoshoots and was also used to photograph the towering Qutb Shahi tombs. On another occasion, in 1998, a seminal exhibition titled 'Other Masters: Five Contemporary Folk and Tribal Artists of India' at the Craft Museum in New Delhi, curated by the anthropologist and art historian Jyotindra Jain, established artisans as the 'other master' in decolonized India's milieu where the traditional and contemporary are enmeshed with the indexical categories like 'folk and tribal artist/primitive artist' in colonial South Asia.

These considerations connect to another crucial issue that remains at the heart of this project: reconfiguring the Deccani *multiplicity*. The widespread institutional and scholarly negligence of Deccani multiplicity was what drove us to make our intervention, which entails two intrinsic components of the idea. At the outset, we explore multiplicity as a methodological tool that resists the dominance of a singular, authoritative narrative drawing on the advocacy of minority histories, drawing on the seminal work of historians Dipesh Chakrabarty and Ranajit Guha (Chakrabarty, 1998: 477, 2000; Guha 2009: 316). Dipesh Chakrabarty argues that the discipline of history is one of the many ways to envision the past (1998: 477). Chakrabarty further elaborates on his argument in his seminal publication *Provincializing Europe: Postcolonial Thought and Historical Difference* (2000). He states,

> The act of championing minority histories has resulted in discoveries of subaltern pasts, constructions of historicity that help us see the limits to modes of viewing enshrined in the

> practices of the discipline of history. Why? Because the discipline of history—as has been argued by many (from Greg Dening to David Cohen in recent times)—is only one among ways of remembering the past.
>
> (2000: 106)

Ranajit Guha's stress on the 'small voices' of history is posed as an antidote to the erasure of unnamed voices from the historical accounts (Guha 2009: 316). Hence, the acknowledgement of the *plurality* of historical resources emerged as a key concept as marginalized voices began to make themselves heard and transformed into more recognizable versions of history writing. Marginalized or neglected historical accounts resist the process of historicization and lead to questions regarding the functioning of the discipline of professional history – predominantly based on tangible evidence.

Acknowledgement of the multiplicity of subject-positions and limitations of institutional narratives call for perceiving histories through multi-sensory engagement (Howes 2003: 56). Another component springs out of this methodological enquiry to address complexities and inherent confusions embedded in the notion of cosmopolitanism. As Walter D. Mignolo and others argue, the notion of cosmopolitanism is understood as a counter to the economic, cultural and political homogenization posed by globalizing processes (Mignolo 2002: 157). The inclusion of the narratives of the marginalized, such as agrarian labours, workers and craftspeople, into this mix does not go far enough to address their contributions. Mignolo instead proposes 'border thinking' or 'the recognition and transformation of the hegemonic imaginary from the perspectives of people in subaltern positions' (Mignolo 2002: 174). Recent scholarly take on the contextuality of colonialism (in regions directly under British rule and princely states) and its impact on communities and artisanal sectors instigate the urgency of prioritizing unheard community voices (Kumar 2022: 15). Whereas the relevance of prioritizing marginalized voices is undeniable, we propose to set up a contextual conversation between archival, object-based, oral and bodily retrievals of the Deccani past. By contextual conversation, we acknowledge the scope of exchanges between more recognized and suppressed historical accounts while not eluding the sociological, cultural and political specificity of the actors involved in our studies. The concepts of tradition and artistic practice appear to be most contentious when their 'margins' are considered critically. The question that unsettles the history of traditional artisans' practices is the 'margin'. Reflecting on the state of textile makers, Tirthankar Roy addresses the role of non-hereditary artisans and the tension between transmission of artisans' skill through hereditary and non-hereditary lineage in geo-colonial South Asia (Roy 2007). This inheritance makes the margin of the tradition of any craft porous and enriches the notion of *multiplicity*.

In the discussions of Chapters 8 and 9, both Syed Omer and Mohammed Salim Pasha, non-hereditary artisans from Hyderabad—as well as other non-hereditary masters—resemble weaver Dubraj from 1900 in Tirthankar Roy's account. Dubraj, a Baluchari weaver belonging to the *Chamar* (shoemaker or tanner or currier by caste) community, learned how to make a *naksha*-loom from an *ustad* (master) who was from a marginalized economic group of the Muslim community. Dubraj was also good at composing music and verses in a musical performance known as *kabir ladai* in Bengal despite being illiterate (Roy 2007: 970). Roy states that after Dubraj died in 1902, 'there was no one in Baluchar to carry on the style that he had initiated'. A similar fate emerged for the weaving workshop of Suraiya Hasan Bose in Hyderabad after the death of Syed Omer in 2019. It remains uncertain whether Mohammed Salim Pasha's descendants will continue to keep their dyehouse thriving after his demise on 18 June 2022. Omer and Salim returned the tradition to the revivalists in post-independence India; they redrew the tradition of artisanal practice. Departing from colonial 'out of the tradition', we suggest that it is the 'afterlife' of a tradition which makes it plural, connected, transitional, non-hereditary, a bricolage, migratory, experimental and cognitive; these give agency to the actors of a tradition (here, artistic practice) to survive and sustain.

In Chapter 6, Hussain Shah Wali Dargāh a living architecture which was built around the Qutb Shahi era (circa early sixteenth to late seventeenth century) in Hyderabad presents an intriguing account of architectural inheritance and contemporary inhabitance in accordance with our ongoing discussion on tradition. The residents around Hussain Shah Wali Dargāh have lovingly taken up the renovation and protection of the structure by incorporating building materials used for making their homes. This eclecticism indicates the porousness of the so-called traditional artistic practices. Thus, the material quality of the old architecture transforms with the introduction of the new materials that stakeholders and donors can afford. Therefore, affordability of any religious architectural care and conservation is a way to understand the healing, reverence and care of the stakeholders and their social lives. For example, straddling between colonial and post-independence metropolis, middle-class and subaltern settlers, the spatial share of sacredness of Kalighat Temple in Kolkata is all about the dissemination of share and care of the concerned community and the stakeholders (Moodie 2018: 106–20). The shrines on the roadside of post-Partition Amritsar are social talismans that the city dwellers hold close to them to heal the memory of separation, distance and division with everyday narratives. The streets, city, religious structures and settlers embody the history and contemporaneity of Amritsar (Snehi 2018). Similarly, smart cities (such as Hyderabad) in recent India accommodate fashionable, creative and ethical socio-religious practices while building religious structures, performing rituals and patronizing varied deities, artisans, urban and migrant devotees.

The contemporary temple architecture in Hyderabad is a collage of canonical architectural forms, recreated with various materials (such as cement, acrylic paint and print) to get the 'look' of traditional temple architecture. The artisans who paint these temples migrate from their villages and earlier professions (often farming or masonry) and are the subject of discussion in the fourth chapter of this anthology. Their painted architectural motifs, drawn from printed books and online images, recreate the historicity of Indian temple architecture and present a compelling case of travelling and floating traditional temple motifs. Tulasi Srinivas addresses such artisanal practice and productivity as 'an anthropology of wonder' of much accustomed, by placing 'creativity' as one of the driving factors. She writes, 'A consideration of wonder shifts our focus from textual treatise and tradition to discourses and practices of emotion, expression, creativity. This allows for the *process* of making, crafting, and manufacturing worlds, possibilities, and dispositions, in its embryonic and collaborative stages' (Srinivas 2018: 6).

Material is one of the most conflictual factors in artistic practice. Coping with the sudden or gradual disappearance of material, and the arrival of the 'new,' is always a challenge to the artisans' practices. Knowledge of a material in craft leads to the exploration of another material. Thus, 'connectedness,' after historian Sanjay Subrahmanyam's theorization of connected histories as a point of departure from segmented and polarized histories to accommodate discussions on materiality, is the centre of cognitive knowledge production of the artisans (Subrahmanyam 1997). Subrahmanyam writes that 'ideas and mental constructs, too, flowed across political boundaries … specific local expression-enable us to see that what we are dealing with are not separate and comparable, but connected histories' (Subrahmanyam 1997: 748). He further argues that uncomfortable edges of our categories provide important clues to define elements of connectedness and transmission (Subrahmanyam 1997: 758–62).

Historical, material, architectural and artistic connectedness are both tangible and intangible, sensorial and physical, symmetrical and contrasting. For example, Michael Meister discusses this connectedness as *kapilī* (juncture wall) in architectural mechanism and aesthetics of coupling and couple sculptures in temple architecture, which mystifies the manifestation of both sculpture and architecture (Meister 1979: 226–34). Lotika Varadarajan identifies the 'connectedness' as *vadhera* in the craft of boat building and its historical trajectories with time and South and Southeast Asia (Varadarajan 1993: 549–54).[11] Bettina Baumer discusses the 'connectedness' as *sandhi* (as junctures of various artisanal practice, knowledge, aesthetics and transition). She writes:

> Space and time … could not be measured, without junctures—a bamboo can be measured by [the] number of knots … These junctures are sensitive and important moments or spaces of transition, taking characteristics from both sides, at the same time separating, thus differentiating the two and uniting them, partly overlapping … The junctures in any field have the purpose of overcoming the fundamental dualities without denying differentiation.
>
> (Baumer 2003: 301)

Thus, the making of doors for the houses, forts and equipment for the farmers by the ancestors of Bhikshamayya Chary and the making of the loom and kalamkari blocks by Bhikshamayya Chary at present in the Weavers Service Centre in Hyderabad are not connected as the indexical category of the objects in institutional record books but by the cognitive knowledge of the raw and processed materials – is at the core of the argument in Chapter 7. The interactive chemistry between the materials is at the core of artisanal knowledge that may produce diverse practices – for example, Bhikshamayya Chary's ayurvedic medicinal and craft (here loom) making practice. Another example is Anwar Chitrakar, whose artistic practice conjoins his expertise in tailoring in the non-branded garment industry of Metiabruz in Kolkata, the production of billboards and murals on city architecture and in the tourism industry rather than the artistic practice by which his community is conventionally and widely recognized—showing painted scrolls and singing narratives. Hansda Sowvendra Shekhar also echoes the similar issue through the character named Mangal Murmu in his book *The Adivasi Will Not Dance* (2015), where Mangal Murmu asserts, '(W)e are like toys—someone presses our "ON" button, or turns a key in our backsides, and we Santhals start beating rhythms on our tamak and tumdak, or start blowing tunes on our tiriyo while someone snatches away our dancing grounds. Tell me, am I wrong?' (Shekhar 2015: loc1909–20). Thus, the artisans' cognitive knowledge of the materials whether raw and processed hardly finds any space in institutional practice, and Bhikshamayya Chary and the Weavers Service Centre in Hyderabad are examples. The artisans' actual practices and experiences are often curtailed to frame them as a representational example of 'Indian craftsman/artisan' and expected to function the way Hansda Sowvendra Shekhar articulates through the character named Mangal Murmu in his book *The Adivasi Will Not Dance*.

However, we would like to remind readers here that the issues raised in the anthology are merely groundwork. We can only hope that this book will open up multiple directions for future research. Some of the methodologies and ideas taken up in the essays we hope will expand and connect with numerous art and sites with the wider histories of social, sensorial and intellectual artistic practice.

Book Plan

The nine essays in this book share an unevenness in critical thinking and a fascination for the interactive and intersected materials and artistic practice. Thus, these essays are clustered and interwoven in ways to engage with collecting, sketching, writing and producing silence, absence and survival. We hope that the interrogations attempted in the essays will be carried out in different directions to understand the process of decolonial knowledge production.

Prajnna Vedavyas's essay in the collection traces the shifting identity of the Telangana State Archaeology Museum in Hyderabad, especially its sacred Buddhist relics and objects, which have witnessed a series of political and social transformations since its inception in the 1930s. An integral section of the museum is the Buddhist collection spread across the Holy Relics Gallery, the Buddhist Sculpture Gallery and the Ajanta Frescoes Gallery, with more than fifty Buddhist sites to its credit, including Amaravati, Nagarjunakonda, Chandavaram, Phanigiri, Bavikonda and Kondapur. As tangible remains of rich histories of Buddhism in the Telugu-speaking region, the Buddhist artefacts have enabled to shape the cultural past of the people of Andhra Pradesh (AP) state after its formation in 1956. Furthermore, the recent state bifurcation of AP into Telangana and (the new) AP in 2014 triggered fresh debates and negotiations around the custody of these artefacts from the museum. Vedavyas delineates that the Buddhist objects in this museum continue to be venerated by Buddhist practitioners, and they were transported to noted Buddhist sites in the past in the undivided state of AP during significant Buddhist events. Plans for the repatriation of these objects, based on the sites of their excavation enmeshed with the regulations set up by the Archaeological Survey, are thus posed with challenges and complexity. Within the State Museum, the Holy Relics Gallery, the Buddhist Sculpture Gallery and the Ajanta Frescoes Gallery present the multifaceted state of Buddhism: from the overlapping of the sacred and the profane to the intertwining of the archaeological excavations and regional politics. The first gallery and the Buddhist sculptures in the museum are the most vulnerable to possible transformations due to the bifurcation. Vedavyas's careful consideration of state bifurcation and its impact on the repatriation of the Buddhist objects allow us to reflect on the origins of archaeological remains and collective identity in the post-independence nation-state.

The museal artefacts in the Health Museum in Hyderabad which was materialized in-between 1947–66 emerges as the protagonist of P. Sindhuri Aparna's compelling essay. The Health Museum as an institution was not unique to Hyderabad. There were other health museums built in various other princely states like Mysore, Baroda, Travancore and Patna, but the one in Hyderabad is the only one that continues to survive. Founded for educational and instructive purposes, the Health Museum, on the one hand, illustrates the impact of Western medicine and its initial application by the Indian princely states and subsequently by the State of post-Independence India; on the other hand, it stands as a confluence of the Nizam's vision of healthcare and the narrative of progress promoted by the independent India's first Prime Minister, Jawaharlal Nehru. The sustained efforts of the Nizam's government to popularize Western medicine, for handling the challenges of the twentieth-century public health better, largely relied on the role of visual and audio-visual media. The tableaus, films and health pavilions at the exhibitions paved the way for a more stable and permanent museum space to convey the state's message on public health. By paying keen attention to the aspects of visuality and visibility of the museum, Aparna sheds light on this understudied institution which, at the age of readily accessible information, has gradually lost its significance in the eyes of the people for whom it was built. While reassessing the foundation and development of this museum, Aparna also reflects on the Nizam's role in popularizing Western medicine and science in the Hyderabad state while employing indigenous methods of disseminating knowledge. Aparna establishes the Nizam's decision to promote Western medicine as a strategic move to prevent the British government's interference in the state's affairs. This calls for further research on the entanglement of Western science, medicine, authority and governance in the context of the Indian princely states.

Although the Islamic architecture of South Asia has garnered much attention from the scholars, *eidgāhs* in South Asia, especially in the Deccan, have remained understudied. An *eidgāh* – an open architectural space consisting of a long *qibla* wall in the direction of Mecca – is primarily constructed to host Eid prayers and the subsequent festivities. *Eidgāh* wall is a space for people to offer *namaz,* but just after *namaz*, it turns into an open ground for celebration, resting, fairs and other festive activities. By building the wall to the west, it becomes possible to expand the use of the space not only during the festival gathering but also throughout the year. This vernacular South Asian Islamic architectural wall offers deep insights into how architecture stands at the crossroads of climate, geography, religion, politics and power structures, as Shaista Anwar's nuanced essay unravels. Her essay presents a comprehensive analysis of the *eidgāh* structures, their representation in the colonial imagery and subsequent documentation in the twentieth-century scholarship. The openness of an *eidgāh*, as opposed to more structured and closed prayer halls, has enabled the use of these spaces not only for religious purposes but for social as well as political gatherings in the early modern times; the very nature of the *eidgāh* served as a metaphor for the vastness of the subcontinent for the colonial artists and chroniclers, destined to be consumed. However, the same openness also contributes to the multifaceted usage of the space by community members, as Anwar proposes in this essay. By exploring multiple connotations of the wall, Anwar tells us of the marginalization of the Qutb Shahi *eidgāh* in the colonial picture production and shared initiatives despite being adjacent to the Quli Qutb Shah's tomb.

The vividly coloured Drāviḍa Hindu temple architecture that attributes a distinctive character to the urban landscape of Hyderabad is made possible by the migrant temple painters who remain at the juncture of the popular, the canonical and the metropolitan. Although the images of the deities and semi-divine beings in the temples follow certain iconographical traits evoking historical connections, one cannot distinguish their visual language from that of the vivid shop signboards and painted adverts on the city walls. The scholarship on the South Indian or Deccani temples emphasizes the patterns of patronage, architecture, trade connections and devotion intersecting at these temple sites. However, the livelihood of the artisans from diverse backgrounds and their experiential aspects remain understudied. By closely following the activities of these temple painters in the city, Bijay Nath presents the suppressed accounts of their practice and identity. As Nath's essay reveals, the painters not only belong to Hindu communities but to Muslim and Christian ones too. The painters—who often work on signboards, commercial hoardings and posters with equal ease—are predominantly Telugu speakers from both Telangana and Andhra Pradesh, but a small fraction of them also arrive from Odisha and elsewhere, as Nath shows. His essay focuses on three prime aspects of the painters' endeavours: their training, their use of paints and the question of ownership over the images. Painting the visuals of gods and goddesses for the public temples demands a fine balance between the knowledge of South Indian Hindu iconography and popular appeal. Nath's essay dedicatedly explores how the temple painters achieve this by bringing together the practitioners' perspectives and peer networks. Further, Nath establishes that networking among temple painters in the city provides them a ground for sharing experiences and companionship; this gradually turns out to be an equally, if not more, constructive form of learning for the painters than the hereditary paradigm.

Keshawram's essay on Family Photo Albums (FPAs) enables us to reconsider the interrelations between home, people, photographs and social relations. Even in the age of rapid digitization and virtual images, FPAs in Hyderabad, as Keshawram delineates, remain significant to certain communities for multiple reasons. FPAs build a sense of affinity between viewers and owners of the albums through an unfolding of oral narratives complemented by snapshots capturing various occasions and functions of the family, such as birthdays, weddings, ritual events, vacations and daily activities. His ethnographic research to comprehend the impact of these albums among their users considers two groups of people: the migrant workers at the University of Hyderabad campus and the residents of the Gopanpally-Tanda area, adjacent to the campus. For the migrant workers, printed photographs operate as tangible reminders of their home and familial relations, which cannot be achieved by the virtual images of mobile phones. For the Tanda residents, the photographs and their careful assemblage into FPAs, during marriage ceremonies for instance, are done as diligently as performing any religious ritual; these albums are then viewed collectively during family gatherings. By flipping through the photographs of their family members, the viewer's sensory memories are rejuvenated; departed relatives are even momentarily brought back to life through this act. A close visual analysis of the photographs, in Keshawram's essay, is complemented by a sensitive reading of the lives of the FPAs—their usage, protection and care in the hands of their owners. This kind of storytelling process, Keshawram proposes, is perhaps a continuation of the storytelling practices through narrative scrolls and allied practices. The notion of care, which primarily indicates the preservation of archival objects, is interpreted as the FPA owners' sensory engagement with them. This charts a trajectory of continuing the lifespan of these mnemonic aids parallel to the measures taken by the photographic archives.

The highly venerated Hussain Shah Wali Dargāh, which lends its name to the locale where it is situated, is regarded as a point of reference for the development of contemporary architecture around the '*dargāh*' area in Sayan Gupta's argument. He argues that the continued devotion centred around this Qutb Shahi Dargāh, the utilization of locally available building materials and the regional economy are the prime factors which enabled the transference of architectural elements between this historical structure and the contemporary residential and public buildings. As opposed to the nearby Golconda Fort and Qutb Shahi tomb complex, the *dargāh* is not a protected monument under the Archaeological Survey of India (ASI); the management committee of the *dargāh* and the locals have thus collectively undertaken the responsibility of repair and renovation works, and this has shaped the identity of the site quite differently from its fellow Qutb Shahi monuments. The local association with and affection for this *dargāh* comes to be reflected in the contemporary buildings in its surrounding area. The replication of Hussain Shah Wali Dargāh's architectural motifs on contemporary architecture indicates that the classical Qutb Shahi architectural style continues to live through the lives of inhabitants around the *dargāh*. Gupta suggests that the architectural transmission between the sacred *dargāh* and the contemporary buildings is rather a reciprocal process, letting the past and present co-exist in this rapidly urbanizing neighbourhood of Hyderabad. We propose that the eclectic nature of the Hussain Shah Wali

Dargāh is explored as the structure allows a flexible exchange of architectural elements with neighbouring constructions through the process of renovation. This eclectic nature, according to Gupta, has helped address and protect the vulnerability of lesser-known structures, including the Hussain Shah Wali Dargāh itself, to the radical urbanization of Hyderabad over the past decades, thus creating a way for these buildings to survive.

The much-debated idea of the 'artisan' heavily rests upon the artisans' expertise in a specific craft sector; in Rajarshi Sengupta's essay, the relevance of craft specialization and the ways to assess the capability of an artisan are revisited. His essay presents a close examination of an artisan, V. Bhikshamayya Chary, based in Hyderabad. It is hard to categorize Chary under one profession as he effortlessly performs woodblock making, woodwork, machinery making and Ayurvedic practice. His interests and multi-layered practice present an alternative account of the more recognized narratives on craft making. Chary's father, Kammari Brahmayya, was well known for woodworks and iron works. Chary's exercise within and outside the institutional space indicates the simultaneity of specialized and diverse craft practices. Chary joined the Weavers Centre in 1980 under a renewable contract. The Hyderabad Weavers Centre provided support and training in the field of fabric and *dhurrie* weaving, kalamkari painting and block printing (both natural and industrial). Here, he remained responsible for the construction of printing tables, a variety of looms and building up a rich repository of carved woodblocks. Within the folds of the institution, surplus knowledge of the craftspeople is removed to give prominence to specialized modes of production. This fails to acknowledge craft practice as part of the social lives of the practitioners, which are continuously evolving. This, as Sengupta argues, is perhaps not an exclusive case study but a reality shared among many Deccani artisans, overshadowed and discouraged by the myth of craft specialization. The figure of a 'transitional artisan' in this account resists this predominant approach in craft scholarship and emphasizes the prime importance of transmission, adaptability and co-existence in the Deccani craft sectors. More importantly, it sheds light on the role of woodworkers in shaping several Deccani crafts, including carving, and loom and machinery making, while reflecting on the possibilities of writing artisanal histories.

Somedutta Mallik's essay reassesses the contribution of a prolific master weaver and teacher, Syed Omer, who was instrumental in the reconstruction of Indo-Persian weaves in Hyderabad. In the grand narratives of craft revival in post-independence India, figures like Omer *sahab* are usually relegated to the margins which resulted in suppressing the scope of writing histories from the artisanal perspectives—a problem that is pertinent in recent scholarship in the field. Whereas entrepreneurs deploy the image of the craftsman at work as an icon of craft revival, Mallik's investigation presents the artisan's perspective on their intimate relationship with materials, tools and mechanisms. Her intimate and in-depth exploration of Omer sahab's five-decade-long career, which began in the 1970s and continued until his death, establishes how he situated himself at the crossroads of multiple organizations, projects and relationships. The accounts of these intricate details and intimate knowledge of weaving and weavers are often missing in the historical studies of South Asian textiles, which often end up posing Omer sahab as a mere draftsman as a result. While being committed to producing textiles and disseminating his knowledge to his fellow artisans, what he enjoyed the most is to stay close to the looms. Omer sahab's command and camaraderie formed a community in the workshop, and his sense of pride was transmitted to others. His presence in the workshop assured the weavers about the functionality of the *loom*. Mallik's sensitive yet critical account proposes that his emotional bond with the weaving looms and textiles cannot be separated from his intellect and indelible contribution as a teacher. Thus, the loom mechanism and instruments in the workshop do not remain distinct from the wanderings of the artisan's mind. Mallik strikes a balance between Omer sahab's biographical details and contextualization of his position against the larger scenario of the late-twentieth-century craft revival in India and offers fresh methodological interventions into studying artisanal histories.

The commitment to sustainable craft practices has renewed the interest in natural dyeing; several crucial questions regarding the notion of sustainability remain underrepresented in scholarly discussions. Tanaya Pashankar's timely and constructive argument about the 'natural' in natural dyeing compels us to interpret sustainability from multiple perspectives. Pashankar situates master indigo dyer Mohammed Salim Pasha (Salimji) from Hyderabad at the centre of her narrative, as Salimji's training, struggle, expertise and teaching over the last four decades present the necessary insights to strengthen her argument. Natural indigo, for its complicated past, limited production and high market value in recent times, has remained a rather intriguing dyestuff in the eyes of scholars and connoisseurs. It has re-emerged as a potent tool for dye producers and consumers who recognize the need for the revival of a simpler, kinder and sustainable future. An integral aspect of practising natural dyeing is the commitment to sustainability, which could be interpreted in different ways from different artisanal perspectives. Pashankar's essay, built upon her thorough ethnographic research at Salimji's workshop as well as rigorous archival study, brings forward fresh perspectives on 'tradition', 'cheating' and 'adulteration' in indigo dyeing and their impact on sustainability. A distinguishing notion of sustainability in regard to indigo dyeing that is intrinsically connected to the challenges of livelihood is conveyed in Salimji's endeavour since his mastery of indigo is not a generational inheritance but a hard-won expertise. Skilled artisans, like Salimji, claim that the lived experience of acquiring the knowledge of dyeing skills is 'natural' or 'cultivated tradition'. Thus, their dye practice reconstructs the 'natural' and 'traditional' with changing times. By dismantling the exoticization of labour, obscuring of caste and gender divisions at work, and the propagation of the machine—handmade binary, Pashankar contributes to a timely and much-needed critique of the notion of 'natural' in craft.

Notes

1 Noted Deccan scholars, Haroon Khan Sherwani, Purshottam Mahadev Joshi and A. R. Kulkarni, are among the ones who received guidance from Ghulam Yazdani.

2 T. W. Haig's report was among the earliest records on the site and construction of Golconda (Haig 1907–8: 23–9; Haig 1907). Sha Rocco's *Golconda and the Qutb Shahs* claimed that the foundation of the Golconda Fort was as early as the Warangal Fort in the thirteenth century (Rocco 1929: 3) Among recent scholars, Marika Sardar attempted to trace the early foundations of the fortress by analysing the stone walls. Sardar identified a significant difference between the inner *Bala Hisar* walls and the outer walls. From this she concluded that the early fortification in this site was refurbished during the Bahmani and Qutb Shahi era (Sardar 2011: 25–50).

3 Along with craft making, oral narratives and social practices, the other categories of intangible heritage recognized by UNESCO are 'performing arts (such as traditional music, dance, and theatre)' and 'knowledge and practices concerning nature and the universe' (Ruggles and Silverman 2009: 2).

4 The Animela inscription reads: '*Ayyavali- mukhyu- laina- chalumula- samastha- yambaiyaru- desala- setti- xc*'. P. Chenna Reddy differentiates

traders from different regions: *desi* (local), *svadesi* (native), *paradesi* (foreigner) and *nanadesi* (from different countries).

5 Anand Raj Varma presents a comprehensive account of the names of various localities of the city. The low-lying areas feature the suffix 'pet', for example, Malakpet. Places around hillocks or hills have 'gutta', 'tekdi' or 'pahad' attached to their names; 'bawli' or well constitutes the latter half of the area names 'Gachibowli' and 'Rethibowli' (Varma 2018: 177).

6 Interview with Suraiya Hasan Bose in Hyderabad, September 2015.

7 See *The Economic Times* (2021), 'National Archives a Heritage Building, Won't Be Demolished; National Museum to Be shifted', 31 May.

8 Also, the aspiration of departing from both the colonial past often reflects in the practice of replacing the names of institutions and civil structures (roads, railway stations) from the colonial period with those of prominent Indian personalities. For example, the Dr. Bhau Daji Lad Mumbai City Museum in Mumbai was formerly known as the Victoria and Albert Museum, Bombay.

9 See Rewati Rau (2021), 'Take a Trip to Mumbai Airport's "Jaya He Museum" Using This App', *The New Indian Express*, 31 January. Anjali Mara (2018), 'Now, Smart Museums to Give Virtual Tours and 3D View of Rare Artifacts', *The Indian Express*, 15 February. Government of India, 'National Digital Repository for Museums of India' in https://www.india.gov.in/spotlight/national-digital-repository-museums-india (accessed 14 February 2023).

10 Objects are treated as an agency of appropriation in decolonized India. See *The Guardian*, 'National Gallery of Australia to Return 14 Artworks Worth $3m to India', 29 July. Furthermore, Richard Davis writes, 'The metonymic relation of collection and modern nation state was drawn even more closely in the other major show of Indian art in the 1985 Festival of India, focusing on objects from 1300 CE to the present, which was simply tilted "India"' (Davis 1997: 25).

11 Varadarajan also shows us the artisans' minute observation of the joinery by depicting it on the representational boat in the Miracle Panel, East Gate Front, South Pillar, Sanchi, Stupa 1, which is dated to the first century BC.

References

Ali, Daud and Emma J. Flatt, eds (2012), *Garden and Landscape Practices in Pre-Colonial India: Histories from the Deccan*, New Delhi: Routledge.

Allchin, F. R. (1963), *Neolithic Cattle-Keepers of India: A Study of the Deccan Ashmounds*, Cambridge: Cambridge University Press.

Amenda C. P., Khadeeja (2018), 'Capturing the Masti ka Baaja in Hyderabad', *Society and Culture in South Asia*, 4 (2): 298–307.

Azam, Kousar J. (2018), *Languages and Literary Cultures in Hyderabad*, London and New York: Routledge.

Bailkin, Jordanna (2015), 'Where Did the Empire Go? Archives and Decolonization in Britain', *The American Historical Review*, 120 (3): 884–99.

Baumer, Bettina, ed. (2003), *Kalātattvakośa: A Lexicon of Fundamental Concepts of the Indian Arts. Space and Time: Deśa-kāla. Vol. II*, New Delhi: Indira Gandhi National Centre for the Arts and Motilal Banarsidass Publishers.

Bhandarkar, Ramkrishan Gopal (1895), *Early History of the Dekkan: Down to the Mahomedan Conquest*, Bombay: Government Central Press.

Bose, Chandan (2019), *Perspectives on Work, Home, and Identity from Artisans in Telangana: Conversations around Craft*, Cham: Palgrave Macmillan.

Chakrabarty, Dipesh (1998), 'Minority Histories, Subaltern Pasts', *Economic and Political Weekly*, 33 (9): 473–9.

Chakrabarty, Dipesh (2000), *Provincializing Europe: Postcolonial Thought and Historical Difference*, Princeton and Oxford: Princeton University Press.

Clifford, James (1997), *Routes: Travel and Translation in the Late Twentieth Century*. Cambridge: Massachusetts Harvard University Press.

Das, Diganta Kumar (2016), 'Sub-national Neoliberalism through City Restructuring and Policy Boosterism: The Case of Hyderabad, India', in June Wang, Tim Oakes and Yang Yang (eds), *Making Cultural Cities in Asia: Mobility, Assemblage, and the Politics of Aspirational Urbanism*, 53–68, Abingdon and New York: Routledge.

Davis, Richard H. (1997), *Lives of Indian Images*, Princeton: Princeton University Press.

Dayal, Subah (2017), 'Vernacular Conquest? A Persian Patron and His Image in the Seventeenth-Century Deccan', *Comparative Studies of South Asia, Africa and the Middle East*, 37 (3): 549–69.

Devare, T. N. (2018), *A Short History of Persian Literature: At the Bahmani, the Adilshahi and the Qutbshahi Courts – Deccan*, Abingdon and New York: Routledge.

Eaton, Richard (2005), *A Social History of the Deccan, 1300–1761: Eight Indian Lives*, Cambridge: Cambridge University Press.

Eaton, Richard M. and Phillip B. Wagoner (2014), *Power, Memory, Architecture: Contested Sites on India's Deccan Plateau, 1300–1600*, Delhi: Oxford University Press.

Faruqui, Munis D. (2013), 'At Empire's End: The Nizam, Hyderabad and Eighteenth-Century India', in Richard M. Eaton, Munis D. Faruqui, David Gilmartin and Sunil Kumar (eds), *Expanding Frontiers in South Asian and World History: Essays in Honour of John F. Richards*, 1–38, New Delhi: Cambridge University Press.

Flatt, Emma J. (2019), *The Courts of the Deccan Sultanates: Living Well in the Persian Cosmopolis*, Cambridge: Cambridge University Press.

Flood, Finbarr Barry (2009), *Objects of Translation: Material Culture and Medieval 'Hindu-Muslim' Encounter*, Oxford and Princeton: Princeton University Press.

Ghosh, Baishali (2019), 'Recovering Local Agency and Technology in the Trans-Roman-Deccani Trade', *World History Connected*, 18 (3). Available online: https://doi.org/10.13021/whc.v18i3.3592 (accessed 14 September 2024).

Government of India, 'National Digital Repository for Museums of India' in https://www.india.gov.in/spotlight/national-digital-repository-museums-india (accessed 14 February 2023).

Green, Nile, ed. (2006), *Indian Sufism since the Seventeenth Century: Saints, Books and Empires in the Muslim Deccan*, New York: Routledge.

Gribble, J. D. B. (1896), A History of the Deccan, London: Luzac & Co.

Granoff, Phyllis (2004), 'Luxury Goods and Intellectual History: The Case of Printed and Woven Multicolored Textiles in Medieval India', *Ars Orientalis*, 34: 151–71.

Guha, Ranajit (2009), 'The Small Voice of History', in Partha Chatterjee (ed.), *The Small Voice of History: Collected Essays*, 304–17, Ranikhet: Permanent Black.

Gullapalli, Praveena (2009), 'Early Metal in South India: Copper and Iron in Megalithic Contexts', *Journal of World Prehistory*, 22: 439–59.

Haidar, Navina Najat and Marika Sardar, eds (2011), *Sultans of the South: Arts of India's Deccan Courts, 1323–1687*, New York: Metropolitan Museum of Art.

Haidar, Navina Najat and Marika Sardar, eds (2015), *Sultans of Deccan India, 1500–1700: opulence and fantasy*, New York: Metropolitan Museum of Art.

Haig, T. W. (1907–8), 'Inscriptions in Hyderabad Golconda', in E. Denison Ross (ed.) Epigraphia Indo–Moslemica Vol. 1, 23–9, Bombay: Education Society Press and The Government of India.

Houghteling, Sylvia (2018), 'Sentiment in Silks: Safavid Figural Textiles in Mughal Courtly Culture', in Kishwar Rizvi (ed.), *Affect, Emotion,* and *Subjectivity in Early Modern Muslim Empires: New Studies in Ottoman, Safavid, and Mughal Art and Culture*, 124–47, Leiden and Boston, MA: Brill.

Howes, David (2003), *Sensual Relations: Engaging the Senses in Culture and Social Theory*, Ann Arbor: The University of Michigan Press.

Hutton, Deborah (2012), 'The Use of Imaginary Landscape in Paintings from Bijapur', in Daud Ali and Emma J. Flatt (eds), *Garden and Landscape Practices in Precolonial India: Histories from the Deccan*, 127–47, New Delhi: Routledge.

Juneja, Monica (2012), 'Preface', in Daud Ali and Emma J. Flatt (eds), *Garden and Landscape Practices in Pre-Colonial India: Histories from the Deccan*, xix–xxii, New Delhi: Routledge.

Kaligotla, Subhashini (2016), 'Beyond Borderland: Claiming a Conceptual Space for Early Deccan Buildings', *Getty Research Journal*, 8: 1–16.

Kanalu, Naveen (2016), 'Pirla Panduga: Muharram Practices of the Deccan Weavers, Their Migrations, Songs and Memories', in Vijaya Ramaswamy (ed.), *Migrations in Medieval and Early Colonial India*, 129–64, London and New York: Routledge.

Khalidi, Omar (2009), *A Guide to Architecture in Hyderabad, Deccan, India*, Cambridge, MA: Aga Khan Programme for Islamic Architecture and Massachusetts Institute of Technology.

Kugle, Scott (2016), *When Sun Meets Moon: Gender, Eros, and Ecstasy in Urdu Poetry*, Chapel Hill: University of North Carolina Press.

Kumar, Amit (2022), *Precious Threads and Precarious Lives: Histories of Shawl and Silk Industries of Kashmir, 1846–1950*, London and New York: Routledge.

Lambourn, Elizabeth A. (2010), 'A Self-Conscious Art? Seeing Micro-Architecture in Sultanate South Asia', *Muqarnas*, 27 (1): 121–56.

Lodhi, Abdulaziz Y. (2008), 'Linguistic Evidence of Bantu Origins of the Siddis of India', in K. K. Prasad and J. P. Angenot (eds), *TADIA, the African Diaspora in Asia, Explorations on a Less Known Fact*, 301–313, Bangalore: Jana Jagrati Prakashana.

Mara, Anjali (2018), 'Now, Smart Museums to Give Virtual Tours and 3D View of Rare Artifacts', *The Indian Express*, 15 February. Available online: https://www.cdac.in/index.aspx?id=pk_itn_spot1098 (accessed 5 October 2021).

Mbembe, Achille (2002), 'The Power of the Archive and its Limits', in Carolyn Hamilton, Verne Harris, Jane Taylor, Michele Pickover, Graeme Reid & Razia Saleh (eds), *Refiguring the archive*, 19–26, Dordrecht: Kluwer Academic Publishers.

Meister, Michael W. (1979), 'Juncture and Conjuncture: Punning and Temple Architecture', *Artibus Asiae*, 41 (2/3): 226–34.

Messier, Philippe (2018), 'Stones and Codes in Hyderabad Building Technologies and the Work of a New State', PhD Thesis, Montreal: McGill University.

Michell, George (1995), *The New Cambridge History of India: Art and Architecture of Southern India, Vijayanagara and the Successor States 1350–1750*, Cambridge: Cambridge University Press.

Michell, George and Mark Zebrowski (1999), *Architecture and Art of the Deccan Sultanates*, Cambridge: Cambridge University Press.

Mignolo, Walter D. (2002), 'The Many Faces of Cosmo-polis: Border Thinking and Critical Cosmopolitanism', in Carol A. Breckenridge, Sheldon Pollock, Homi K. Bhabha and Dipesh Chakrabarty (eds), *Cosmopolitanism*, 157–87, Durham, NC, and London: Duke University Press.

Mittal, Jagdish (2013), *Deccani Scroll paintings in the Jagdish and Kamla Mittal Museum of Indian Art*, Hyderabad: Jagdish and Kamla Mittal Museum of Indian Art.

Mohammad, Afsar (2013), *The Festival of Pirs: Popular Islam and Shared Devotion in South India*, Oxford: Oxford University Press.

Moodie, Deonnie (2018), The *Making of a Modern Temple and a Hindu City: Kālīghāṭ and Kolkata*, Oxford: Oxford University Press.

Morrison, Kathleen D. (2016), 'On Putting Time in its Place: Archaeological Practice and Politics of Time in Southern India', *Cambridge Archaeological Journal*, 26 (4): 619–41.

Mukherjee, Anushyama (2017), 'Gulf Migration and the Flows of Social Remittances: A Study of Barkas in Hyderabad', *Sociological Bulletin*, 66 (1): 91–103.

Nanisetti, Serish (2019), 'Link to city's evolution snapped', *The Hindu*, 16 July. Available online: https://www.thehindu.com/news/cities/Hyderabad/link-to-citys-evolution-snapped/article28454264.ece (accessed 14 September 2024).

Nochlin, Linda (1989), *The Politics of Vision: Essays on Nineteenth-Century Art and Society*, New York: Harper & Row, Publishers.

Overton, Keelan, ed. (2020), *Iran and the Deccan: Persianate Art, Culture, and Talent in Circulation, 1400–1700*, Bloomington: Indiana University Press.

Patel, Alka (2012), 'Mercantile Architectural Patronage in Hyderabad, Late 18th–19th Centuries', in Alka Patel and Karen Leonard (eds), *Indo-Muslim Cultures in Transition*, 139–64, Leiden and Boston, MA: Brill.

Perks, Robert and Alistair Thomson, eds (2015), *The Oral History Reader*, London: Routledge.

Prakash, Om (2004), 'The Indian Maritime Merchant, 1500–1800', *Journal of the Economic and Social History of the Orient*, 47 (3): 436–50.

Purushotham, Sunil (2015), 'Internal Violence: The "Police Action" in Hyderabad', *Comparative Studies in Society and History*, 57 (2): 435–66.

Rafi, Ashraf (2018), 'Dakhni Literature: History, Culture and Linguistic Exchanges', in Kousar J. Azam (ed.), *Languages and Literary Cultures in Hyderabad*, 155–62, London and New York: Routledge.

Ramachandraiah, C. and Sheela Prasad (2004), 'Impact of Urban Growth on Water Bodies: The Case of Hyderabad', Working Paper No. 60, Centre for Economic and Social Studies, Hyderabad.

Ramaswami, Preeti Bahadur and Kavita Singh (2015), *Nauras: The Many Arts of the Deccan*, New Delhi: National Museum.

Rao, M. Pratap (1990), *Planning for Metropolitan Cities: A Suggestive Approach*, New Delhi: Concept Publishing Company.

Rewati, Rau (2021), 'Take a Trip to Mumbai Airport's "Jaya He Museum" Using This App', The New Indian Express, 31 January. Available online: https://www.newindianexpress.com/nation/2021/jan/31/take-a-trip-tomumbai-airports-jaya-he-museum-usingthis-app-2256330.html (accessed 5 October 2021).

Reddy, P. Chenna (1991), *Guilds in Medieval Āndhra Dēśa: A.D. 1000 to A.D. 1500*, New Delhi: Sandeep Prakashan.

Rizvi, Kishwar, ed. (2018), *Affect, Emotion, and Subjectivity in Early Modern Muslim Empires: New Studies in Ottoman, Safavid, and Mughal Art and Culture*, Leiden and Boston, MA: Brill.

Rocco, Sha (1929), *Golconda and the Qutb Shahs*, Hyderabad–Deccan: Government Central Press, 1929.

Roy, Tirthankar (2007), 'Out of Tradition: Master Artisans and Economic Change in Colonial India', *The Journal of Asian Studies*, 66 (4): 963–91.

Ruggles, D. Fairchild and Helaine Silverman, eds (2009), *Intangible Heritage Embodied*, New York: Springer.

Sardar, Marika (2011), 'The Early Foundations of Golconda and the Rise of Fortifications in the Fourteenth-Century Deccan', *South Asian Studies*, 27 (1): 25–50.

Sen, Aloka Parasher (2020), *Settlement and Local Histories of the Early Deccan*, New Delhi: Monohar.

Sengupta, Rajarshi (2019), 'Performing Histories: Enduring Dyes and Waterways in Artisanal Lives', *Journal of Textile Design Research and Practice*, 8 (3): 335–57.

Seremetakis, Constantina Nadia, ed. (1994), *The Senses Still: Perception and Memory as Material Culture in Modernity*, Boulder, CO: Westview Press.

Sewell, Robert (1900), *A Forgotten Empire (Vijayanagar): A Contribution to the History of India*, London: Swan Sonnenschein.

Shaheen, Shagufta and Sajjad Shahid (2018), 'The Unique Literary Traditions of Dakhni', in Kousar J. Azam (ed.), *Languages and Literary Cultures in Hyderabad*, 89–154, London and New York: Routledge.

Shalem, Avinoam (2012), 'What Do We Mean When We Say "Islamic Art"? A Plea for a Critical Rewriting of the History of the Arts of Islam', *The Journal of Art Historiography*, 6 (AS/1): 1–18.

Sharma, R. S. (2018), 'A Tentative Paradigm for the Study of Languages and Literary Cultures in Hyderabad City', in Kousar J. Azam (ed.), *Languages and Literary Cultures in Hyderabad*, 21–34, London and New York: Routledge.

Shekhar, Hansda Sowvendra (2015), The *Adivasi Will Not Dance: Stories*, Kindle version, New Delhi: Speaking Tiger. (downloaded 5 May 2016).

Snehi, Yogesh (2018), 'Spatiality, Memory and Street Shrines of Amritsar', *South Asia Multidisciplinary Academic Journal*, 18. Available online: https://doi.org/10.4000/samaj.4559 (accessed 5 May 2021).

Sohoni, Pushkar (2018), 'Imbrication and Implication: Early Maratha Architecture and the Deccan Sultanates', *Archives of Asian Art*, 68 (1): 33–46.

Srinivas, Tulasi (2018), *The Cow in the Elevator: An Anthropology of Wonder*, Durham, NC: Duke University Press.

Srinivasan, Sharada (1994), 'Wootz Crucible Steel: A Newly Discovered Production Site in South India', *Institute of Archaeology*, 5 (1): 49–59.

Subbarao, Bendapudi (1955), 'Chalcolithic Blade Industry of Maheshvar (Central India) and a Note of the History of the Technique', *Bulletin of the Deccan College Research Institute*, 17 (2): 126–49.

Subbarao, Bendapudi (1958), *The Personality of India: A Study in the Development of Material Culture of India and Pakistan*, M.S. University Archaeology Series 3, Baroda: Faculty of Arts, Maharaja Sayajirao University of Baroda.

Subrahmanyam, Sanjay (1997), 'Connected Histories: Notes towards a Reconfiguration of Early Modern Eurasia', *Modern Asian Studies*, 31 (3): 735–62.

Subramanyam, Sanjay (2017), *Europe's India: Words, People, Empires, 1500–1800*, Cambridge, MA, and London: Harvard University Press.

Taussig, Michael (1993), *Mimesis and Alterity: A Particular History of the Senses*, London and New York: Routledge.

Tayob, Huda (2021), 'Unconfessed Architectures', *e-flux Architecture*, June. Available online: https://www.e-flux.com/architecture/survivance/386349/unconfessed-architectures/ (accessed 27 October 2023).

The Economic Times (2021), 'National Archives a Heritage Building, Won't Be Demolished; National Museum to Be Shifted', 31 May. Available online: https://economictimes.indiatimes.com/news/india/national-archives-a-heritage-building-wont-be-demolished-national-museum-to-be-shifted/articleshow/83117409.cms (accessed 5 October 2021).

The Guardian, 'National Gallery of Australia to Return 14 Artworks Worth $3m to India', 29 July. Available online: https://www.theguardian.com/australia-news/2021/jul/29/national-gallery-of-australia-to-return-14-artworks-worth-3m-to-india (accessed 5 October 2021).

Tiwari, Mayank (2021), 'Hidden in Plain Sight', *The New Indian Express*, 13 July. Available online: https://www.newindianexpress.com/hyderabad/2021/Jul/13/hiddenin-plain-sight-2329249.html (accessed 14 September 2024).

TNN (2015), 'Archaeologists to Spread Out for More Iron Age Proof', *The Times of India*, 19 May. Available online: https://timesofindia.indiatimes.com/city/hyderabad/archaeologists-to-spread-out-for-more-iron-age-proof/articleshow/47336026.cms (accessed 14 September 2024).

Turner, Victor W. and M. Edward, eds (1986), *The Anthropology of Experience*, Urbana: University of Illinois Press.

Varadarajan, Lotika (1993), 'Indian Boat Building Traditions. The Ethnological Evidence', *Topoi*, 3 (2): 547–68.

Varma, Anand Raj (2018), 'Localities as Reflections of Linguistic Cultures of Hyderabad', in Kousar J Azam (ed.), *Languages and Literary Cultures in Hyderabad*, 171–86, London and New York: Routledge.

Wagoner, Philip B. (1996), '"Sultan among Hindu Kings": Dress, Titles, and the Islamicization of Hindu Culture at Vijayanagara', *Journal of Asian Studies*, 55 (4): 851–80.

Wagoner, Philip B. and Laura Weinstein (2017), 'The Deccani Sultanates and Their Interregional Connections', in Finbarr Barry Flood and Gülru Necipoğlu (eds), *A Companion to Islamic Art and Architecture*, 777–804, Hoboken, NJ: Wiley Blackwell.

Wheeler, R. E. M., A. Ghosh and Krishna Deva (1946), 'Arikamedu: An Indo-Roman Trading-Station on the East Coast of India', Ancient India: Bulletin of the Archaeological Survey of India, 2 (July):17–124.

Wheeler, R. E. M. (1984), 'Brahmagiri and Chandravalli 1947: Megalithic and Other Cultures in Mysore State', Ancient India: Bulletin of the Archaeological Survey of India, 4 (July 1947–January 1948):181–310.

Yazdani, Ghulam (1917), *The Antiquities of Bidar*, Calcutta: Baptist Mission Press.

Yazdani, Ghulam (1930), *Guide to Ajanta Frescoes*, Hyderabad: Archaeological Department H.E.H. The Nizam's Government.

Yazdani, Ghulam (1944), *Hyderabad: A Souvenir*, Hyderabad: Government Central Press.

Yimene, Ababu Minda (2007), 'Dynamics of Ethnic Identity among the Siddis of Hyderabad', *African and Asian Studies*, 6 (3): 321–45.

1

Buddhist Material at the State Museum, Hyderabad: Between Negotiation and Repatriation

Prajnna Vedavyas

Introduction

At the heart of Hyderabad's Public Garden Complex stands the Telangana State Archaeology Museum, formerly known as the Hyderabad Museum and then as the Dr. Y. S. Rajasekhara Reddy Andhra Pradesh State Museum. In this chapter, I simply address it as the State Museum (Figure 1.1) while I discuss the immediate impact of Andhra Pradesh (hereafter AP) state bifurcation on the museum. An integral section of the museum is the Buddhist collection spread across the Holy Relics Gallery, the Buddhist Sculpture Gallery and the Ajanta Frescoes Gallery, with more than fifty Buddhist sites to its credit, including Amaravati, Nagarjunakonda, Chandavaram, Phanigiri, Bavikonda and Kondapur. The long Buddhist legacy left a deep impact on the socio-cultural aspects and material culture of the Deccan; simultaneously, the bifurcation of AP and the formation of Telangana as a new state in 2014 transformed the State Museum's Buddhist collection into a contested subject. My fieldwork from 2013 to 2015 happened just after the bifurcation of the state; whomever I met in the Museum and its library had curiosity and sneaking suspicion because of the effect of the bifurcation. Set against this backdrop of the AP state bifurcation in

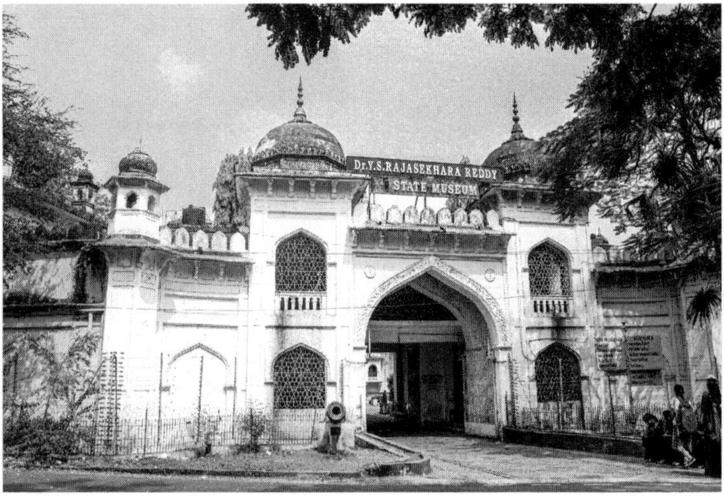

Figure 1.1 The Former Dr Y. S. Rajasekhara Reddy Andhra Pradesh State Museum, Now Telangana State Archaeology Museum (Front View), Public Gardens, Hyderabad-Deccan. Courtesy: Rituparna Roy, 2022.

2014, this chapter[1] examines the relationship between the formation of the Buddhist galleries and the formation of states, while focusing on the Buddhist past of the region, object histories and the display strategies of this government-run State Museum.

The Telugu and Marathi speaking regions of the Deccan witnessed the flourishing of Buddhism during the reign of the Buddhist Mauryan king Ashoka in the third century BCE (Singh 2008: 321–53), and of the Sātavāhanas or Andhras who effectively ruled the northern Deccan from the first century BCE to the third century CE (Omvedt 2003: 119–20; Shimada 2013: 1). The later Sātavāhanas ruled from Amaravati (the ancient city of Dhānyakaṭaka) in the Krishna River plains; they reconstructed the Great Stupa of the Ashokan era at Amaravati and developed the city as the prime Buddhist centre in the Deccan (Shimada 2013: 15–16; 2016: 1). The contribution of the Sātavāhanas in constructing Buddhist site in their metropolitan district attracted a large number of Buddhist merchants that perhaps had helped their region to prosper (Zin 2016: 46). Once, addressing a press conference, the then Andhra Pradesh Chief Minister Chandrababu Naidu highlighted the significance of Buddhism and the glory of the Sātavāhanas, and justified his claim to elect Amaravati as the site of the new state capital as a reminder to the people about their rich Buddhist heritage.[2] Under the Īkṣvāku dynasty, Nagarjunakonda, another key Buddhist site, rose to prominence (Shimada 2013: 47). The seventh-century Chinese traveller Xuanzang's travelogue confirms the rise of Shaivism and the existence of numerous Hindu temples in *Āndhradeśa* – the land inhabited by the Andhras; however, he also noted that the significance of Amaravati as a Buddhist site persisted (Omvedt 2003: 150, 156).

After a prolonged gap, during the colonial period, the renewal of the Buddhist histories was prompted by major archaeological excavations in South Asia, including the excavation of the Amaravati Stupa by Colonel Colin Mackenzie in 1797 (Howes 2002: 53–6). The expedition to the Ajanta caves, supervised by John Smith, a British Army official, in 1819 further expanded the scope of reclaiming Buddhist material culture in the Deccan (Sharma 2006: 121). A systematic documentation of this site, first by James E. Alexander and James Fergusson, and later by the then Director of the Archaeological Survey of India (ASI), Sir John Marshal, drew the Nizam's interest to this site. This led Ghulam Yazdani, the first Director of Archaeology of the Nizam's state, to further study and copy the murals of Ajanta in the early twentieth century (Yazdani 1930b; Sharma 2006: 128–31). Yazdani also published photographic reproductions of the Ajanta frescoes, bringing them to global audiences (Sharma 2006: 128).

Simultaneously, the revival of Buddhism in the late nineteenth century was also employed as a tool for social change. A Sri Lankan Buddhist revivalist, Anagarika Dharmapala, visited India in 1891 and played a pivotal role in restoring Bodh Gaya and taking Buddhism to a global platform by addressing the Parliament of World Religions in Chicago (Omvedt 2003: 234). Jyotiba Phule, an anti-caste social reformer from the Marathwada region, contested the Hindu ideology, opposed Brahmanical superiority, and demanded free and compulsory education for children from Dalit communities (Omvedt 2003: 231). The fight for social justice was further strengthened by Bhimrao Ambedkar's activism and its inseparable connection to Buddhist thought (Omvedt 2003: 235). After his intervention, Buddhism was renewed as 'Navayāna' and aligned with the three major sects of Buddhism: Hinayana, Mahayana and the Vajrayana (Omvedt 2003: 2). Bhagya Reddy Verma, BS Venkat Rao and Arigay Ramaswamy were important Dalit leaders in the Nizam's state (Omvedt 2003: 240; Ratnam 2008: 4). Bhagya Reddy Verma, a staunch supporter of Ambedkar, celebrated *Buddha Jayantī* (birthday of Buddha) in 1913 (Ratnam 2008: 4). As the struggle to overthrow the caste system continues, Buddhist teachings and thought remain relevant today in the Deccan and beyond. Thus, the entanglement of history, archaeology and regional politics imbued specificity to the development of Deccani Buddhism in the twentieth century. The establishment of the Archaeology Department of the princely state of Hyderabad in 1914 and subsequently the creation of a permanent display space for Buddhist relics and artefacts further intensified the ground for future debates in this area.[3]

The Museum of Shifting Identities

A palace built to restore the antiquities recovered from the Nizam's dominion in 1920 was converted into the Hyderabad Museum after Yazdani's suggestion in 1931 (Luther 2006). After the princely state was annexed to India, the Telangana region was joined with the Telugu-speaking regions of the Madras Presidency to form the state of Andhra Pradesh (AP) in 1956 (Sherman 2007: 489–516). Following this, the Hyderabad Museum acquired a new name, the Andhra Pradesh State Archaeology Museum. In 2009, the State Museum was renamed as the Dr. Y. S. Rajasekhara Reddy Andhra Pradesh State Museum (Figure 1.1) to honour the then recently deceased chief minister of the state who had died in a helicopter crash (Mungara 2013). Meanwhile, historian and heritage activist Sajjad Shahid demanded that the State Museum be named after Ghulam Yazdani as a reminder of his dedication to Deccani histories and archaeology (Shahid 2011). However, after the state bifurcation in 2014, the museum was renamed again – this time as the Telangana State Archaeology Museum.

The museums in South Asia, as Monica Juneja delineates (2015: XIII), are sites of 'specific negotiations, conceptual tensions, improvisations, and unpredictable affective resonances' due to our complicated relationship with the Western European modernity. Saloni Mathur and Kavita Singh foreground the ideas of the indigenization of museum spaces, by nurturing both the ritualistic connotations of historical objects as well as the promise of delivering education wrapped in wonderment, heavily contributed to the dynamism of these spaces. Museums such as the one under consideration, depart from the framework of Victorian pedagogy and the sovereignty of neoliberal states by remaining vulnerable to the political shifts in the region (Mathur and Singh 2015: 2–5). The museum stands between the secular state with its non-religious and civic symbols and the religious communities whose beliefs are embodied in specific museum artefacts. For example, since 2005, museum authorities have allowed Buddhist monks to worship the Buddhist relics from the collection on the occasion of *Buddha Pūrṇimā* (also known as *Buddha Jayantī*) every year within the gallery space. Now, owing to the state bifurcation, Buddhist communities residing in Andhra Pradesh have made claims over the holy Buddhist relics and other artefacts recovered from sites within the perimeter of their newly formed state (Mungara 2014). The tussle for repatriation of the Buddhist antiquities ties up the formation of new political identities of both states and claims over the rich Buddhist past of the region. While portable historical objects from the museum invited much debate in recent years, it is the site of the museum which silently bears witness to the contingent socio-political shifts.

The demand for repatriation of antiquities has strong links with the displacement of the remains of the Great Stupa, Amaravati; the majority of the Amaravati Stupa's remains are now dispersed across the British Museum and the Government Museum in Chennai. The near impossibility of bringing them back to AP has contributed to the urgency for transporting the Buddhist antiquities from the neighbouring state. In June 2014, Chandana Khan, the then special chief secretary (Tourism and Culture) for AP, convened a meeting in Hyderabad to frame guidelines for bifurcation of artefacts in various museums (Mungara 2014). The meeting concluded that to split museum artefacts, there was to be formed a special committee with a senior official of the Archaeological Survey of India and representatives from Telangana and AP. However, the process plunged into uncertainty as the committee was unable to find a native of Andhra or Telangana who could assume the role of a chairperson by winning the approval of both states (Pisharody 2014; Sankar 2015). The erstwhile Director of the Department of Archaeology and Museums of AP, G. V. Ramakrishna Rao, suggested that the states divide the artefacts as per their records in the accession register whether it was excavated, received as donation, purchased or found as treasure trove. He also suggested that in cases of unknown provenance, artefacts could be divided as per a bifurcation ratio. The distribution of the artefacts or the claim on the Buddhist pasts of the Deccan by both states came to rely upon the acquisition records and the year of foundation of AP. As several artefacts in the State Museum stand on the verge of another displacement, there is a compelling case to reassess the politics of belonging shaped by geographical perimeters.

Conundrums of Repatriation

Within the State Museum, the Holy Relics Gallery, the Buddhist Sculpture Gallery and the Ajanta Frescoes Gallery (Figure 1.2) present the multifaceted state of Buddhism: from the overlapping of the sacred and the secular to the intertwining of the archaeological excavations and regional politics. The first gallery and the Buddhist sculptures in the museum are the most vulnerable to possible transformations due to the bifurcation. My attempt here will be to furnish these entangled narratives connecting the acquisition of the artefacts, their display, viewers' engagement and the demands for repatriation.

The Holy Relics Gallery (Figure 1.3) is a rectangular south-facing hall that displays the relics of Buddha from the site of Mahācaitya (a large congregational site with one or mulitple stupas) at Bavikonda, Vishakhapatnam: a Khondalite stone reliquary encasing an earthen urn from the south of Mahācaitya, and three urns excavated from the other three cardinal directions. Belonging to the third century BCE, the urns contain charcoal, ash, gold and silver caskets, precious and semi-precious beads, and a piece of bone – possibly belonging to Shakyamuni (Prasad and Pachauri 1993: 4–9). Posed in the backdrop of a white marble sculpture of Buddha placed at the centre of a large relief depicting a stupa on the northern wall of the gallery, the sacred urns from Bavikonda

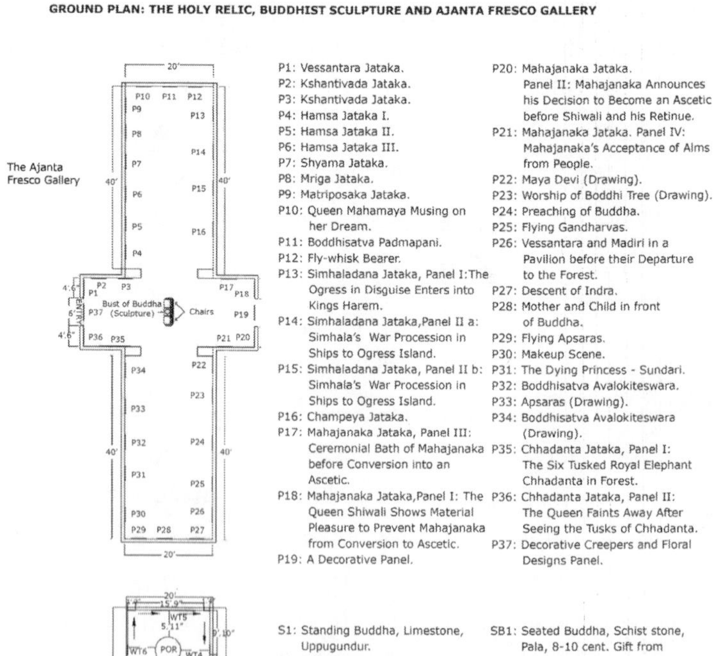

Figure 1.2 The Ground Plans of the Three Buddhist Galleries in the State Museum. Courtesy: D. S. Jayaprakash, Bijay Nath and Prajnna Vedavyas, 2021.

are presently displayed inside a bulletproof glass replica of the stupa placed on a circular white marble platform evoking the bases of the hemispherical stupas. On the marble platform, the urns are arranged

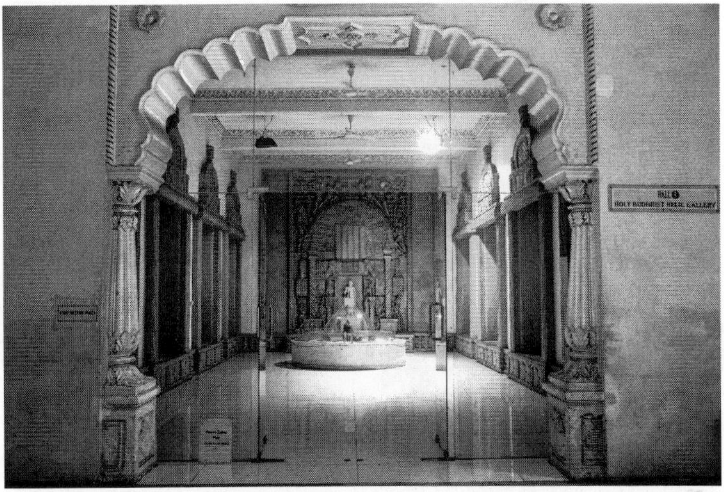

Figure 1.3 The Holy Relics Gallery (Outside and Inside View), The State Museum, Hyderabad-Deccan. Courtesy: Rituparna Roy, 2022.

according to their placement at the site of excavation, while the stone reliquary is positioned at the centre. Upon the marble slab, thin rectangular boards wrapped in sacred saffron cloth constitute the bases for the urns (Figure 1.4). The overall display closely resembles a Buddhist stupa, perhaps to nurture a strong tie between the site of Mahācaitya at Bavikonda and the State Museum. The holy relics were not put on display until they were first permitted to be worshipped on *Buddha Pūrṇimā* at the State Museum on 23 May 2005.[4] A text with information pertaining to this history is also displayed on the eastern interior wall near the entrance of the Holy Relics Gallery. On the occasion of *Buddha Pūrṇimā*, the relics were taken out of the State Museum in a procession by the Buddhist monks around the city. Soon thereafter, on 2 January 2006, the relics were covered with the bulletproof glass dome presently on display, and their public viewing was inaugurated by His Highness the Dalai Lama.[5] Since then, Buddhist monks worship the relics within the gallery on *Buddha Pūrṇimā* every year by adorning the protective glass stupa with flowers and lighting lamps.[6] While the

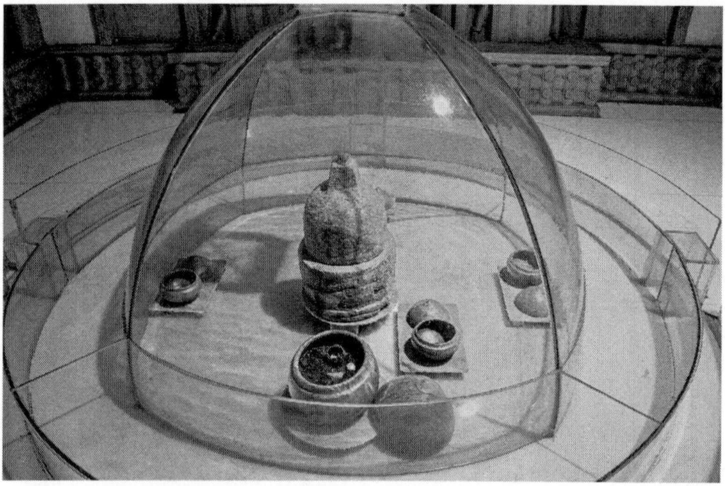

Figure 1.4 The Buddhist Relics inside the Glass Dome, The State Museum, Hyderabad-Deccan. Courtesy: Rituparna Roy, 2022.

archaeological relevance of the excavated material is acknowledged, it is the sacred aspects of the antiquities which are celebrated in this gallery; this is why entering the gallery with footwear is prohibited.

The sanctity of the key object of veneration in this gallery is further enhanced by the relief depicting the stupa, the standing Buddha, and wall hangings containing information on Buddhism as well as the sites. The complementary relationship between these objects within the space would be disrupted if the holy relics are removed. As these relics belong to the Andhra region and were acquired long after 1956, there is a strong possibility of their repatriation to AP, more so because the public and religious practitioners support this claim. During an interview, a Buddhist monk, Ven Khemachara Thero, stated that a large number of monks from the ancient *Āndhradeśa* had participated in the historic third Buddhist Council around 250 BCE; since then, the Andhra region has played a crucial role in shaping Buddhist histories (Interview with Ven Khemachara Thero in Hyderabad, February 2015). Whereas his comment on historicity cannot be separated from the narratives furnished by the modern states, it prompted envisioning an alternative display plan for the gallery. Meanwhile, an earthen urn with a silver container was excavated from the Mahācaitya of Phanigiri, Telangana, in 2015 (Akbar 2015). The container carried, according to B. Srinivas, at the time the Director of the former Department of Archaeology and Museums (at present known as Department of Heritage, Telangana) a few personal belongings of a chief Buddhist monk, such as eleven miniature beads, three silver and three thin flower petals (Akbar 2015). Srinivas also noted it was the first time that a Buddhist antiquity of such stature was excavated from the Telangana region (Akbar 2015). One cannot help but ask – will the excavated urn from Phanigiri in Telangana region emerge as a potential replacement of the relics from Bavikonda? Will the identity of this gallery be negotiated if the repatriation is implemented?

The north-facing Buddhist Sculpture Gallery has the same dimensions as the Holy Relics Gallery. The corridor between these two galleries houses four Buddhist sculptures, setting up a palpable visual connection between the two exhibition halls. Out of the fifty-seven Buddhist sculptures displayed in the museum, fifty-one are situated in the Buddhist Sculpture Gallery. The sculptures are arranged in three straight rows and placed above cement pedestals, except the Gandhara and Pala sculptures from the middle row, which are showcased in glass boxes supported by wooden pedestals (Figure 1.5). The sculptures are randomly displayed – neither according to their provenance nor according to their time period. Based on their acquisition records, the distribution of the sculptures in this gallery might not be affected if repatriation is underway; nevertheless, the provenance records of the sculptures from the museum collection present enthralling narratives of their acquisition, traversing through the recently drawn boundaries of the two Telugu-speaking states of southern India.

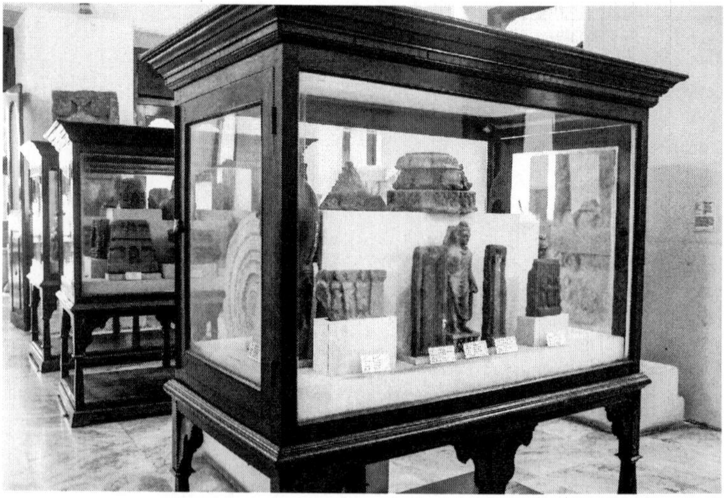

Figure 1.5 The Buddhist Sculptures from the Gandhara and Pala Period Preserved in the Glass Boxes Framed and Supported by Wooden Leg-pedestals in Buddhist Sculpture Gallery, The State Museum, Hyderabad-Deccan. Courtesy: Rituparna Roy, 2022.

Among the fifty-seven Buddhist sculptures in the museum, forty-six were acquired as gifts (Kedareswari 2005: 3). There are six Amaravati sculptures, gifted by the Madras Presidency; fifteen Gandhara sculptures (schist stones, second century BCE) and twenty-five Pala sculptures (schist stones and sandstones, ninth to tenth century CE) were gifted by the Indian Museum, Calcutta. They all were received during the Nizam's rule in 1919–20, so the possibility of their redistribution can be ruled out. Unlike them, four sculptures (dome panels, first century BCE to the third century CE) excavated between 1972 and 1975 at Chandavaram, Andhra Pradesh (Kedareswari 2005: 5–7), and two limestone sculptures from Uppugundur, Andhra Pradesh, might be considered for repatriation. Out of the two sculptures of Uppugundur, there is a mighty Standing Buddha acquired in 1961 (Ghosh 1964: 108, PLATE CLIX A), whereas the other one is a 'Dome Panel' with no excavation records.

The sculptures from Nelakondapalli and Phanigiri show the deep impact of Buddhism on the Telangana region. Two exhibited sculptures (one limestone and one marble) of Standing Buddha (third century CE) from Nelakondapalli were possibly excavated during 1976–82 (Thapar 1980a: 5; Thapar 1980b: 3; Kedareswari 2005: 7–8). Among the two sculptures from Phanigiri, there is an extraordinary vertical 'Buddhist Panel' (Figure 1.6), known as the 'Turban Relief of Phanigiri' (A/c no. 2003-270) dating back to the first century CE, which was excavated in 2003 (Ahuja 2021: 188).

Divided in three horizontal registers, the 'Turban Relief of Phanigiri' (Figure 1.6) intricately modelled panel depicts Buddha in two narrative scenes; the bottom register shows his departure from the royal palace; the middle register above depicts Buddha seated in the *sukhasana* posture being venerated by devotees and the register above transforms into a crown shape that depicts some euphoric people carrying the crown which prince Siddhartha had tossed away in order to reject his life as a prince according to the familiar story 'The Great Departure' (Ahuja 2021: 188). After this panel was excavated, it was stolen from Phanigiri in September 2003, but later recovered by the police from Dachepalli (Guntur district, Andhra Pradesh) in October 2003 (Becker 2015: 92–4; Ahuja 2021: 206–7). Unfortunately, it was found broken and had to be reassembled before relocating it to the State Museum. This magnificent antiquity was also uniquely preferred as if a jewel in the crown to become a part of display in the *India and the World Exhibition* at Chhatrapati Shivaji Maharaj Vastu Sangrahalaya, Mumbai in 2017–18 (Ahuja 2021: 207). Another displayed sculpture from Phanigiri is a 'Railing Piece', belonging to the first century CE, was found during an excavation at the site in 1941 (Subrahmanyam et al. 2008: 3–5). Even though these sculptures of Nelakondapalli and Phanigiri are not considered for redistribution, they ask us to rethink the relationship between the notion of *Āndhradeśa* and the present-day boundaries of states.

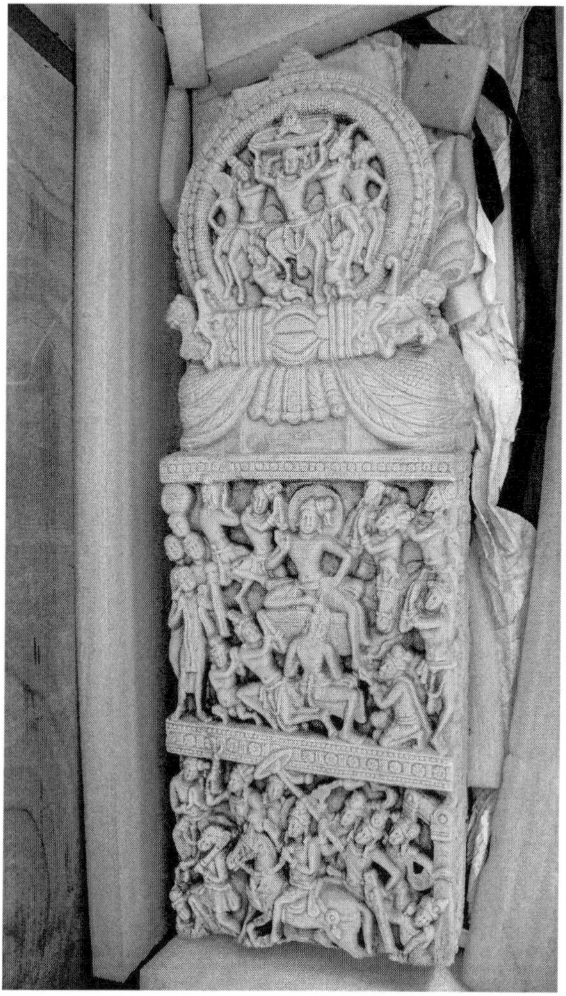

Figure 1.6 The Buddhist Panel, Known as the 'Turban Relief of Phanigiri', First Century CE, Limestone, 127 × 43 cm, Phanigiri, Nalgonda District, Telangana (Accession Number: 2003–270), The State Museum, Hyderabad-Deccan. Courtesy: Rituparna Roy, 2022.

Annual Buddhist rituals and events entail the moving of antiquities between Hyderabad, Amaravati and Nagarjunakonda, which gained momentum in the light of the bifurcation. Amaravati is considered sacred as it is widely believed that Lord Buddha initiated the *Kālacakra* (wheel of time) tantric teaching at this very site. During the annual commemoration of this sacred event on 7 December 2005, thirteen Amaravati sculptures from the State Museum were lent to the Amaravati Museum.[7] Despite their AP provenance, the Amaravati sculptures are claimed to return to the State Museum as they were gifted by the Madras Presidency in the year 1919–20 during the reign of the Nizam (Suares 2014). It is anticipated that these thirteen sculptures will be returned to the State Museum. Upon examination, it was also found that a total of ninety-five Buddhist sculptures, including some gift-sculptures of Amaravati, along with the Gandhara and Pala sculptures and others, excavated by the AP Archaeology Department, had been shifted from the State Museum to the Buddha Vanam Project Museum, Nagarjunakonda, AP, on 31 March 2013.[8] Concerning some complaints about the suspicious shift of Buddhist sculptures, the then Assistant Director of the Buddha Vanam Museum, D. Ramulu Naik, confirmed that all the ninety-five sculptures were safe and had been put on display at their new venue (Interview with D. Ramulu Naik, at that time the Assistant Director of the Buddha Vanam Museum in Hyderabad, January 2015).

Unlike the two connected galleries discussed above, the Ajanta Frescoes Gallery (Figures 1.2 and 1.7) embodies a distinct flavour. Thirty-seven carefully mounted direct eye-copies of the Ajanta frescoes made under the patronage of the seventh Nizam of Hyderabad are on display here. The gallery consists of two rectangular chambers, attached on either side by a rectangular corridor. Each of the chambers exhibits thirteen Ajanta-copy paintings on canvas and the corridor has additional eleven paintings. The images in the paintings are not that clearly visible due to insufficient light, ironically echoing the dimly lit interiors of the grottoes. Whereas the Holy Relics Gallery has a strong ritualistic implication, and the sculpture gallery is somewhat in between the sacred and the secular, the frescoes gallery narrates a specific history of the Hyderabad

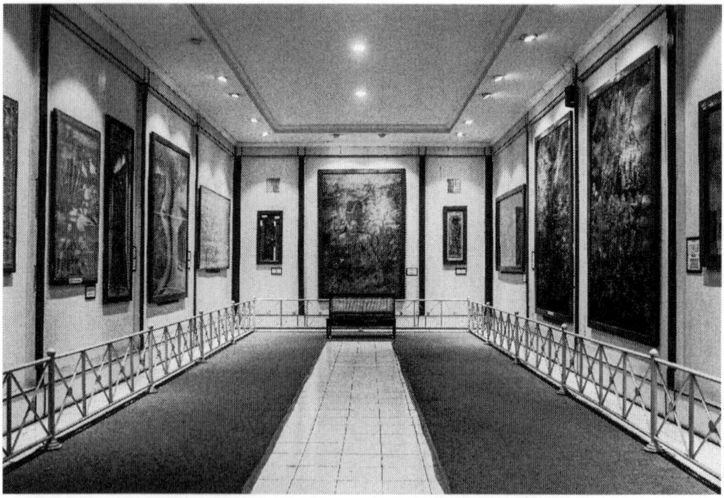

Figure 1.7 Ajanta Frescoes Gallery (Right Chamber), The State Museum, Hyderabad-Deccan. Courtesy: Rituparna Roy, 2022.

State's involvement in retrieving the architectural and artistic pasts of Ajanta. With deep concern for the deteriorating state of the Ajanta frescoes, Sir John Marshal, the then Director General of Archaeological Survey of India, visited Ajanta in 1915 and examined the paintings for conservation (Yazdani 1916: 5). In 1918, Signor L. Cecconi from Italy was given the responsibility of restoring the historic frescoes. In the same year, there were discussions on the conservations by three colour photographic reproductions of the frescoes (Yazdani 1920: 7–8). Signor L. Cecconi and his assistant Count Orsini began the restoration process of the cave-paintings in 1920 and continued till 1922 (Yazdani 1923: 14; 1926a: 7). This time around (1921–4) an artist named Syed Ahmad was employed to trace the outline drawings of Ajanta frescoes (Yazdani 1926b: 13). By 1926, his drawings became available in postcard size in the press at Oxford, where his skill was highly appreciated (Yazdani 1926b: 13–14; 1930a: 15). In 1936, Syed Ahmad was assisted by other two artists Jalal Uddin and Maulavi Nazir Muhammad (Yazdani 1939: 21–68).

Ghulam Yazdani has been credited with employing these artists to produce copies of the Ajanta cave-paintings for the Department's record, as it was he who persuaded the Nizam to employ them (Khan 2013). Between the years 1930 and 1955, Yazdani also produced his four-volume work, *Ajanta: The Colour and Monochrome*. The work reflects a complete history of Buddhist paintings of *Jataka* stories in the Ajanta caves and reproduction of Ajanta frescoes based on photography with illustrations and photographs. They also include some drawings of Syed Ahmad (Sharma 2006: 128). Yazdani could comprehend the great moral Buddhist ideologies; he pointed out in one of his volumes that the Buddhist teachings on the high ideals of self-control and depth of vision were deteriorating even as he clearly conveyed the *Jataka* stories embedded with morals of life, which are depicted on the Ajanta caves' walls (Sharma 2006: 129).

The reproduction of the Ajanta frescoes in fact was initiated by Robert Gill, commissioned by the Royal Asiatic Society, London, between 1844 and 1863. Unfortunately, they were destroyed in a fire in 1866 (Patel and Costaras 2006). After this, the Government of Bombay commissioned John Griffith to copy the frescoes (1872–85), but most of them were again destroyed in a fire in 1885. Finally, assisted by artists Nandalal Bose, Asit Kumar Haldar and Samarendranath Gupta from Bengal, Dorothy Larcher from England, and Syed Ahmad and Muhammad Fazl-ud-din from Hyderabad, Christiana Jane Herringham undertook the copying of the Ajanta frescoes in 1914–15 (Sharma 2006: 126). Syed Ahmad's dedication prompted Yazdani to produce a set of eye-copies of the frescoes (these eye-copies are presently on display at the gallery). The nineteenth-century copies of the frescoes by Robert Gill and John Griffith had been gutted by fire, and the rest of the copies are preserved at the Victoria and Albert Museum,

London (Patel and Costaras 2006). Yet, the paintings produced under Ghulam Yazdani's supervision hold their original virtue for posterity in India.

The Ajanta Frescoes Gallery does not face uncertainty over the bifurcation, because all the works are the 'copy works' of Buddhist sites produced under Hyderabad-based Nizam dominion. The remaining Buddhist artefacts' future, however, remains uncertain due to the dire state of preservation and unprepared transportation of the works to the Kalachakra Museum, Amaravati, and the Buddha Vanam Museum, Nagarjunakonda (Khan 2013; Sur 2018). The problems specific to these paintings allow us to comprehend that the threat of damage and displacement posed to the museum objects are not only due to the issue of redistribution but also might indicate deep-rooted problems within the management, which perhaps draw negligible public attention.

Conclusion

Through my analysis, I have argued that the basis of bifurcation or redistribution of antiquities is far more complicated than simply following their acquisition or excavation records. By allowing both pedagogical and ritualistic endeavours to flourish at the venue, the State Museum of the undivided and divided Andhra Pradesh, with the formation of the new state Telangana, assumed a unique identity based on negotiations. On account of their religious association, there is tremendous appeal in the idea of repatriating the Buddhist antiquities in the State Museum to their original sites. However, we must interpret the notion of origin with caution since, much like the State Museum, the idea of origin remains vulnerable to notions of statehood and collective identity.

Notes

1 I thank Kirtana Thangavelu, Sita Reddy, Santosh Sakhinala, B. Srinivas, V. Shuguna Sharma K. Vasanthi, D. S. Jayaprakash, Bijay Nath, A. Vijayashree, Tapan Kumar Pati, Amulya Kumar Mall and Rituparna Roy for their help during my fieldwork, and the editors for their critical edge, which inspired me to bring forth this essay.

2 *The New Indian Express* (2015), 'Its Official, New Andhra Pradesh Capital Is Named Amaravathi', 2 April.

3 The Department of Heritage Telangana, 'State Museum Hyderabad'. https://heritage.telangana.gov.in.

4 *The Hindu* (2005), 'Gearing up for Kalachakra', 24 May.

5 *The Hindu* (2005), 'Buddha's Relics to Add Attraction to State Archaeological Museum', 31 December.

6 *The Hindu* (2008), 'Buddhist Relics on Display at State Museum', 21 May.

7 The Head Office Letter No. H2/3353/2005 dated 5 December 2005, and State Museum Letter No. A/319/05 dated 7 December 2005.

8 Information as per the (1) Head Office Memo. No. F1/2058/2012 dated 22 February 2013, and (2) GO No. 965 of YAT & C (PMU) Dept. dated 22 December 2012, and the office of the Assistant Director Dr YSR AP State Museum Letter. No. Rc. No. A/22/2013 dated 19 March 2013.

References

Ahuja, Naman P., ed. (2021), *Phanigiri Interpreting an Ancient Buddhist Site in Telangana,* Mumbai: Marg Publications and Department of Heritage Telangana.

Akbar, Syed (2015), 'Rare Buddhist Relics Discovered in Nalgonda District', *The Times of India*, 8 January. Available online:https://timesofindia.indiatimes.com/city/hyderabad/rare-buddhist-relics-discovered-in-nalgonda-district/articleshow/45813715.cms (accessed 17 June 2024).

Becker, Catherine (2015), *Shifting Stones, Shaping the Past: Sculpture from the Buddhist Stupas of Andhra Pradesh*, New York: Oxford University Press.

Ghosh, A. (1964), *Indian Archaeology 1961–1962: A Review*, New Delhi: Archaeological Survey of India.

Howes, Jennifer (2002), 'Colin Mackenzie and the Stupa at Amaravati', *South Asian Studies*, 18 (1): 53–65.

Juneja, Monica (2015), 'Preface', in Saloni Mathur and Kavita Singh (eds), *No Touching, No Spitting, No Praying: The Museum in South Asia*, xiii–xiv, New Delhi: Routledge.

Kedareswari, J., ed. (2005), *The Buddhist Gallery Companion Guide Book*, Hyderabad: Department of Archaeology and Museums, Government of Andhra Pradesh.

Khan, Mir Ayoob Ali (2013), 'Museum's Ajanta cave paintings need upkeep', *The Times of India*, 11 May. Available Online: https://timesofindia.indiatimes.com/city/hyderabad/museums-ajanta-cave-paintings-need-upkeep/articleshow/19994905.cms (accessed 18 June 2024).

Luther, Narendra (2006), 'The Romance of Public Garden – I', *Narendra Luther Archives*, 6 December. Available online: http://narendralutherarchives.blogspot.com/2006/12/romance-of-public-garden-i.html (accessed 7 May 2020).

Mathur, Saloni and Kavita Singh (2015), *No Touching, No Spitting, No Praying: The Museum in South Asia*, New Delhi: Routledge.

Mungara, Sunil (2013), 'Telangana Effect: Hyderabad's Oldest Museum Faces Division', *Times of India*, 6 August. Available online:https://timesofindia.indiatimes.com/city/hyderabad/telanagana-effect-hyderabads-oldest-museum-faces-division/articleshow/21636203.cms (accessed 18 June 2024).

Mungara, Sunil (2014), 'For a Slice History', *The Times of India*, 1 July. Available online: https://timesofindia.indiatimes.com/city/hyderabad/for-a-slice-of-history/articleshow/37551126.cms (accessed 18 June 2024).

Omvedt, Gail (2003), *Buddhism in India: Challenging Brahmanism and Caste*, New Delhi & London: Sage Publications.

Patel, Divia and Nicola Costaras (2006), 'Conserving the Copies of the Ajanta Cave Paintings at the V&A', *Conservation Journal*, 52: 6–8.

http://www.vam.ac.uk/content/journals/conservation-journal/issue-52/conserving-the-copies-of-the-ajanta-cave-paintings-at-the-v-and-a/ (accessed 18 June 2024).

Pisharody, Rahul V. (2014), 'Now AP and TS Quarrel over Artefacts Sharing', *The New Indian Express*, 8 December. Available online:https://www.newindianexpress.com/states/telangana/2014/dec/08/Now-AP-and-TS-Quarrel-over-Artefacts-Sharing-691504.html (accessed 17 June 2024).

Prasad, NRV and S. K. Pachauri (1993), *Recent Buddhist Discoveries in Vishakhapatnam District A.P. Relic Caskets at Bavikonda*, Hyderabad: Department of Archaeology and Museums, Govt. of Andhra Pradesh.

Ratnam, K. Y. (2008), "The Dalit Movement and Democratization in Andhra Pradesh', *East-West Centre Washington Working Papers*, 13, Washington, DC: East-West Center. Available online: https://scholarspace.manoa.hawaii.edu/items/0b57f0d7-ca27-4f2f-acd2-b52ffae56816..

Sankar, KN Murali (2015), 'Andhra Pradesh, Telangana yet to Share Artefacts', *The Hindu*, 25 March. Available online: https://www.thehindu.com/news/national/andhra-pradesh/andhra-pradesh-telangana-yet-to-share-artefacts/article7030733.ece (accessed 18 June 2024).

Shahid, Sajjad (2011), 'Outstanding Scholar of Archaeology Ignored', *The Times of India*, 12 December. Available online: https://timesofindia.indiatimes.com/city/hyderabad/outstanding-scholar-of-archaeology-ignored/articleshow/11076258.cms (accessed 18 June 2024).

Sharma, Mandira (2006), 'Disquisitions on the Paintings of Ajanta', in Parul Pandya Dhar (ed.), *Indian Art History Changing Perspectives*, 126–9, New Delhi: DK Printworld.

Sherman, Taylor C. (2007), 'The Integration of the Princely State of Hyderabad and the Making of the Postcolonial State in India', *The Indian Economic and Social History Review*, 44 (4): 489–516.

Shimada, Akira (2013), *Early Buddhist Architecture in Context: The Great Stūpa at Amarāvatī (ca. 300 BCE-300 CE)*, Leiden: Brill.

Shimada, Akira (2016), 'Discovery of the Amaravati Stupa: Early Excavations and Interpretations', in Akira Shimada and Michael Willis (eds), *Amaravati: The Art of an Early Buddhist Monument in Context*, 188–207, London: The British Museum.

Singh, Upender (2008), *A History of Ancient and Early Medieval India, from the Stone Age to 12th Century*, Delhi: Pearson.

Suares, Coreena (2014), 'Return Telangana Artefacts, Demand Activists', *Deccan Chronicle*, 2 June. Available Online; https://www.deccanchronicle.com/140602/nation-current-affairs/article/return-telangana-artefacts-demand-activists (accessed 18 June 2024).

Subrahmanyam, B., J. Vijaya Kumar, G.V. Ramakrishna Rao and K.S.B. Kesava (2008), *Phanigiri A Buddhist Site in Andhra Pradesh (An Interim Report 2001–2007)*, Hyderabad: Department of Archaeology and Museums, Govt. of Andhra Pradesh.

Sur, Aihik (2018), 'Ajanta Cave Paintings of Nizam Era Lie in a State of Neglect', *The New Indian Express*, 8 July. Available online: https://www.newindianexpress.com/cities/hyderabad/2018/Jul/03/ajanta-cave-paintings-of-nizam-era-lie-in-a-state-of-neglect-1837405.html (accessed 18 June 2024).

Thapar, B. K., ed. (1980a), *Indian Archaeology 1976–1977: A Review*, New Delhi: Archaeological Survey of India.

Thapar, B. K., ed. (1980b), *Indian Archaeology 1977–1978: A Review*, New Delhi: Archaeological Survey of India.

The Department of Heritage Telangana, 'State Museum Hyderabad'. https://heritage.telangana.gov.in (accessed 7 May 2020).

The Hindu (2005), 'Buddha's Relics to Add Attraction to State Archaeological Museum', *The Hindu*, 31 December. Available online: https://www.thehindu.com/todays-paper/tp-national/tp-andhrapradesh/buddhas-relic-to-add-attraction-to-state-archaeological-museum/article27545705.ece (accessed 17 June 2024).

The Hindu (2019), 'Gearing up for Kalachakra', *The Hindu*, 31 May. Available online: https://www.thehindu.com/todays-paper/tp-national/tp-andhrapradesh/gearing-up-for-kaalchakra/article27371941.ece (accessed 30 June 2024).

The Hindu (2016), 'Buddhist Relics on Display at State Museum', *The Hindu*, 9 October. Available online: https://www.thehindu.com/todays-paper/tp-national/tp-andhrapradesh/Buddhist-relics-on-display-at-State-Museum/article15226589.ece# (accessed 17 June 2024).

The New Indian Express (2015), 'It's Official, New Andhra Pradesh Capital Is Named Amaravathi', *The New Indian Express*, 2 April. Available online: https://www.newindianexpress.com/nation/2015/Apr/02/it%E2%80%99s-official-new-andhra-pradesh-capital-is-named-amaravathi-736977.html (accessed 7 May 2020).

Yazdani, Ghulam (1916), *Annual Report of the Archaeological Department of His Highness the Nizam's Dominions 1914–1915*, Calcutta: Baptist Mission Press.

Yazdani, Ghulam (1920), *Annual Report of the Archaeological Department of His Exalted Highness the Nizam's Dominions 1918–1919*, Calcutta: Baptist Mission Press.

Yazdani, Ghulam (1923), *Annual Report of the Archaeological Department of His Exalted Highness the Nizam's Dominions 1920–1921*, Calcutta: Baptist Mission Press.

Yazdani, Ghulam (1926a), *Annual Report of the Archaeological Department of His Exalted Highness the Nizam's Dominions 1921–1924*, Calcutta: Baptist Mission Press.

Yazdani, Ghulam (1926b), *Annual Report of the Archaeological Department of His Exalted Highness the Nizam's Dominions 1924–1925*, Calcutta: Baptist Mission Press.

Yazdani, Ghulam (1930a), *Annual Report of the Archaeological Department of His Exalted Highness the Nizam's Dominions 1927–1928*, Calcutta: Baptist Mission Press.

Yazdani, Ghulam (1930b), *Ajanta. The Colour and Monochrome Reproductions of the Ajanta Frescoes Based on Photography*, Oxford: Oxford University Press.

Yazdani, Ghulam (1939), *Annual Report of the Archaeological Department of His Exalted Highness the Nizam's Dominions 1936–1937*, Calcutta: Baptist Mission Press.

Zin, Monika (2016), 'Buddhist Narratives and Amaravati', in Akira Shimada and Michael Willis (eds), *Amaravati: The Art of an Early Buddhist Monument in Context*, London: The British Museum.

2

A Review of the Nizam's *Numāish-gāh Sehat*

P. Sindhuri Aparna

Introduction

A pink building, a stone's throw away from the Telangana State Archaeology Museum (formerly known as the Dr. Y. S. Rajasekhara Reddy Andhra Pradesh State Museum) in Hyderabad's *Bagh-e-Aam* (Public Gardens), bears evidence of a lesser-known facet of the princely state of Hyderabad: the effort it made to popularize Western medicine. A blue signboard at the entrance of the pink building announces in four languages—this is the Health Museum in English, *Numāish-gāh Sehat* in Urdu, *Ārogya Pradarśanalaya* in Hindi and *Ārogya Pradarśanaśālā* in Telugu—indicating the linguistic orientations of its expected audiences. All the instructions inside the museum are also written in these four languages. Visiting the museum in 2017, a strong smell of rotten flesh, expired chemicals and years of dust immediately hit me as I entered a spacious hall with lofty ceilings through the doorway. I was greeted by a middle-aged woman behind a desk placed at the threshold of another massive door guarding the remains of the forgotten initiative of the Nizams' Medical Department. Upon entering the hall, I am immediately asked to enter my contact details in a register. Overlooking the room is a painting of Hygeia (Figure 2.1), the Greek goddess of health and well-being. Below, at

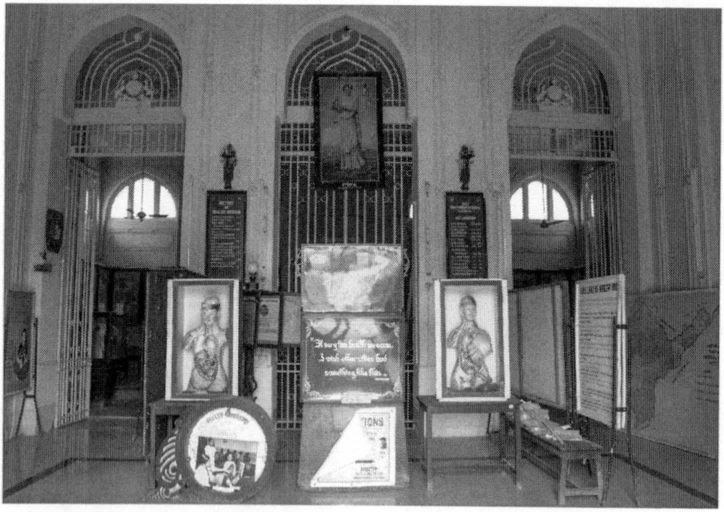

Figure 2.1 The Foyer of the Health Museum, Hyderabad-Deccan. Courtesy: P. Sindhuri Aparna, 2017.

eye level, a black and white photograph of former Prime Minister Jawaharlal Nehru visiting the museum in 1953 is on display. It is as if Hygeia sends blessings from the heavens, whereas Nehru, posing as her messenger on earth (read post-independence India), spreads her message of health and well-being. The exhibits of the building (Figure 2.2) reveal that the museum was set up to spread awareness of various diseases among the residents of Hyderabad, educate them on preventive measures and promote a healthy lifestyle based on proper sanitary measures (Figures 2.3 and 2.4). The artefacts displayed and their accompanying informative texts bear an uncanny resemblance to the illustrative texts and images of textbooks widely used in primary and middle schools across India – for example, the book titled *Looking Around: Environmental Studies for Class 3* (National Council for Education and Training 2019a) and *Science: Textbook for Studies' for Class 6* (National Council for Education and Training 2019b).

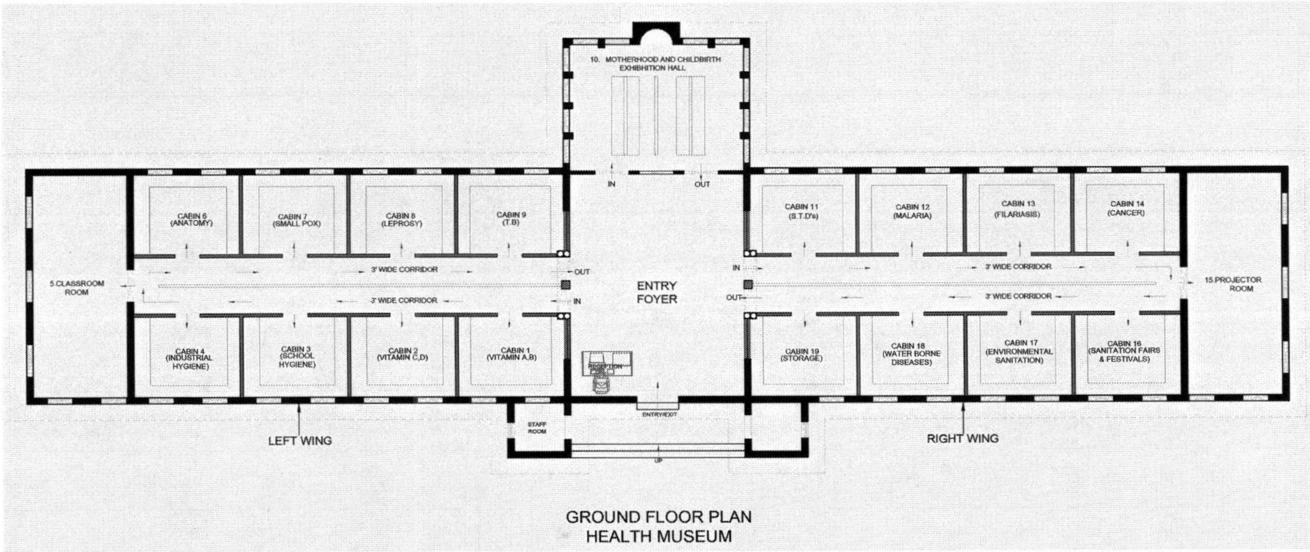

Figure 2.2 Map of the Display in the Health Museum, Hyderabad-Deccan. Courtesy: Anu Kumari and P. Sindhuri, 2021.

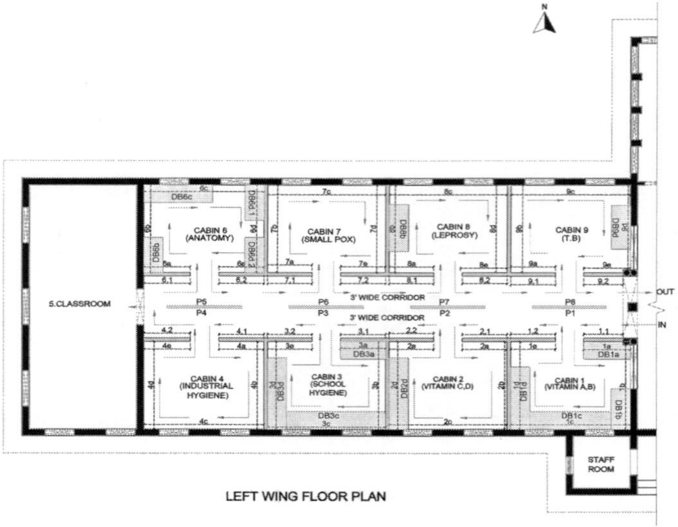

1a- Deficiency Diseases Vitamin A, DB1a- Protective food, 1b- Eat this way for Vitamin, DB1b- Rich in Vitamin A and Body Building Food, 1c- Vitamin D, B,A Deficiency, DB1c- Body Building Food and Energy Producing Food, 1d- Deficiencies of Vitamin B complex, 2a- Vitamin C&D sources, 2b- Vitamin C & D Deficiencies, 2c- Calorie requirements, 2d- Vitamin A deficiency, DB2d- Protective Food, 2e- Effects of cooking, 3a- Children learn what they live, Db3a- Model School, 3b- Healthy Habits and School Hygiene, 3c- School Hygiene, DB3c- Child deformities, 3d- School Hygiene, DB3d- Teeth, 3e- Healthy children, 4a- empty, 4b- Proper care in industries, 4c- Food adulteration, 4d- Common adulterants in foods, 4e- What is food adulterations, 6.1- Why Health Education, 6a- Anatomy of foot, palm, brain, 6b- Anatomy of Eye, DB6b- Eye, 6c- Human Organs, 6d- Anatomy, Db6d.1- Human skeleton, DB6d.2- Plastic human heart, 6.2- Foetal circulation, 7.1- What is Diabetes?, 7a- Small Pox 1962 eradication, 7b- Polio, diphtheria, 7c- Photographs of Diphtheria, Polio, 7d- Ideal immunization schedule, 7e- Stages of Chicken pox and small pox, 7.2- Diabetic Diet, 8.1- Tools of treatment, 8a- Leprosy can be easily cured, 8b- National Leprosy Eradication Programme, 8c- Symptoms of Leprosy, 8d- Prevention of Lung Diseases, P1 & P2- The Work of Greens, P3& P4- Diet for Nursing Mothers & Preschool Children, P5- Protection against Deficiency Diseases, P6- Goitre, P7- Nutrition for Pregnant Women, P8- Marasmus, Pellagra.

Figure 2.3 Detailed Display Plan of the Left Wing of the Health Museum, Hyderabad-Deccan. Courtesy: Anu Kumari and P. Sindhuri Aparna, 2021.

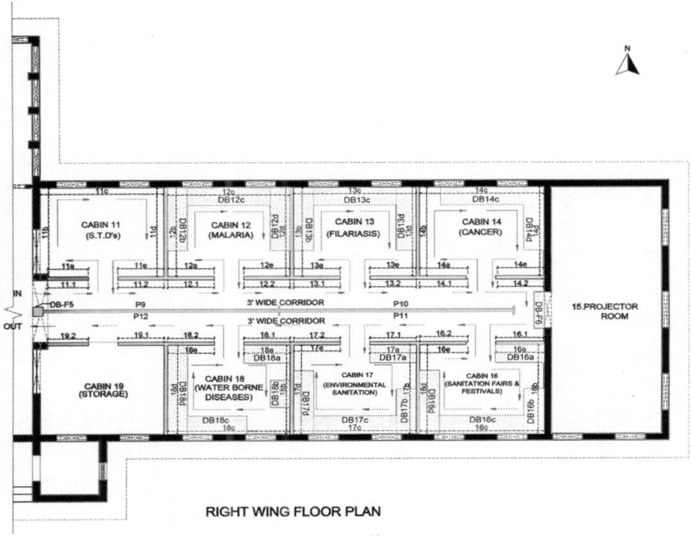

11.1- SexuallyTransmitted Diseases 11a- V.D, 11b- Rat flea, 11c- Types of Syphillis, 11d- Medically Important Order of Insects, 11e- YAWS. 11.2- Scrabies, 12.1- Malaria, 12a- Difference between Malaria control and eradication. DB12b- Our Insect Foes, Our Microbic Enemies, DB12c- Treating of Breeding places of Mosquitoes, DB12d- Sandfly, 12e- Life History of Culex, 12.2- You Can Prevent Mosquito Breeding, P9- Dignitaries who visited Health Museum, P10- Scientist and Discoveries, 13.1- You can prevent mosquito breeding, 13a- Probable Natural Cycle of Encephalitis in India, DB13b- Breeding Places of Malaria, DB13c- Japanese Virus Encephalitis in AP, DB13d- Elephantiasis of scrotum, 13e- The Killer on the Prowl, 13.2- Modified strategy in Malaria, 14.1- Danger signals of cancer, 14a- Cancer types, 14b- Cancer types, DB14e- Danger signals of Cancer (English and Telugu), DB14d- Cancer affected body parts, 14e- Progress at Cancer Hospital, Hyd. , DBF6- Snakes, 16.1- How to detect poisonous snakes, DB16a- Hygienic House, DB16b- Clean Sweet-Neat Shop, DB16c- Sanitary Arrangements of the Jatra, DB16d- Sanitary and insanitary Villages, 16e &16.2- Good and Bad environment, P11- Scientists and Discoveries, P12- Dignitaries who visited the Health Museum, DB17a- Environmental Sanitation, DB17b- Good Environments Ensure Good Health, DB17c- Bore Hole Latrine, Soakage Pit, DB17d- Sanitary Well, Insanitary Well, 17e- Disinfection for Small Community Water Supplies, 17.2- Medical Officers, 18.1- Routes of Transmission of Diseases, DB18a- Cholera Mode of Spread, DB18b- Sanitary Cowshed, DB16c- Life cyclye of Ascaris lumbricoides, DB18d- House fly and its breeding place, 18e- Classification of Food Borne Diseases.

Figure 2.4 A Display Plan of the Right Wing of the Health Museum in Hyderabad-Deccan. Courtesy: Anu Kumari and P. Sindhuri Aparna, 2021.

The dissemination of awareness about hygiene and health and the circulation of certain types of images and text that are seen as the best suited for education go hand in hand. Set up during the transition from Nizam's rule to modern Indian statehood (1947–8), the Health Museum embodies both the ethos of the Nizam government's deep interest in Western scientific education and the promises of a newly independent India. First built at Chikkadpally in 1948, the Health Museum was moved to the Trophy Hall (presently known as Jawahar Bal Bhawan) in 1952, where it was inaugurated by M. K. Vellodi, the Counsellor of the Government of Hyderabad. In 1966, the museum was relocated to its present location: the Ajanta Pavilion (Figure 2.5). The building used to host the exhibition of copied paintings of the Ajanta murals. In 1915, the Archaeological Department of Hyderabad had appointed Syed Ahmad to copy the paintings of Ajanta to document the original murals, which were in a deteriorating state. The façade of the building even incorporates Ajanta's iconic *gabākṣa* or *candraśālā* motif to symbolize the site's original architecture. In July of 1966, the copied paintings along with other artefacts were dismantled from the pavilion, and many of those paintings found space in the display at the Dr. Y. S. Rajasekhara Reddy Andhra Pradesh State

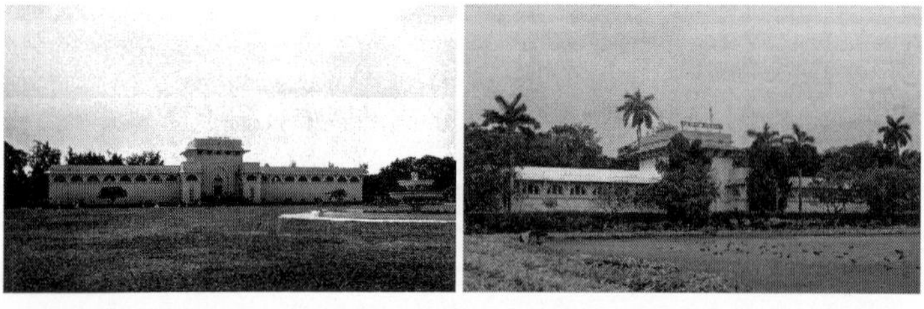

Figure 2.5 (Left) Raja Deen Dayal's Photograph of the Health Museum, Hyderabad-Deccan. 1900s. Courtesy: Wellcome Collection. **(Right)** Today's Health Museum, Hyderabad-Deccan. Courtesy: P. Sindhuri Aparna, 2017.

Museum (present Telangana State Archaeology Museum) (Ghosh 1996: 5). Today, Ajanta's iconic architectural feature of *gabākṣa* or *candraśālā* at the entrance facade of the building is the only remnant of the copied Ajanta paintings exhibition history. Thus, the building of today's Health Museum received the name 'Ajanta Pavilion'. Near the entrance of the present venue, a wooden board titled the 'History of the Health Museum' records Jawaharlal Nehru's visit to the museum in 1953, with a photograph from the visit on display. The Health Museum as an institution was not unique to Hyderabad. There were other museums built in various other princely states like Mysore, Baroda, Travancore and Patna (Ernst et al. 2018), but the only Hyderabad one continues to survive. As a connecting piece in history, the Health Museum draws its lessons and knowledge from Western medicine and blends into Nehru's scientific and modern newly independent India.

In this chapter,[1] I shed light on visual discourses on health, diseases and body developed by the Health Museum in Hyderabad for educational and instructive purposes, targeting the general public. A serious lack of literature on this institution, which once served as an important site for health education in the Nizam's state, prompts my endeavour to situate this museum within the historiography of health in South Asia and reflect on its pedagogical framework. The historiography of medicine and public health in the past three decades has emerged as one of the most important themes in South Asian studies. The literature in this field predominantly focuses on the colonial legacy of public health in India and its dissemination. David Arnold (2016: 3) calls attention to the problem of considering the practice of Western medicine in colonial India as monolithic. Whereas the imposition of colonial science heavily transformed the socio-political parameters of the subcontinent, the diversity of the population and the approach of regional governing bodies resisted a uniform distribution of

British medicinal practice. Arnold (1993: 7) also questions the appropriateness of the term 'public health' in the Indian context, preferring to employ the term 'state medicine' instead. He points to the creation of a state-centred system of scientific knowledge and power, rather than the more diffused and generalized forms of knowledge and power Michel Foucault (1976) described in his writings. This approach encourages further investigation to assess the negotiations between Western science and its application by Indian states. The scholarship in the field has also established public health measures as a strategy by which the colonial government aimed to know and control its subjects. However, the literature on the colonial healthcare in the subcontinent exclusively focuses on regions under the direct rule of the British – often rendered in pink on the colonial maps. These works therefore fail to acknowledge two-fifths of the region, which were administered by Indian agencies (Ernst et al. 2018: 1). Around 600 princely states operated during the colonial rule, but the residents of these states were not considered British subjects. Furthermore, states were differentiated as 'progressive' (such as Travancore) or 'backward' (such as the states in Odisha) based on their inclination to comply with the colonial interests (Ernst et al. 2018: 3). Given that the British exerted indirect rule over Indian states, several issues arise in relation to the role of medicine as a means of justifying British overlordship in the states ruled by the indigenous rulers with diverse backgrounds and political inclinations. Hence a thorough understanding of the state of public health in princely states is essential to expand the perimeters of this burgeoning field of study.

In this chapter, I also attempt to shed light on three crucial aspects of this subject: Firstly, what was the nature of medical services in Indian princely states? Can we imagine 'indigenous western healthcare' operating in these states? Secondly, how did hegemony and its legitimization play out between indigenous rulers and their subjects? Thirdly, did the princely states opt for Western healthcare as a strategic tool to please the British and minimize their interventions in state affairs? I will unravel the complexity of this layered topic while limiting my analysis to the former princely state of Hyderabad. In the first section of this chapter, I trace the establishment of the public health department under the Nizam government. In the second section, I discuss the establishment of the Health Museum, its concept and how the public health department's mandates are reflected in the museum. The final section of the chapter describes in detail the contents of the museum – its sections – while discussing the socio-cultural nature of the display.

Perception of Health in the Nizam's Dominions

Hyderabad was the fourth-largest city in South Asia and the largest princely state in the subcontinent during British rule (Beverley 2015: 17). The arrival of Western medicine in Hyderabad is linked to an incident involving the fourth Nizam of Hyderabad, Nawab Nasir-ud-Daullah:

> Nawab Nasirud-Dawlah fell ill (Probably he was suffering with Diabetes) in 1842/43 A.D. and he did not recover for quite some time under the treatment of Unani Hakeems, as all the people in Hyderabad had belief in Unani Medicine and no one practised Allopathic Medicine here before 1846 A.D. Mr. Fraser the then British Resident in Hyderabad recommended treatment of the ailing Nizam by the Residency surgeon Dr. William Campbell Maclean. He treated the Nizam by adjustment in his daily diet, without any medicine, as the Nizam wanted that he must be cured without having to eat or drink any Allopathic Drug. The King followed the diet schedule as prescribed by Dr. Maclean and

> recovered within a period of three months. The western system of medicine thus appears to have gone high in his estimate and so, he ordered for the establishment of the medical school in Hyderabad in the same year.
>
> (Ali and Ramachari 1996: 120)

Alongside the medical school, a medical department was established, which remained associated with the school until 1853. In 1866, Salar Jung I, Sir Nawab Turab Ali Khan Mukhtar-ul-Mulk Bahadur established the Afzalgunj Hospital (presently known as Osmania General Hospital), a public hospital on the northern bank of the river Musi, for the benefit of the sick and the betterment of Western medical studies (Ali and Ramachari 1996: 122). The year, the Medical Department was reorganized and became fully functional under the guidance of the residency surgeon, who was Surgeon Major or Colonel of the British army. The Medical Department's Director was made the superintendent of the Afzal Gunj Hospital (Rao 2015: 110). The Nizam's deep reliance on the British paved the way for Western medical science and allopathy gaining prominence for care and relief in the Nizam Dominions (Rao 2015: 313).

By the end of the nineteenth century, there were three allopathic hospitals managed by the Hyderabad state: Afzal Gunj Hospital, Central Police Hospital and the Chanchalguda Jail Hospital (Baru 1992: 98). While the British were reluctant to pay attention to the specificities of women's health, the Nizam's state established specialized hospitals for women, such as the Victoria Zenana Hospital in Hyderabad and the Rani Sharnapalli Women Hospital in Gulbarga; additionally, the state provided qualified lady doctors to all city and district hospitals, and female wards in the general hospitals (Rao 2015: 89–118). Though the focus of the Nizam's medical department was on curative services, preventive measures were also stressed on, given the plague, malaria and floods of 1908 that disrupted the well-being of the Nizam's beloved city (Baru 1992: 101). In 1322 Faslī /1912–13, a separate public health unit under the control of the Director of the Medical Department was established. In the same year, the Sanitation Department was created and the Director of the Medical Department was given its additional charge (Baru 1992: 98). The Nizam's state was divided into two circles, each under the charge of a Deputy Sanitation Commissioner. The Medical Department also appointed civil surgeons who acted as district sanitary officers, and assistant surgeons as sanitary assistants, who had the control of the travelling dispensaries. In 1331 Faslī /1921–2, the Public Health Department and the Medical Department were separated (Rao 2015: 111). However, in 1343 Faslī /1933–4, the Public Health Department was merged again with the Medical Department and reorganized to suit the local conditions of the Nizam's Domain. With this, the Medical Department was renamed the Medical and Public Health Department. The functions of the Public Health Department (Rao 2015: 112) were specified as follows:

1. To adopt measures and design to improve the physical well-being of the population, maternity and child welfare work, medical inspection of school children, physical education, diet surveys, suggestions to improve the nutritional levels of the population and rural reconstruction.
2. To prevent and control preventable diseases and epidemics.
3. To improve the general environmental conditions in both urban and rural areas.
4. To undertake health education of the masses with a view by obtaining their active cooperation in the health measures taken up by the medical and health department.
5. Survey and control of malaria, leprosy, yaws, guinea worm and filariasis.
6. Overlooking the sanitary arrangements for all *Urs-s* and *Jatrās* in the Nizam's Dominions.
7. Prevention and control of tuberculosis.

There was an urgent need to combat epidemics and mobilize awareness among the population. Thus, it brought into play a range of knowledge and techniques of sanitation, laws, tactics, studies of diseases and strategies to control the epidemic with the use of statistics, vaccination, quarantine, hospitalization and municipal governmentality. As will be seen in the next few sections, the health museum is a physical manifestation of these functions specified for the public health department.

Display and Departure

The administration of the Medical and Sanitation Department of H.E.H. of the Nizam's Government always had a public health initiative as its mandate concerning the ignorance of common people about issues of diseases, health, and the environment. H.E.H. the Nizam's Government published the report of the Medical and Sanitation Department in Urdu and English. One of the reports mentions that 'little progress in social amelioration can be made by thrusting Public Health improvements on an unwilling community and in order to obtain the active cooperation of the people, health education is essential' (H.E.H. the Nizam's Government 1939: 32). However, the district health staff implemented this mandate by presenting health talks, exhibiting posters and using the magic lantern for demonstrations. The scope was broadened with the introduction of cinema cars in 1342 Faslī /1923–33. A customized van with a projector and other equipment such as lights and motors was popularly known as a 'cinema-car' in the Nizam's Dominions. It was used to tour to the remote villages for visual education purposes. The cinema cars were equipped with a projector and a separate motor as the power generator. They would show films like *Plague: The Destroyer*, *Rural Uplift*, *Malaria* and *Kumbha Melā*

(H.E.H. the Nizam's Government 1934: 142; Mahadevan 2015: 60). In 1938, an artist was employed to prepare posters and slides; as a result, sets of 200 coloured slides were prepared on infectious diseases in Urdu, Telugu, Marathi and Kanarese (Kannada) (H.E.H. the Nizam's Government 1939: 32). In 1349 Faslī /1939–40, a health stall was inaugurated at the Industrial Exhibition at Public Gardens (H.E.H. the Nizam's Government 1940: 219). In 1351 Faslī / 1941–2, a 'nutrition museum', containing models of vegetables, fruits and grains, along with framed posters and coloured charts, was set up (H.E.H. the Nizam's Government 1942: 224). A Bureau of Health and Education and Industrial Hygiene was proposed by the Nizam's Government in 1942, and was finally established in 1948. According to a report of the Medical Department, the establishment of the health publicity bureau seemed essential because 'the State may provide elaborate health services, but the people, through ignorance or suspicion, may refuse to avail themselves of these services or make insufficient use of them' (H.E.H. the Nizam's Government 1939: 32). The idea of a health museum was conceived in 1939. In May 1948, the Health Museum was established under the canopy of the Bureau of Health and Education and Industrial Hygiene. The sustained efforts of the Nizam's government to popularize Western medicine, for handling the challenges of the twentieth-century public health better, largely relied on the role of visual and audio-visual media. Tableaus, films and health pavilions at exhibitions paved the way for a more stable and permanent museum space to convey the state's message on public health.

Gyan Prakash (1999: 64) argues that the 'staging of science' in British India was performed through museums and exhibitions, where artefacts, plants, animals and people were catalogued and displayed to dislocate the binaries of civilized and savage, and science and magic. It was employed to appeal to the natives; science had to be exhibited through magic and wonder: the establishment of science's power is through its estrangement. Similarly, in Hyderabad, the Health Museum acted as a space for the visual orientation and popularization of scientific medicine and of a modern body to the Hyderabad Deccan residents. It provided the general audience with knowledge and advice on how to manage their own body in line with Western norms. In order to wield its transforming power, health was tropicalized, brought down to the level of the people and imposed upon them. Public health went 'native' in this museum that displayed the wonders of medicine and therefore appealed to the imagination and superstition as much as to the reason. Delineating the function of such institutes, Bruno Gebhard (1946) argues,

> Health museums are nothing less than science museums specialising in human biology, personal and public health. They are a natural bridge between preventive and curative medicine. As is the case with all science museums, health museums are made; they are manufactured – they are not collected.
>
> (Gebhard 1946: 1013)

Gebhard stresses on the challenges of making preventive services and public health concerns visible, as protective and preventive measures are hard to visualize for general audiences. Hospital as a structure is a tangible expression of medical services; however, a health museum stands as a symbol of public health, while separating medical facilities from educational purpose (Gebhard 1946: 1014). Should this institution be called a museum then? As Gebhard notes, 'there are disadvantages in using the word "museum" which for too many people sounds like "mausoleum"' (Gebhard 1946: 1013).

A response to his concern is perhaps reflected in the signboard text at the Health Museum, which seeks to justify the need for such places. The text in the signboard reads: 'Learning by looking is much easier and less time-consuming, and what they have learnt in this way, they do not forget so quickly (seeing is not only believing but also reliving). Our exhibits, which show causes and means of cure of disease, lessen the fear complex of the patients that springs from the "unknown."'

From the Ill to the Healthy Body

James Elkins critiques the practices in art historical studies while examining 'informational images'. He argues that art history ignores a whole panorama of non-art images, such as graphs, charts, maps, seals and stamps, astronomical and astrological charts, and a range of scientific images that are used in the domain of science. Elkins points out that these images serve a more utilitarian purpose than artistic and are hence treated as 'informational images'. He writes, 'In general, the studies in art history set its boundaries by working on popular culture, medieval and non-Western images. However, the domain of images is substantially larger. In particular, there is a group of images that seem to have neither religious nor artistic purpose, and that is the images principally intended … to convey information' (Elkins 1999: 4).

The three keys of Elkins's argument on why these informational images are worthy of consideration for art history have offered me a framework to probe the display of 'informational images and text' at the Health Museum. He argues that, first, through their stylistic features, the informational images bear the socio-cultural value system of an era; secondly, they represent complex questions of representation, convention, medium, production, interpretation and reception for their dialectical position between educational and fine art practices; thirdly, their expressive capability is enlivened through public interactions which work differently for fine art objects or artefacts (Elkins 1999: 45; Marshall 2004: 137).

A survey of the museum reflects that the museum is a physical manifestation of the mandates of the Nizam's Public Health Department. Hence, one can see dedicated displays about nutrition, industrial and school hygiene, diseases, motherhood and childbirth, sanitation during fairs and festivals, and environmental sanitation at the museum. This is achieved with a range of objects, including wax models, anatomical specimens, posters, photographs and statistical graphs. While a portion of the museum illustrates 'normal' or 'ideal anatomy', a major portion illustrates deformity, disease and ignorance (Figure 2.6 Right). As the human body in the nineteenth-century European context emerged 'as something docile that could be subjected, used, transformed and improved', its reflection is persistent in the display strategy here (Armstrong 1983: 3). Assessing healthy bodies employs a series of surveillance techniques: bodies should be inspected to judge their status; they need to be analysed to identify their deficits and monitored to evaluate their functioning. The museum displays an excerpt from the Constitution of India, which states that health is a basic right of citizens and that improving public health conditions is the primary duty of the government.

The Health Museum claims that the human body is a meticulously made machine, which requires as much preservation and care as any other machine. The objects on display showcase the perils of neglect and ignorance, as well as educate visitors about preventive measures. In an attempt to orient the behaviour of its visitors, the museum has displayed various objects, including anatomical specimens like a hydrocephalic abnormal foetus and a cancerous uterus; there is also a cubicle where sexual diseases such as syphilis are illustrated. For effective transmission of these ideas through objects, the written material is displayed not only in English but also in the regional languages – Telugu and Urdu.

A healthy body or a body without disease is also on display to persuade visitors to aim for one by following healthy habits and eating nutritious food, incorporating nutrients and vitamins in their diet regularly (Figure 2.6 Left). The museum display notifies viewers about various diseases, their symptoms and preventive measures. For example, tuberculosis is showcased as a disease of contact and social space. The medical gaze identifies and constructs a social and sanitized area between individuals with their knowledge about the disease. Tuberculosis is therefore shown as a disease that could be transmitted through 'respiratory contact'.

Another section of the museum addresses food adulteration; milk, ghee, mustard oil and wheat flour – staple items in South Asian households and of unique economic, social and cultural significance – have been targeted for adulteration, leading to health hazards. Food adulteration in colonial India did not create the kind of striking visuality of horror resulting from famines. Yet it raised crucial questions around the consumption of edibles and health to the extent that food adulteration became synonymous with anxieties about the body, community and nation.

The exhibited section on public health and the individual showcases sub-themes such as mother and child, school and industrial hygiene, and health education. The body of a child especially holds great significance as childhood is seen as a state that can be manipulated and transformed towards a healthy future.

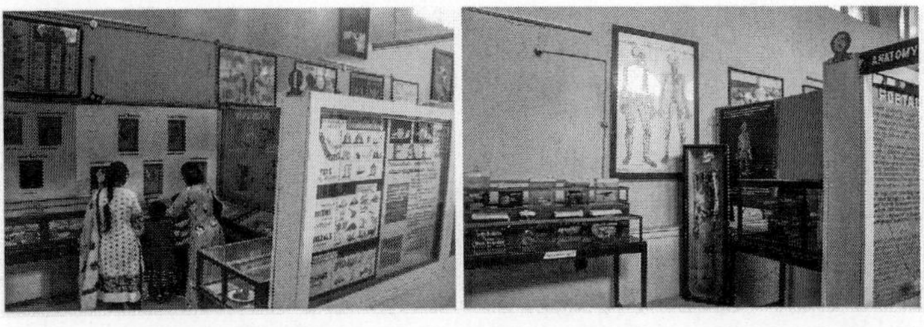

Figure 2.6 (Left) Visitors in Section-1 of the Health Museum in Hyderabad-Deccan Learning about Vitamins and Their Deficiencies, 2017. **(Right)** Anatomical Section with Specimens. Courtesy: P. Sindhuri Aparna, 2017.

As per what is displayed in the museum, pure air, a rational diet and free movement give strength and symmetry to a child's body. Under the section on hygiene at the school, it is recommended that the usually dark and enclosed halls of schools be made to feature large windows to allow fresh air during lessons. Fresh air, temperature, humidity and movement are also suggested to increase industrial efficiency. Overall, hygienic spaces with ample air and light are shown as therapeutic and nurturing a healthy body.

The gendered nature of hygiene practice is clearly observed in the displays. Health and hygiene agendas were produced as ideologies in and through the deployment of the gendered responsibilities of women (Prasad 2015: 111). Srirupa Prasad underscores that preventive medicine and health education became the prime focus in the early twentieth century. In India, more often than not, hygiene was considered a woman's responsibility in the domestic space because of the roles that women had to take on as wives and mothers. Even in the medical profession, women were often portrayed as midwives (Prasad 2015: 105). Thus, gender-specific intrusive health education for mothers and children, developed in the twentieth century, is distinctively reflected through the exhibits.

A section titled *Motherhood and Childbirth* represents the reproductive body and a 'birth atlas' (Figure 2.7). The atlas depicts the organization of a three-dimensional body on a two-dimensional plane. The atlas depicts the body as a transparent film, allowing the observer to decipher and differentiate the structure and changes in the reproductive organs during the various stages of pregnancy. The museum also sought to provide information on midwives, facilities such as maternity hospitals, and so on (Figure 2.8). The museum also displays sexual bodies and tries to provide sex education, but it is limited to providing brief information on sexually transmitted and venereal diseases. Srirupa Prasad points out that the visual media of epidemics in early-twentieth-century India operated

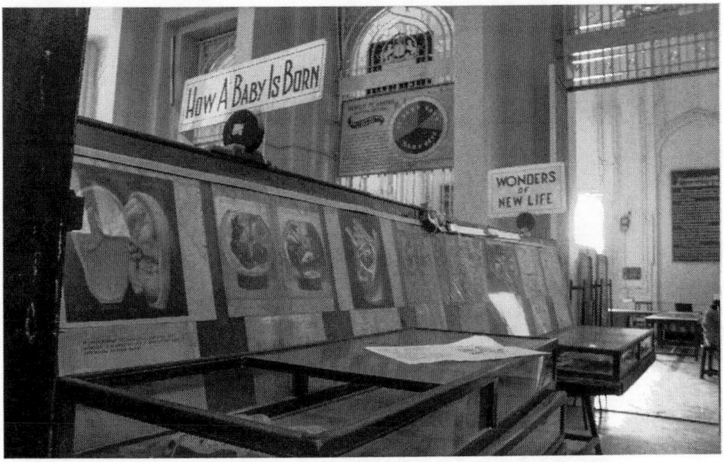

Figure 2.7 Display and Models Showing 'How a Baby Is Born'. Courtesy: P. Sindhuri Aparna, 2017.

by 'evoking a controlled form of fear and anxiety for purposes of rational governance over personal and/or national life' (Prasad 2015: 28).

The museum display also establishes a close connection between infectious diseases and vital statistics of populations. The vast quantities of information about diseases and health that began to be archived in statistical and scientific forms, and through the development of medical agencies, were often employed as a tool of governance. The statistical charts in the museum inform approximations of patterns of disease and mortality, and medical interventions in changing patterns of mortality across the state. In pre-colonial India, health and medical care were matters of individual initiative or, at most, community effort. Under colonial rule, they became part of a more comprehensive process of state regulation (Rao 2015: 311). The justification of governmental control over public health is implied through this process. The coexistence of concepts of public health from both the nineteenth and twentieth centuries allows us to recognize the shift in priorities.

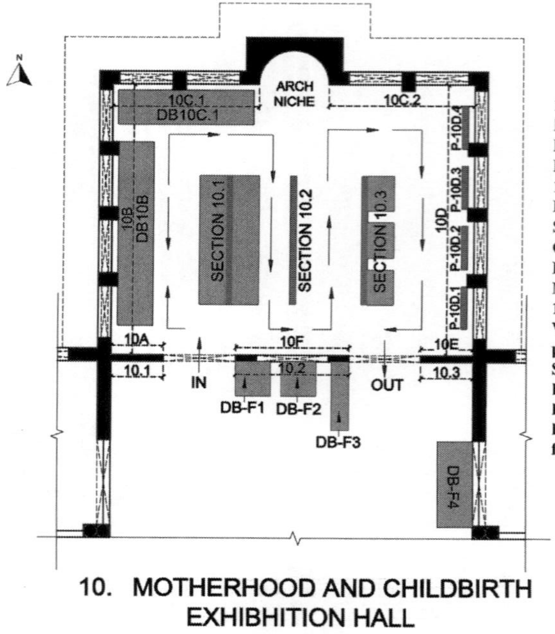

10.1- History of Health Museum, 10.2- Painting of Hygiea, DB-F1 Anatomical model, DB-F2- Photograph of Nehru's visit to Health Museum, DB-F3- Anatomical model 10A& 10B- Child care & development, DB10B- Delivery Clinic, Child Clinic, Antenatal clinic, Section 10.1- How a baby is born, 10C.1- Care of problem children, DB10C.1- Development of the Foetus at Different Months, Section 10.2- use of contraceptives, 10C.2-Heart diseases, P-10D.4& P-10D.3- Vascular changes in eyes due to high blood pressure, P-10D.2& P-10D.1- Eye Diseases, Section 10.3- World Health Day Themes, Family Welfare Programme in Andhra Pradesh, Ill Effects of Tobacco in Human Body, 10E- Prevent Blindness, DB-F4- A to z for Health and Happiness.

Figure 2.8 Detailed Display Plan of the Central Hall and Motherhood and Childbirth Hall in the Health Museum, Hyderabad-Deccan. Courtesy: Anu Kumari and P. Sindhur, 2021.

In the nineteenth century, the emphasis was on 'sanitarianism' – the perils of contamination of the environment, and the impurities in air and water. On the other hand, in the twentieth century, the notions of individual responsibility and risk emerged. Health and well-being were gradually defined as moral projects wherein the policing and disciplining of the individual and social bodies were paramount (Rao 2015: 20).

As discussed above, the visuality and visibility of public health concerns in the Nizam's Dominions have been explored in terms of both temporary visuals and stable permanent artefacts. While institutionalizing these responsibilities, stressing on the term 'museum' sets up the institute's relationship with colonial, anthropological and archaeological repositories of knowledge. The signboards, models and tableaus within the institute become comparable to precious historical remains. Thus, these have educational and application values. A survey of the exhibited objects makes the Health Museum's drive to promote awareness about health and hygiene quite evident.

Conclusion

It is observed that the Health Museum echoes the public health policies of the colonial and Nizam government. The design and direction of the Medical Department of the Nizam state were given by British Indian Medical Service officers. Yet, its indigenous nature is reflected in its dissemination – the exhibited materials in the Health Museum resonate with it. While the British government focused on providing healthcare facilities primarily to the British residents in India, the Nizam government extended its services to people across gender and class in Hyderabad Deccan. The state of Hyderabad also became a centre of learning, training and research in Western medical science and technology during the colonial era with the support of the Nizam government. In the medical schools and the Health Museum, the dissemination of medical knowledge was carried out in local languages (Urdu and Telugu) to reach and attract a wider audience from the city. For the Nizam and his government, encouraging Western medicine had obvious advantages. On the one hand, they were able to demonstrate their 'modernizing stance' to the British. On the other hand, Western medicine was also a useful tool to diffuse the idea of a 'charitable ruler', which in turn contributed to the legitimization of the Nizam's rule. There was a steady increase in the number of dispensaries and hospitals supported by the Nizam government in the form of state-owned and -aided institutions. The budgetary allocation for the development of Western medical science and technology was increased from year to year for the purchase of medical stores, provision of infrastructure, hiring of medical professionals and for the education and training of medical professionals. The support rendered by the Nizam government played an important role in the introduction and penetration of Western medical science and technology into the state of Hyderabad.

The Health Museum is indicative of the development of medicine that focused on health instead of disease in the post First World War. In order to bring about effective changes in health-related social behaviour and to reduce the chances of people contracting diseases, educating general audiences and teaching them how to maximize their health seemed essential. This idea was institutionalized at the end of the British Raj and in post-Independence India in a new academic discipline that came to be known as Social and Community Medicine which was enhanced by the Health Museum. The period after the First World War saw the popularization of health education through the celebration of health weeks, health talks by supervisors, medical inspections, film shows and exhibitions in all of which the Health Museum actively participated.

We may observe the assimilation of health education, industrial exhibitions and scientific fora at the Health Museum. The museum follows a colonial pedagogy in that it exhibits congenital diseases and classifications of diseases, organized and authorized by science, by displaying morbid anatomies and three-dimensional mode, although the ideas and concepts of Western medicine were indeed made available to natives. In the time of interactive exhibitions, the visitor here must still walk the dusty galleries of this museum with its 'Don't touch' signs. The museum preserves in itself the development of public health policies, research and propaganda during the nineteenth and twentieth centuries.

Note

1 I thank the editors who ploughed through several preliminary versions of my text, making critical suggestions and posing challenging questions. I also thank Dr Dheeraraju, Training Officer, Health Museum, Hyderabad for giving permission to photo documentation.

References

Ali, Momin and A. Ramachari (1996), 'One Hundred Fifty Years of Osmania Medical College (1846–1996)', *Bulletin of The Indian Institute of History of Medicine (BIIHM)*, XXVI (1 and 2): 119–42.

Armstrong, David (1983), *Political Anatomy of the Body: Medical Knowledge in Britain in the Twentieth Century*, Cambridge: Cambridge University Press.

Arnold, David (1993), *Colonizing the Body: State Medicine and Epidemic Disease in the Nineteenth-Century India*, Berkeley: University of California Press.

Arnold, David (2016), *Toxic Histories: Poison and Pollution in Modern India*, Cambridge: Cambridge University Press.

Baru, Rama Vaidyanathan (1992), 'Some Aspects of the Private Sector in Medical Care and Its Inter-relationship with the Public Sector: A Study of Hyderabad-Secunderabad', PhD diss., Jawaharlal Nehru University, New Delhi.

Beverley, Eric Lewis (2015), *Hyderabad, British India, and the World: Muslim Networks and Minor Sovereignty, c. 1850–1950*, Cambridge: Cambridge University Press.

Elkins, James (1999), *The Domain of Images*, Ithaca, NY: Cornell University Press.

Ernst, Watraud, Biswamoy Pati and TV Sekher (2018), *Health and Medicine in the Indian Princely States, 1850–1950*, New York: Routledge.

Foucault, Michel (1976), *The Birth of the Clinic: An Archaeology of Medical Perception*, Translated from French by A. M. Sheridan, London: Tavistock Publications Limited.

Gebhard, Bruno (1946), 'What Good Are Health Museums?' *American Journal of Public Health and the Nation's Health*, 36 (9): 1012–15.

Ghosh, A. (1996), *Ajanta Murals: An Album of Eighty-Five Reproductions in Colour*, New Delhi: Archaeological Survey of India.

Mahadevan, Sudhir (2015), *A Very Old Machine: The Many Origins of the Cinema in India*, New York: SUNY Press.

Marshall, Julia (2004), 'Articulate Images: Bringing the Pictures of Science and Natural History into the Art Curriculum', *Studies in Art Education*, 45 (2): 135–52.

National Council for Education and Training (2019a), *Looking Around: Environmental Studies for Class 3*, New Delhi: National Council for Education Research and Training.

National Council for Education and Training (2019b), *Science: Textbook for Studies for Class 6*, New Delhi: National Council for Education Research and Training.

Prakash, Gyan (1999), *Another Reason: Science and the Imagination of Modern India*, Princeton: Princeton University Press.

Prasad, Srirupa (2015), *Cultural Politics of Hygiene in India, 1890–1940*, London: Palgrave Macmillan.

Rao, Prasad Thota (2015), 'Medical Science, Technology and Colonial Power: Study on Nizam state of Hyderabad 1800 to 1948', PhD diss., Osmania University, Hyderabad.

H.E.H. The Nizam's Government (1934), *The Administration Report of the Medical and Sanitation Department of H.E.H. The Nizam's Government*, Hyderabad-Deccan: Government Central Press.

H.E.H. The Nizam's Government (1939), *The Administration Report of the Medical and Sanitation Department of H.E.H. The Nizam's Government*, Hyderabad-Deccan: Government Central Press.

H.E.H. The Nizam's Government (1940), *The Administration Report of the Medical and Sanitation Department of H.E.H. The Nizam's Government*, Hyderabad-Deccan: Government Central Press.

H.E.H. The Nizam's Government (1942), *The Administration Report of the Medical and Sanitation Department of H.E.H. The Nizam's Government*, Hyderabad-Deccan: Government Central Press.

3

Qutb Shahi *Eidgāh*: An Analysis on Manifestation of South Asian Islamic Architecture

Shaista Anwar

Introduction

A long freestanding wall facing west (Figure 3.1), either alone or adjacent to Sufi shrines, fascinated many colonial travellers, photographers and artists. This came to be reflected in their paintings, drawings and photographs. The wall is often marked by two columns – one on either side, situated on a plinth with arches or cusped arches, and a *mimber* (a pulpit from which the sermon is delivered) often rising taller than the *mihrab* (a prayer niche in a *qibla* wall indicating the direction of Mecca used by Muslims as the direction of prayer or *namaz*). This architectural wall is known as an *eidgāh*[1] in South Asia (Anwar 2023: 51). The Muslims commonly utilize an *eidgāh* on an open ground for gatherings to perform the *salat* (prayer) of Eid (Eid ul-Fitr and Eid al-Adha), but not in the same way as daily prayer mosques and congregational (Friday) mosques. An *azan* (a muezzin's call for prayer) is used to gather people to offer *namaz* in daily prayer and congregational mosques, but no call to prayer is made for the Eid prayer. On the eve of Eid, after witnessing the *ćāṅd rāt* (night of moon-sighting), Eid *namaz* is offered at the *eidgāh* ground in a congregation that symbolizes the togetherness of family, friends, neighbours, relatives

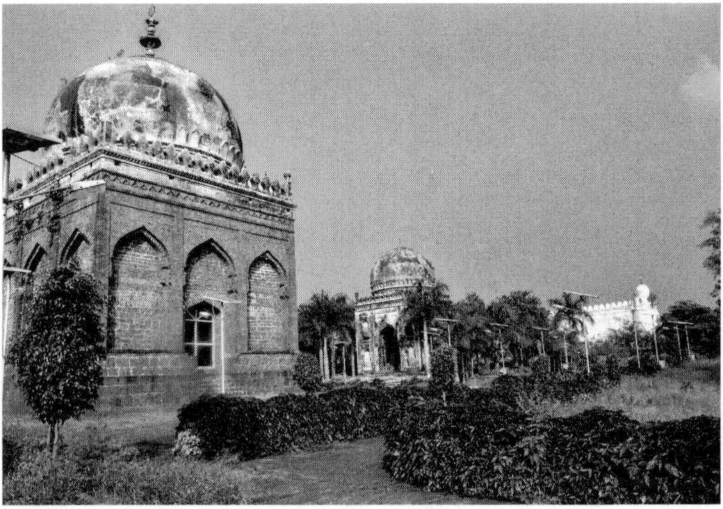

Figure 3.1 The *Eidgāh* at the Rear End, the Barid Shahi Tombs Complex in Bidar, Karnataka, Sixteenth Century. Courtesy: Shaista Anwar, 2015.

and the community, although Eid namaz is not *fard* (obligatory or compulsory like daily prayers that every Muslim must perform).

The question arises here is – why do South Asian Muslims build *eidgāhs* in addition to daily prayer mosques and congregational mosques? I suggest that daily prayer and congregational mosques cannot accommodate large gatherings for an entire community celebration in a town or village. If the congregational or Jama mosques are considered an enlarged version of the daily prayer mosques, then an *eidgāh* is a further expansion of the congregational mosques. An *eidgāh* ground is an open space for people to offer *namaz*; after *namaz*, it turns into an open ground for celebration, resting, fairs and other festive activities. *Eidgāhs* are usually built on the peripheries of the towns and villages. For example, Timur (1336–1405 CE) held an open-air court meeting in the Kharera *eidgāh* in Delhi, indicating multiple purposes of an *eidgāh* ground. Another example is a miniature painting, dated 1635 CE, painted perhaps during the reign of the Mughal Emperor Shah Jahan, titled

'*Shah Jahan and Three Sons*', which is now in the collection of South and South East Asia at the Victoria and Albert Museum, London. The painting depicting the Mughal Emperor Shah Jahan with his three sons mounted on elephants approaching the *eidgāh* of Ajmer further supports the claim. The painting depicts the *eidgāh* stands on a low plinth facing a vast open ground, which is canopied by a brilliant red tent referring to the itinerant nature of the assembly. The off-white *qibla* wall indicates marble, the signature material of Shah Jahan's architecture. The painting is framed by a painted enclosure wall; the plinth is covered by a carpet. The presence of a Sufi saint, his disciples, the Emperor and non-Muslims is enough to suggest an acculturated spatiality of the *eidgāh*. Historians M. A. Qaiyum and Sajjad Shahid mentioned that the *eidgāh's* open-air ground (*sahen*) might have also been used for army tents as their resting place (M. A. Qaiyum and Sajjad Shahid, interview, October, 2015).

However, *eidgāh*s consist of two broad categories: those based on *sahen* (an open area) with a minaret, plinth, *mimber* and *qibla* wall, and those with similar architectural features except for the addition of the *qibla* wall with small chambers. An *eidgāh* with and without chambers suggests a hierarchy in spatial usage. An *eidgāh's chamber* is generally reserved for upper-ranked people. An *eidgāh* without a chamber with plinths intends for the higher officials and sultans. Furthermore, considering the hot and humid climate in the expansive geo-local of the Indian subcontinent, an open-aired *eidgāh* is meant to offer accommodation for large gatherings on religious occasions and otherwise.

On the basis of my archival research and fieldwork[2] I find that *eidgāh* as an architecture remains on the margins of the Islamic art and architecture studies. The existing literature on the Islamic architecture in the Deccan (Safrani 1992; Farooqui 2008; Michell and Zebrowski 2008; Lambourn 2010; Philon 2011; Sardar 2011; Husain 2012; Eaton and Wagoner 2014; Parodi 2014;

Haider and Sardar 2015; Sardar 2015; Michell and Philon 2018), and my field research which involves engaging conversations with various stakeholders such as heritage activists, archaeologists, conservationists, masons, cleaners devotees, tourist guides and archival research in the Department of Archaeology and Museum (now Department of Heritage, Telangana) in 2016–20 encourage me to critically engage with the *eidgāh* on the Qutb Shahi Tomb (henceforth QST) premises in Hyderabad. The first section of this chapter traces the study of *eidgāh* in the historiography of South Asian Islamic architecture. The following section analyses the visual manifestations of *eidgāh* in the colonial artistic production. The third section traces the QST *eidgāh* as a distinct cultural manifestation of architecture-making. Finally, I discuss the underrepresentation of *eidgāh* in the Islamic art and architecture studies and its expressions as manifested in the reports and artistic production of colonial and postcolonial South Asia. The *eidgāh* in the chronicles of the travellers and scholars presents a fresh perspective to reflect upon the idea of a 'wall'. I borrow the methodological framework from Elizabeth Edwards, who proposes that photographs (or images) represent a strong narrative as they 'reinforce a sense of being, of possession, of identity and of belonging … ' (Edwards 2015: 322). I also derive from Homi Bhabha's argument on 'mimicry' to probe the picturesque compositions of the paintings and photographs discussed in this chapter (Bhabha 1984: 132).

Eidgāh in the Historiography of Islamic Architecture

Ghulam Yazdani, the first director of the Department of Archaeology and Museums (DAM), Hyderabad, established in 1914 by the seventh Nizam Mir Osman Ali Khan, reports the *eidgāh* in

Koilkonda (presently in Mahbubnagar, Telangana) (Yazdani 1935: 5). Enhanced by two bulky columns on either side with significant girth due to staircases leading to a *jharokhā* (a balcony on which one can stand) on the upper level, the *eidgāh* is situated on a plinth with cusped arches, the *mimber* taller than the *mihrab*. In his study of Bidar's architecture, Yazdani mentions that the Bidar *eidgāh* was constructed at the end of the courtyard of Qasim Barid II's tomb (Yazdani 1944: 165–6). The *eidgāh* wall facing the *Kaaba*[3] has seven arched niches, including *mihrab* and *mimber*. John Burton-Page mentions the Bahmani *eidgāh* at Bijapur, the Chanderi *eidgāh* in Malwa, an *eidgāh* in Burhanpur and three from Gulbarga. He observes a close resemblance between the *eidgāh* structures of Malwa, Gulbarga (now renamed Kalaburagi), Bidar, Bijapur (now known as Vijayapura) and the Farooqi dynasty (1382–1601 CE) buildings in Burhanpur (Burton-Page 2008: 175–6). However, their study does not offer a socio-spatial understanding of Deccani *eidgāh* architectural walls.

The *eidgāhs* of the Delhi Sultanate from the thirteenth to the mid-sixteenth century and the Mughal era between the mid-sixteenth and nineteenth centuries gained reasonable scholarly attention. For instance, Muhammad Mokhlesur Rahman's study, especially of the Samsi *eidgāh* (1202–9 CE) in Badaun, and the *eidgāh* built during the Khalji dynasty (1290–1320 CE) in Rapri, near Agra in Uttar Pradesh (Rahman 1988: 267–8; Porter 2018: 281–92). The Rapri *eidgāhs* is an expansive brick structure with a plain voluminous tower at each end. However, the bright blue glazed tiles ornamentation on both *eidgāh*s remains the centre of attraction (Porter 2018: 281–92). Catharine Asher's study of the Mughal *eidgāh*, specifically the *eidgāh* in Merta (in present Rajasthan) built in the seventeenth century during Shah Jahan's reign, reflects the stylistic interaction between Mughal and Rajput architecture (Asher 2017: 223). The Patna *eidgāh* built in 1628 was patronized by Saif Khan. Its shallow arched *mihrab* is surmounted by a cusped *kangurā*, a decorative undulating pattern on arches (Asher 2017: 237). The *eidgāh* at the Ajmer Sharif patronized by Nawab Mirza Chaman Beg in 1773–4 and the *eidgāh* in Agra are built after Shah Jahan's Diwan-e-Aam (public pavilion) (Asher 2017: 312–13). The Agra *eidgāh* in red sandstone features a cusped entrance under the high arch within a tall *pīshṭāq* (centrally situated a high portal or entrance), a distinct Shah Jahan's architectural feature found as in the Machchi Bhawan (the Fish Chamber) in the Agra fort (Asher 2017: 250–60). The Sultanate and Mughal *eidgāh*s embody a spirit of experimentation with the architectural elements as well as local materials and broaden the scope of assimilation in the architectural landscape of South Asia. The *eidgāh*s also bear the Iranian, Turkish and Rajput architecture features. For instance, the Bidar *eidgāh*'s spiral pillars resemble the mosque's pillars in Samarra, Iraq and the Delhi Sultanate architecture, such as the mosque of Mubarak Khalji in Daulatabad Fort (Manohar 2021: 66–9). The Koilkonda *eidgāh* features *kangurās*, common in Mughal architecture. Thus, an eclectic combination of the standardized elements and the regional preferences enriches the architectural vocabulary of the South Asian *eidgāh*s. Thus, we find that the studies on *eidgāh*s are based on the formal architectural form and materials that are often linked with imperial and local feudal patronage. Any architectural studies hardly foregrounds the basic socio-spatial character of an *eidgāh* wall which is an open architectural wall with shifting usage and purposes based on common people's need.[4]

The *eidgāh*s are also responses of climatic condition of South Asia. The climate variation across South Asia makes the *sahen* of the *eidgāh* shaded with regional perennial trees such as tamarind or mango, considering it's a wall on open ground and is used for prayer and fair and other congregation purposes (Anwar 2023: 56).

Thus, the perennial trees around the *eidgāh* wall are a registration of people's participation, care and conservation of space and structure. We often find images of bushy and bulky trees around the *eidgāhs* in the colonial drawings, paintings and prints.

Eidgāh as a Motif in the Colonial Artistic Production

In the mid-eighteenth century, as the sovereignty of the British Raj expanded, so did their interaction with locals, leading to enmeshed acculturation. Among the group of colonial travellers and settlers in the subcontinent were also painters and photographers who had diverse interests ranging from political motivations to documenting and narrating the native lives. Thus, we see the images of the *eidgāhs* in the colonial paintings and photographs; they witnessed the festivals and celebrations along with natives or merely observed from afar. The colonial pictures thus offer several interesting facets, such as the abandoned and lonely features of *eidgāh*s, which fascinated the painters. These permit us to notice their relationship with the *eidgāh*s and their own aesthetic sensibilities, representing the nature of their artistic practice in visualizing the 'other' (Said 2003: 222). The seemingly evidential quality of the images indicates the presence of the painters on site; by doing so, they function as a sophisticated colonial strategy. The colonial artworks reinforce a sense of confusion and chaos for onlookers rather than invoking a resemblance to the reality of the sites. For example, Thomas Daniell's non-chambered *eidgāh in Amroha* (1810), now in the Tate Modern, London, was painted in European naturalism; it shows the *eidgāh* in a lush green with two octagonal Turkish pillars and a conical pointed dome on a vast plinth. He paints the worshippers performing their ablution near the fountain, people wearing skull caps heading towards the *eidgāh* and standing near the *qibla* wall. Thomas

Daniell's *Eedgah Barelli* (1790), which is now in the collection of the British Library, London is a drawing of the non-chambered *eidgāh* in Bareilly. The drawing depicts an onion-shaped dome and the arch, minarets and gateway in Mughal style. Philip Meadows Taylor's drawing of the non-chambered *eidgāh* in Burhanpur from the collection of the British Library, London (Figure 3.2), shows the decorative *mihrab*, Iranian niches with *muqarnas* (rhythmic stalactite vaulting), and a small tomb at the corner.

Linnaeus Tripe's photograph (1858) in the collection of the British Library shows the non-chambered *eidgāh* with a tomb in the background at Rayakottai in Salem district; it presents the brick structure with stucco work. It is open from all four sides with the *qibla* wall seeming almost like a curtain drawn over the landscape. Sita Ram's painting (1814–15) shows the chambered

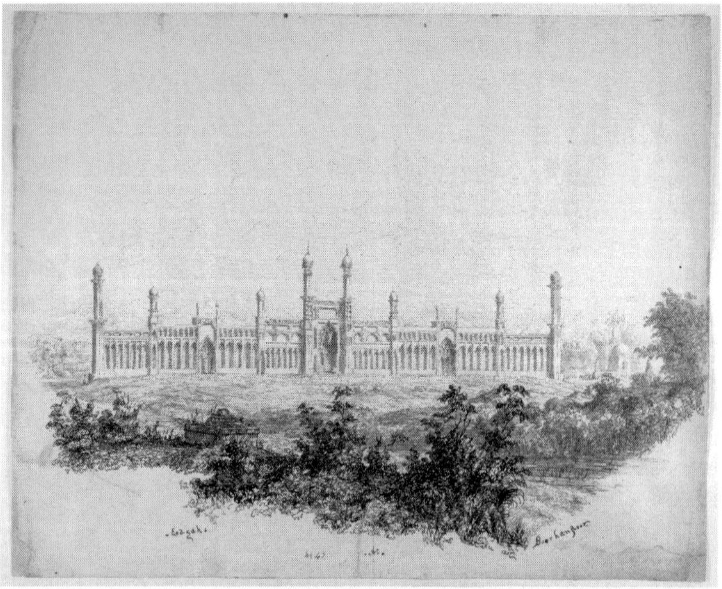

Figure 3.2 An Exotic Representation of the *Eidgāh*, Burhanpur, Madhya Pradesh, India. Courtesy: Philip Meadows Taylor 1837, and The British Library.

eidgāh in the middle with a plinth close to the ablution area and a *pīshṭāq* on the left. The *eidgāh*'s three onion-shaped domes and cusped entrances in red sandstone have stylistic affinities with Mughal mosques such as the Jama Mosque, Delhi, and the Badshahi Mosque, Lahore. James Hunter's print (1804) from the British Library is one of the chambered *eidgāh* in Mysore, with its four pillars – one in each corner – resembling the buttresses at the mausoleum of Sheikh Rukn-ud-Din Abul Fateh from the Tughlaq period. The upper part of the pillars is octagonal, perhaps inspired by the pillars at the Mahmud Gawan Madrasa in Bidar, Karnataka. The print displays people, including sepoys of the British army, shown speaking to the natives. William Henry Baker's photograph (1865) of a chambered *eidgāh* at Multan in the collection of the British Library presents the ruin in red sandstone of Mughal style.

Christiane Gruber and Sune Haugbolle argue that 'images are always produced within the dynamics of power as well as within arenas of conflicting ideologies' (Gruber and Haugbolle 2013: xxi). I suggest that the standalone *eidgāh*s in South Asian landscapes were visual reminders of differences and strangeness and were hence perceived as *exotic* by the Europeans. Their acquaintance with the Walls of Babylon (in modern Iraq), the Great Wall of China, Hadrian's Wall of England, and the Western Wall of Jerusalem did not equip them to understand the *eidgāh* walls in the subcontinent. Fortification, protection, separation, bifurcation and division were characteristic of these walls, such as the Babylon Wall, China Wall and Hadrian's Wall, but the *eidgāh* does not serve the same purpose. However, the European artists probably confused seeing the *eidgāh* wall in the open field as a standalone structure and the transformation of this structure on the day of Eid. This challenged their knowledge production about the walls, which are usually known to stand for division, partition, defence and barrier.

The *Eidgāh* Next to the Qutb Shahi Tombs and Its Absence in the Pictorial Representation

From the mid-fourteenth century, during the Bahmani Sultanate, Deccan received attention as a land of opportunities for many communities, including Central Asians (Sherwani and Joshi 1974; Khalidi 1999; Shakeb 2017; Simpkins 2019; Manohar 2021). Maritime trade provided a bridge for commerce and the fluid cultural, artistic and material exchanges. However, after the decline of the Bahmani in the late fifteenth century, the Qutb Shahi dynasty was one of the five sultanates, who rose to power. By the mid-sixteenth century, the dynasty, during the reign of Muhammad Quli Qutb Shah, developed Hyderabad into a cosmopolitan city.

The *eidgāh*, close to Ibrahim Quli Qutub Shah's tomb, behind the tomb of Muhammad Quli Qutb Shah, intrigues me because of its architectural and historical complexities. Marika Sardar delineates that this structure was built by Sultan Quli Qutb Shah (Sardar 2015: 94). Whereas Robert Alan Simpkins's map (Simpkins 2014: 37) shows the *eidgāh* inside the boundary wall of the complex, which was built by Sir Mir Turab Ali Khan, popularly known as Salar Jung I in Hyderabad, most influential nobleman and minister in Asaf Jahi Dynasty – Nizams of Hyderabad (1724–1948). However, considering the *eidgāh* as a standalone wall on the open field (*sahen*) it is difficult to imagine with a boundary wall as it can be seen in Simpkins's map (Simpkins 2014: 37). During my fieldwork, I witnessed thousands of people come from far away for Eid *namaz* and celebrate their Eid. The *eidgāh* inside the boundary wall cannot serve the purpose because of its functionality mentioned earlier.

The DAM carried out the renovation works in the QST complex over the years and preserves photo documentation of the site, but none of the DAM's Annual Reports mentions about the QST *eidgāh* (Yazdani 1916, 1917, 1919, 1922, 1923, 1926, 1928, 1935,

1942; Deshpande 1974, 1975 and 1978; Thapar 1979; Sastry 1985, 1986, 1988a, b, c; Kedareshwari 2003; Aga Khan Trust for Culture 2014, 2016; Sardar 2015).[5] In the report of DAM in 1920–1, a large plan of the Golconda Tomb and extended site of the QST is printed (Figure 3.3) and the *eidgāh* remains absent in the plan. Syed Ali Asgar Bilgrami, the Director of DAM (1922–4), mentioned another *eidgāh* at Sultan Nagar built by Muhammad Qutb Shah VI which remained incomplete due to his untimely death. However, we do not find any mention of the QST *eidgāh* in Syed Bilgrami's study (1927: 46). In 2004–5, the *eidgāh* wall had minor restoration. In 2009, DAM and the Andhra Pradesh government sent a dossier of the QST, including the *eidgāh*, to UNESCO. In 2012, the Andhra Pradesh State Waqf Board, the Quli Qutb Shah Urban Development Authority and DAM restored the *eidgāh* pavement with the Shahabad stone (draft of the dossier, 2012).

Furthermore, the QST *eidgāh* continues to be absent in different pictorial production in the nineteenth century. Robert Melville Grindlay's print (1813) in the Aga Khan Visual Archive, one of the earliest visuals of the QST site, depicts Abdullah Qutb Shah's tomb appears at the centre. The other tombs are smaller in size, are visible in the rear background. Sultan Quli Qutb Shah's tomb is recognizable in the background. However, the *eidgāh* is barely seen as it is behind Quli Qutb Shah's tomb. Alexandre De Bar's drawing of the QST (*c*. 1862–4) in bird's-eye view depicts the abandoned royal burial land in wild bushes. Louis Rousselet's drawing dated 1877 displays the *hammam* bath in the QST premise in Albertian perspective. The *hammam* is opposite to Muhammad Quli Qutb Shah's Tomb and the *eidgāh* behind is not visible in the drawing. Here, the artist also draws a ruin in dense, wild vegetation. Another drawing of an unknown artist dated 1876–7 showcases Sultan Quli Qutb Shah's Tomb in the abandoned landscape where bushes grow till the parapet.

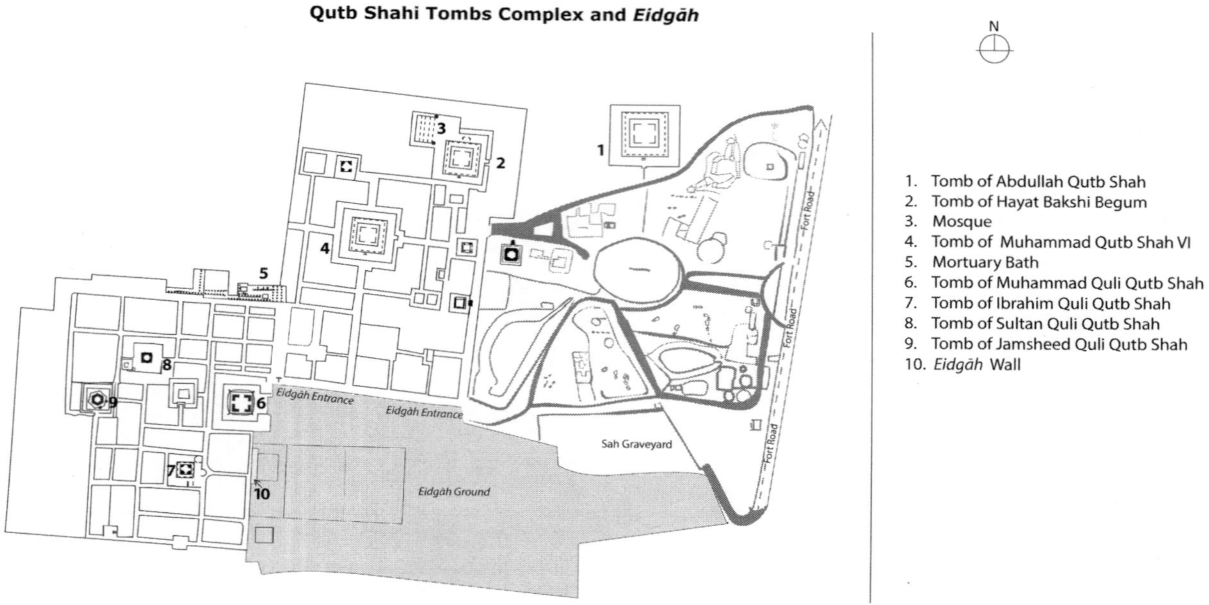

Figure 3.3 The Ground Plan of the Qutb Shahi Tombs Complex and *Eidgāh*. Courtesy: Bijay Nath 2025. Sources: The Report of the Archaeological Department of H. E. H. Nizam's Dominions, 1920–1 and Shaista Anwar.

Edward Said argues that Orientalism was based on generalizations and stereotypes which every traveller from Europe produced consciously or unconsciously (Said 2003: 166). The colonial art discussed in this chapter demonstrates the lack of human life and activity around the landscape. The ruin in the abandoned landscape with wild vegetation is an example of the stereotype. Sayed Farid Alatas says, 'Visual Orientalism ... refers to the use of selective imagery that acts as a representation of an Orientalist thought-style ... Orientalist art is not merely a reflection of the political economy of Western domination but was produced in the context of cross-cultural interaction, between the colonizer and colonized' (Alatas 2018: 20). Using Alatas's framework, I suggest that the QST *eidgāh* in colonial art is *visual orientalism*, a stereotypical representation of deserted landscapes, embodying backwardness and primitiveness.

> Now all Asia's land
> Moans in Emptiness.
> Xerxes led forth, oh oh!
> Xerxes destroyed, woe woe!
> Xerxes' plans have all miscarried
> In ship of the sea.
>
> (Said 2003: 57)

This extract from a poem by Aeschylus, a Greek dramatist, evokes a sense of despair about Asia. Here, 'Asia' is a metaphor referring to the Persians; Aeschylus has described them as weak and pathetic, signifying the Greeks as a superior race. Said explains that this shows the imaginative geography, classification and hierarchy among the Europeans. He says that in the European imagination, the Orient was divided into the realms of visited and conquered (Said 2003: 58). I suggest that colonial textual (here DAM Reports)

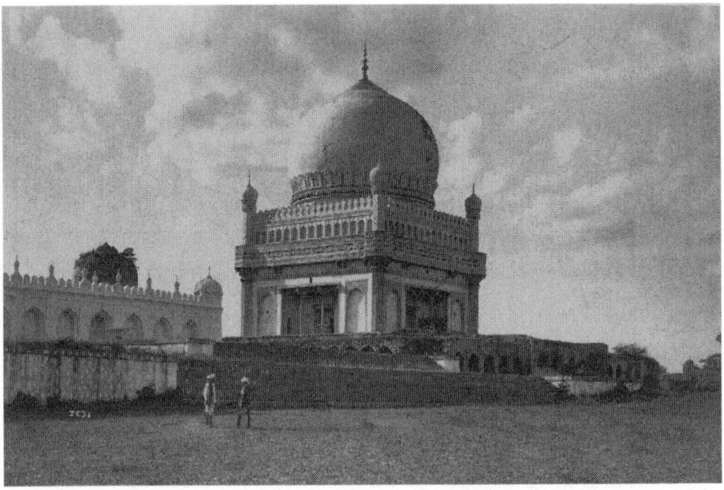

Figure 3.4 The QST *Eidgāh* (Which Is Visible Accidentally in the Photographer's Frame on the Right), the Qutb Shahi Tombs Complex, Hyderabad-Deccan, Sixteenth-Century *Eidgāh*. Courtesy: Raja Deen Dayal, 1988, and The British Library.

and pictorial productions (photographs, prints) of the QST as an uninhabited and ruined complex and the colonial drawings of *eidgāh* resonate with Said's argument.

Raja Deen Dayal's photographs showcase the elites of the Hyderabad princely state from 1887 to 1902 (Dewan and Hutton 2013: 42–3). His photographs portray the Nizam's well-governed state, diverse heritage and elites' leisure and activities such as hunting and hospitality. It looks like the QST *eidgāh* appears accidentally with Muhammad Quli Qutb Shah's Tomb (Figure 3.4) in one of Dayal's photographs (1888) from the collection of the British Library. This picture brings forth a different understanding of power. Why does the QST *eidgāh* fail to appear in the frame of the photograph and the photographer? Dayal's photograph depicts his attentiveness to the beauty of the royal tomb (here Muhammad Quli Qutb Shah's Tomb). The QST *eidgāh* next to the royal tombs looks ordinary and mundane. Compared to the colonial art discussed earlier, Dayal's photograph depicts a distinct shift. The sense of alienation that prevails in the European traveller's pictures has been replaced by a sense of familiarity in Dayal's photographs. One can notice that the past is weak and defeated in the European representation of the QST site as if space has become an asset of the colonial power. Two men standing near the *eidgāh* plinth in local attire in Dayal's photograph show that the place is no more a ghostly space; its belonging to the princely state suggests the state's strength and architectural prowess. Another photograph by Dayal showing a more than a mile-long procession of the troop on the elephants is a visual trope of the Nizam's power and wealth in the colonial period. A banner hung over the bridge pushes our sight further back to the Charminar. Thus, Charminar in the background and the gigantic tomb of Quli Qutb Shah in Dayal's photos for the Nizam is the visual appropriation of the ownership of Hyderabad, built by Qutb Shahs.

Two photographs (credit: Mansell) in the Life Photo Collection, New York, present two different angles of the QST *eidgāh* site. In both photographs, the *eidgāh* appears almost unnoticed, as the photographer's vantage point is the ruins of Golconda Fort. Thus, the *eidgāh,* which was hitherto unseen in the historiography of South Asian Islamic architecture, is seen and documented in 1975 for the first time in a direct photograph (Figure 3.5). Thomas Lüettge, the photographer, has captured the *eidgāh* (1975) from the south with Ibrahim Quli Qutb Shah's tomb clearly visible at the far right. However, I do not wish to focus on this set of photographs in terms of composition, but on the dynamic way in which the *eidgāh* seems to be telling viewers about its existence in ruins. Arjun Kamal Mangaldas's photograph of the *eidgāh* in 1986 depicts the tombs of Sultan Quli Qutb Shah, Jamsheed Quli Qutb Shah, Ibrahim Quli Qutb Shah, Muhammad Quli Qutb Shah and the *eidgāh.*

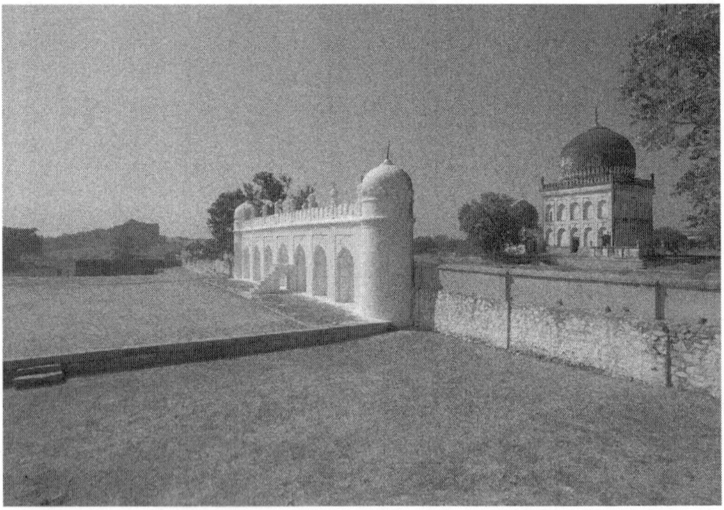

Figure 3.5 A View of the QST *Eidgāh* (Ibrahim Quli Qutb Shah's Tomb Is Visible at the Right Corner) in the Qutb Shahi Tombs Complex, Hyderabad-Deccan, Sixteenth Century. Courtesy: Thomas Lüettge, the Photographer, 1975 and Aga Khan Visual Archive, MIT Library.

The Qutb Shahis had a stronghold on power in Deccan and became an important centre of wealth during Ibrahim Quli Qutb Shah. His patronization of temples, Telugu literature and large-scale irrigation initiatives like those of Kakatiyas made him come to be known by the title 'Ibharama cakravarti' (Eaton 2005: 142). It was almost as if the Kakatiya dynasty (twelfth–fourteenth century) had been reborn during his time with a Perso-Islamic veneer (Eaton 2005: 156) which led to the development of Perso-Islamic culture infused with Telugu aesthetics (Eaton 2005: 142–3). I suggest that the QST *eidgāh* perhaps is the witness of cohabitation of regional, local, royal and commoners, bearing the architectural insignia of Ibrahim Quli Qutb Shah's ideologies and carried forward by his successors (Sardar 2014: 17; Fischel 2020: 69, 96 and 152).

Conclusion

The *eidgāhs* seen today across the landscape of South Asia are relevant to the history of Islamic architecture from the perspectives of its shared socio-spatial practices. The *eidgāh* walls on the open field are the embodiment of pluralistic fluid architecture, land and spaces by their very nature, blurring the presumed boundaries of rituals and traditions in Islamic practice. In this chapter, I have explored the *eidgāh* and its historiography in South Asia to discuss the colonial picture on the muted representation of the QST site. I have also discussed the agency of framing strategy in the photographs, which are distinctively different from the colonial picture productions. Raja Deen Dayal did not emphasize the void and loneliness of the open space which was visibly common in the colonial pictures. Instead, the close proximity between Quli Qutb Shah's tomb and the *eidgāh* is employed to display the power of the princely state. Later images of the *eidgāh*, after the 1960s and 1970s, depict and represent it as a 'potent symbolic and affective source of cultural identity' (Bhabha 1994: 140).

During my research, I found that the QST complex is a socially shared architectural site, but the *eidgāh* does not draw much attention of the crowd. While navigating through the complex, the visitors often overlook the *eidgāh*, similar to Deccan studies, and the reports of the institutional custodians. The institutions such as DAM, the Waqf Board of present Telangana and the Aga Khan Development Network, and skilled individuals who temporarily or permanently work in the site, such as masons, craftsmen, engineers and conservationists exercise their power to control the site, which continuously generates new and counter-narratives about the QST complex. This keeps my critical enquiry active as more facets open up each time, I visit the site.

Notes

1 The word *eidgāh* is derived from the Arabic and Persian languages. Eid is derived from the Arabic word – *aúwda* meaning custom or repeat, celebrated as a festival among Muslims. *Gāh* is a Persian word, meaning space. *Eidgāh* therefore implies a place or space for celebration.

2 I thank Sir Dorabji Tata Trust travel grant for supporting my field work, the Department of Archaeology and Museums (now Department of Heritage, Government of Telangana), George Michell, Sanjay Subodh, Janab M. A. Qaiyum, Janab Sajjad Shahid, Yousuf Saeed, Baishali Ghosh, Rajarshi Sengupta and Irfan Zuberi for their insights and suggestions, and Thomas Lüettge for giving access to his photographs.

3 The Kaaba, meaning cube, is the centre of the Holy Mosque in Mecca. It is draped in a silk curtain adorned with calligraphy in gold which is replaced annually (Petersen 1996: 142–3).

4 This issue is addressed in the article, titled 'Eidgah – Multifunctional Open Architecture as a Shared Space for Memory and Emotion' (Anwar 2023: 51–61).

5 The known and lesser-known structures in the QST complex provide an insight into the Golconda courtly culture. Some architectural elements altered with time and some got hidden or buried under the sprawling explanation of recent urban settlement which remaps the land and alters the local landscape. However, the buried and lost structure survives through the ephemeral and intangible lives of objects, and humans. Thus, some local tourist maps used for the foreign visitors for the heritage walk in the QST complex mark the QST *eidgāh* in their walk routes. One such local tourist map reads, 'This *eidgāh* is one of the times of Qutb Shahi King. Adjacent to this, there is a well – built and strong. This well is known as *Eidgāh Bowli* and it is worth visiting.' [*sic*]

References

Alatas, Sayed Farid (2018), 'The Arrest of Diponegoro: Visual Orientalism and Its Alternative', in Sanaz Fotouhi and Esmaeil Zeiny (eds), *Seen and Unseen: Visual Cultures of Imperialism*, 17–33, Leiden: Brill.

Aga Khan Trust for Culture (2014), 'Qutb Shahi Heritage Park Conservation and Landscape Restoration, Annual Report 2014', *Architexturez South Asia*, https://architexturez.net/doc/az-cf-179028 (accessed 3 May 2021).

Aga Khan Trust for Culture (2016), 'Report of the Excavations Carried out at Qutb Shahi Heritage Park at Hyderabad: 2014–16, in Qutb Shahi Heritage Park: Conservation and Landscape Restoration', *Architexturez South Asia*. https://architexturez.net/doc/az-cf-184415 (accessed 3 May 2021).

Anwar, Shaista (2023). 'Eidgah: Multifunctional Open Architecture as a Shared Space for Memory and Emotion', in Hussein Rashid and Kristian Petersen (eds), *The Bloomsbury Handbook of Muslims and Popular Culture*, 51–61, London: Bloomsbury Academic.

Asher, Catherine B. (2017), *Architecture of Mughal India*, Delhi: Cambridge University Press.

Bhabha, Homi (1984), 'Of Mimicry and Man: The Ambivalence of Colonial Discourse', October, 28: 125–33, www.jstor.org/stable/778467 (accessed 3 May 2021).

Bhabha, Homi K. (1994), *The Location of Culture*, London and New York: Routledge.

Bilgrami, Syed Ali Asgar ([1927] 1992), *Landmarks of the Deccan: A Comprehensive Guide to the Archaeological Remains of the City and Suburbs of Hyderabad*, Hyderabad-Deccan: Government Central Press.

Burton-Page, John (2008), *Indian Islamic Architecture: Forms and Typologies, Sites and Monuments*, George Michell (ed.), Vol. 20, Leiden and Boston: Brill.

Dewan, Deepali and Deborah Hutton (2013), *Raja Deen Dayal: Artist-Photographer in 19th-Century India*, Ahmedabad: Mapin Publishing.

Deshpande, M. N., ed. (1974), *Indian Archaeology 1970–71: A Review*, New Delhi: Archaeological Survey of India, Government of India.

Deshpande, M. N., ed. (1975), *Indian Archaeology 1971–72: A Review*, New Delhi: Archaeological Survey of India, Government of India.

Deshpande, M. N., ed. (1978), *Indian Archaeology 1972–73: A Review*, New Delhi: Archaeological Survey of India, Government of India.

Eaton, Richard M. (2005), *A Social History of the Deccan 1300–1761: Eight Indian Lives*, Delhi: Cambridge University Press.

Eaton, Richard M. and Phillip B. Wagoner (2014), *Power, Memory, Architecture: Contested Sites on India's Deccan Plateau, 1300–1600*, New Delhi: Oxford University Press.

Edwards, Elizabeth (2015), 'Photographs as Strong History', in Caraffa Costanza and Tiziana Serena (eds), *Photo Archives and the Idea of Nation*, 321–30, Berlin: De Gruyter.

Farooqui, Salma Ahmed (2008), *Multicultural Dimensions of Medieval Deccan*, New Delhi: Primus Books.

Fischel, Roy S. (2020), *Local States in an Imperial World: Identity, Society and Politics in the Early Modern Deccan*, Edinburgh: Edinburgh University Press.

Gruber, Christiane and Sune Haugbolle, eds (2013), *Visual Culture in the Modern Middle East: Rhetoric of the Image*, Bloomington: Indiana University Press.

Haider, Navina Najat and Marika Sardar, eds (2015), *Sultans of Deccan India, 1500–1700: Opulence and Fantasy*, New York: The Metropolitan Museum of Art.

Husain, Ali Akbar (2012), *Scent in the Islamic Garden: A Study of Literary Sources in Persian and Urdu*, Karachi: Oxford University Press.

Kedareshwari, J. (2003), *The Qutb Shahi Tombs: A Companion Guide*, Hyderabad: Department of Archaeology and Museums.

Khalidi, Omar (1999), *Romance of the Golconda Diamonds*, Ahmedabad: Mapin Publishing.

Lambourn, Elizabeth A. (2010), 'A Self-Conscious Art? Seeing Micro-Architecture in Sultanate South Asia', *Muqarnas*, 27 (1): 121–56.

Manohar, Mohit (2021), 'A Victory Tower Built by a Slave: The Chand Minar at Daulatabad in Deccan India, *Muqarnas*, 38 (1): 35–76.

Michell, George and Mark Zebrowski (2008), *Architecture and Art of the Deccan Sultanates*, Cambridge: Cambridge University Press.

Michell, George and Helen Philon (2018), *Islamic Architecture of Deccan India*, Woodbridge: ACC Art Books.

Parodi, Laura E. (2014), *The Visual World of Muslim India: The Art, Culture and Society of the Deccan in the Early Modern Era*, London and New York: I.B. Tauris.

Petersen, Andrew (1996), *Dictionary of Islamic architecture*, London: Routledge.

Philon, Helen (2011), 'Deccani Gardens and Architectural Landscapes in the Fourteenth and Fifteenth Centuries', *South Asian Studies*, 27 (2): 157–84.

Porter, Yves (2018), 'The Shahi `Idgah of 1312 at Rapri (Uttar Pradesh): A Landmark in Indian Glazed Tiles', *Muqarnas*, 35 (1): 281–92.

Rahman, Muhammad Mokhlesur (1988), 'A Khalji Idgah at Rapri (1312): Reflections on Its Glazed Tile Decoration', *Islamic Studies*, 27 (3): 267–68. www.jstor.org/stable/20839900 (accessed 3 May 2021).

Safrani, Shehzeb ed. (1992), *Golconda and Hyderabad*, Bombay: Marg.

Said, Edward W. (2003), *Orientalism*, Gurgaon: Penguin Random House India.

Sardar, Marika (2011), 'The Early Foundations of Golconda and the Rise of Fortifications in the Fourteenth-Century Deccan', *South Asian Studies*, 27 (1): 25–50.

Sardar, Marika (2014), 'Circular Cities of Deccan', in Laura E. Parodi (ed.), *The Visual World of Muslim India: The Art, Culture and Society of the Deccan in the Early Modern Era*, 3–30, London: I.B. Tauris.

Sardar, Marika (2015), *Hyderabad, Golconda*, Mumbai: Jaico Publishing House.

Sastry, V. V. Krishna, ed. (1985), *Annual Report of the Department of Archaeology & Museums, Andhra Pradesh, 1971–1972*, Hyderabad: The Government of Andhra Pradesh.

Sastry, V. V. Krishna, ed. (1986), *Annual Report of the Department of Archaeology & Museums, Andhra Pradesh 1975–1976*, Hyderabad: The Government of Andhra Pradesh.

Sastry, V. V. Krishna, ed. (1988a), *Annual Report of the Department of Archaeology & Museums, Andhra Pradesh 1979–1980*, Hyderabad: The Government of Andhra Pradesh.

Sastry, V. V. Krishna, ed. (1988b), *Annual Report of the Department of Archaeology & Museums, Andhra Pradesh 1982–1983*, Hyderabad: The Government of Andhra Pradesh.

Sastry, V. V. Krishna, ed. (1988c), *Annual Report of the Department of Archaeology & Museums, Andhra Pradesh 1984–1985*, Hyderabad: The Government of Andhra Pradesh.

Shakeb, M. Z. A. (2017), *Relations of Golkonda with Iran*, Delhi: Primus Books.

Sherwani, H. K. and P. M. Joshi (1974), *History of the Medieval Deccan (1295–1724), Vol. I & II,* Hyderabad: The Government of Andhra Pradesh.

Simpkins, Robert Alan (2019), 'Inferring Road Networks and Social Change through Elite Monuments of the Golconda Kingdom', *South Asian Studies*, 36 (1): 1–19.

Simpkins, Robert Alan (2014), 'Golconda's Mosques and Tombs: Distribution, Chronology and Meaning', in Laura E. Parodi (ed.), *The Visual World of Muslim India: The Art, Culture and Society of the Deccan in the Early Modern Era*, 31–52, London: I.B. Tauris.

Thapar, B. K., ed. (1979), *Indian Archaeology 1973–74: A Review*, New Delhi: Archaeological Survey of India, Government of India.

Yazdani, Ghulam (1916), *Annual Report of the Archaeological Department of His Exalted Highness the Nizam's Dominions 1914–1915*, Calcutta: Baptist Mission Press.

Yazdani, Ghulam (1917), *Annual Report of the Archaeological Department of His Exalted Highness the Nizam's Dominions 1915–1916*, Calcutta: Baptist Mission Press.

Yazdani, Ghulam (1919), *Annual Report of the Archaeological Department of His Exalted Highness the Nizam's Dominions 1917–1918*, Calcutta: Baptist Mission Press.

Yazdani, Ghulam (1922), *Annual Report of the Archaeological Department of His Exalted Highness the Nizam's Dominions 1919–19120*, Calcutta: Baptist Mission Press.

Yazdani, Ghulam (1923), *Annual Report of the Archaeological Department of His Exalted Highness the Nizam's Dominions 1920–1921*, Calcutta: Baptist Mission Press.

Yazdani, Ghulam (1926), *Annual Report of the Archaeological Department of His Exalted Highness the Nizam's Dominions 1921–1924*, Calcutta: Baptist Mission Press.

Yazdani, Ghulam (1928), *Annual Report of the Archaeological Department of His Exalted Highness the Nizam's Dominions 1925–1926*, Calcutta: Baptist Mission Press.

Yazdani, Ghulam (1935), *Annual Report of the Archaeological Department of His Exalted Highness the Nizam's Dominions 1931–1933*, Calcutta: Baptist Mission Press.

Yazdani, Ghulam (1942), *Annual Report of the Archaeological Department of His Exalted Highness the Nizam's Dominions 19137–1940*, Calcutta: Baptist Mission Press.

Yazdani, Ghulam (1944), *Bidar: Its History and Monuments*, Oxford: Oxford University Press.

4

Chronicles of the Temple Painters in Hyderabad

Bijay Nath

Introduction

When travelling in the city of Hyderabad, one cannot possibly ignore the numerous neighbourhood temples that enliven the cityscape with their bright contrasting colour scheme. Temples built in the Drāviḍa temple architectural style are a common sight all over Hyderabad (Figure 4.1). The features and fragments of Dravidian temple architecture and painted murals have generated a robust body of scholarship, which has delved into the patterns of patronage, architecture, trade connections and devotion intersecting at these temple sites (Talbot 1991; Leonard 2011; Branfoot 2013). The role of artisans in making temples has been confronted in two different trajectories. Firstly, the details of temple building and mural painting are discussed from a reconstructionist's perspective, with limited stress on the artisanal livelihood and knowledge system (Sinha 2000). Secondly, the genealogical and generational frameworks are prioritized to contextualize the link between historical and contemporary modes of temple building and painting (Appadurai 1974; Parker 2003). These considerations, however, do not adequately address the complexity of the practice of temple painting in a burgeoning metropolis like Hyderabad.

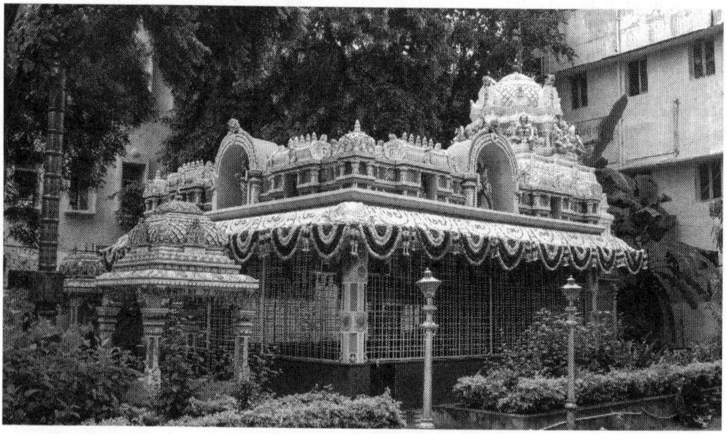

Figure 4.1 The multicoloured Gopura – The Superstructure over the Entrance-Gate to the Precinct of a Temple in Southern India, Sivalayam of Public Garden in Hyderabad-Deccan. Courtesy: Bijay Nath, 2012.

Urban temple painters lie at the crossroads of contemporaneity and histories – popular, canonical and metropolitan. Although the images of the deities and semi-divine beings in the temples follow certain iconographical traits evoking historical connections, one cannot distinguish their visual language from that of the vivid shop signboards and painted adverts on the city walls. Who then are the painters, and how do we assess the shared authorship of the painted images created by them? How do the artisans learn to paint? Is it strictly a hereditary skill or is it acquired? In this chapter, I attempt to put forward a chronicle of the temple painters of Hyderabad, highlighting these concerns while emphasizing the role of craftsmanship and artisanal networks.

My argument rests on my fieldwork[1] from 2012 to 2017 which involves the interviewing of the ninety-one temple painters in Hyderabad, most of whom have migrated from different parts of Telangana, Andhra Pradesh, Tamil Nadu, Odisha and Maharashtra, the family members of the temple painters, patrons and visual documentation of the temple painting projects in Hyderabad (Figure 4.2).[2] The Telugu-speaking painters hailed from Medak, Nalgonda, Karimnagar, Warangal, Khammam, Mahbubnagar and Ranga Reddy districts in Telangana, and East Godavari, West Godavari, Prakasam, Guntur and Kurnool in Andhra Pradesh. While the majority of the painters are Hindu, including a fraction of them from Schedule Caste communities, especially Madiga, there are Muslim and Christian artisans too.

Among my interviewees, there was Krishna Remidala from Kodada, Nalgonda, who was Christian and Madiga. He received training in painting from Mohammed Jani, Hyderabad (Interview with Krishna Remidala, Hyderabad, May 2013). Sheikh Arsadullah from Marteru, East Godavari, learned temple painting from several practising artisans in Hyderabad, including Ravi Kumar, Shankar and Suresh, and has a rental settlement in Uppal; he painted the interior and the superstructure of the Mahakali temple in Kavadiguda, Secunderabad (Interview with Sheikh Arsadullah, Hyderabad, March 2013). There were also hereditary artisans such as Naga Babu Katta, who hailed from the Gouda community of Bhimavaram, West Godavari. He was trained under the keen eye of his father, Katta Venugopala Rao (Interview with Naga Babu Katta, Hyderabad, May 2013).

More than 500 painters reside or work in Hyderabad and have contributed to around 1,000 temples, of which 600 are under the Endowments Department (presently in Telangana).[3] These temples are dedicated to regional goddesses (such as Pochamma, Yellamma and Maisamma), pan-Indian goddesses and gods (such as Durga, Kali, Shiva, Rama and Vishnu) and interregional gods (like Jagannatha of Puri in Odisha).

Mostly, the temple authorities give commissions to the painters. However, there are also contractors who function as intermediaries between the authorities and the artisans. The contractors or

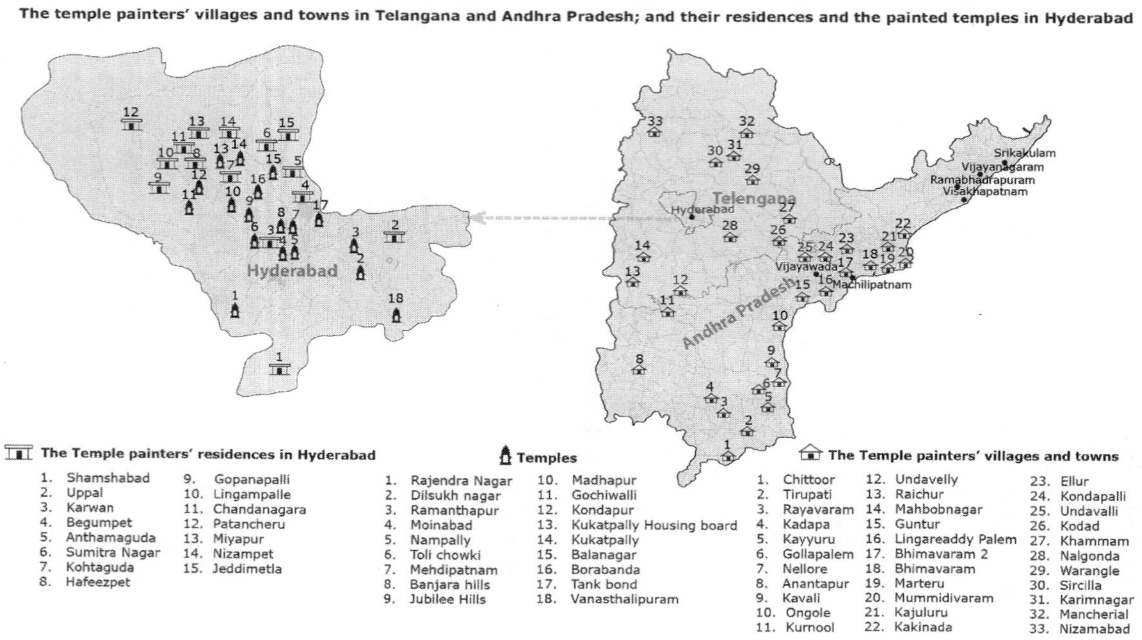

Figure 4.2 The Map Shows the Temples Painters' Home-Villages and Towns in Present Telangana and Andhra Pradesh, and Their Rented Residences and the Painted Temples in Hyderabad-Deccan. Illustration Credit: Bijay Nath, 2021.

intermediaries are mostly concerned about the monetary aspects and not the aesthetics pertaining to the style and composition of the temple painting. The painters are aware that the contractors keep a significant part of the payment with them. For example, Gola Ramulu, a contractor as well as a mason, pays from Rs 500 to 800 per day to a painter, and Rs 50 to 400 per day to the assistants depending upon skill and years of experience. If a painter manages to secure a painting job directly from the temple authorities, they earn between Rs 700 and 1000 in a day, and the assistants fetch Rs 300 to 600 per day. As the contractors do not play a significant role in developing the visual appearances of the temple paintings, the painters do not consider them integral to their network. Once the painters understand the mediators' role, they leave their name and contact details in the corners of temple murals to attract the attention of the viewers and future patrons directly (Figure 4.3).

The painters' names also appear on their bills and tenders at the Endowments Department, Hyderabad. The network of temple painters in Hyderabad thrives on intra-communal connections and painters' associations, such as the Housing Board Artist and Painters Association in Kukatpally that consists of seventy members, and the Jaya Durga Artists and Painters Association, which has forty members. The members of the Kukatpally Housing Board (KPHB) played a significant role in forming the Housing Board Artist and Painters Association as they put them in touch with numerous clients and guided them to build a welfare and working mechanism in the 1980s. These associations collect a fixed amount of Rs 100 every month from the members to maintain a corpus fund that serves the painters when they fall sick or meet with an accident. The interconnections within communities and the challenges posed by every temple painting project make the painters aware of their collective as well as individual identity. As I progressed with my ethnographic research, two predominant means of networking

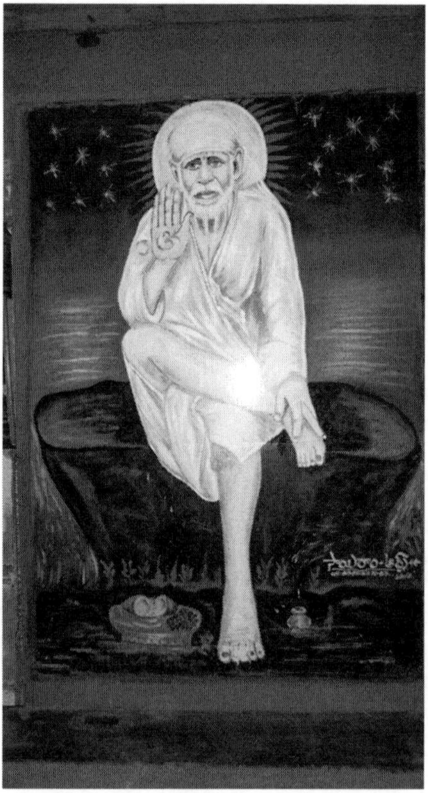

Figure 4.3 The Painter Wrote His Name and Contact Details after Completion of the Paintings on the Walls of Sai Ram Temple, Kukatpally, Hyderabad-Deccan. Courtesy: Bijay Nath, 2012.

within the painter community came to be revealed: one was centred on the Endowments Department in Hyderabad and the other one – perhaps more effective and widespread – on the intra-community bonding between the artisans.

When I initiated my fieldwork at the Hanuman Temple in Rajendranagar, which is under the Endowments Department, upon asking the priest, devotees and the temple committee, I was directed to the Endowments Department. The department calls for tenders to execute the repairing or repainting works in the temples. After their initial assessment, the department employs the painters for the designated job with clear instructions on the nature of paintings expected and the colour scheme chosen. They maintain a record of the artisans for whom they facilitate the procurement of temple painting tenders and the sanction of bills for the assigned works. Thus, only two painters' names consistently appear in the record of their finance registry. The person in charge of the assessment and renovation works, *sṭhāpati* (master craftsman and architect) Venugopal, plays the decision-making role; he appoints painters for the jobs assigned in the temples under the Board. Two painters – A. Velu, a local artist, and Kunja Jayaraman, from Tamil Nadu – are preferred by Venugopal. All painting assignments are usually reserved for them. This dedicated group of three people represents a fraction of the painters' network; the majority of the artisans in the city remain undocumented in the records provided by the Board.

I therefore had to seek to identify alternative means of networking among the artisans. This led me to increasingly focus on the names, signatures and the brief contact details left behind by the painters at the corners of their murals on the temple walls. Using these contact numbers gradually revealed the city-wide intra-communal web of the artisans responsible for brightening the cityscape with their brush strokes. Starting from Gachibowli, I travelled across the city, connecting the dots to find a large network of the temple painters, sculptors, masons, contractors and priests. I found that the masons and sculptors often recommend the painters to the organizing committees of the city temples or individual patrons. Thus, the painters remain dependent on the makers of the temples for their livelihood. Simultaneously, the temple committees also refer the painters to other temple trusts if they carry out their tasks satisfactorily. Even though individual painters keep a record book of their projects and contacts, the intertwined networks, connecting patrons, masons and temple painters thrive orally and through the phone contacts.

Learning Temple Painting

As noted above, practitioners from diverse regional and caste backgrounds participate in enlivening temple walls and interiors with lifelike paintings of deities and semi-divine beings. I have also stressed that the scholarship on temple makers is often within the fold of 'tradition' and therefore tends to overlook non-hereditary artisans (Parker 2019: 114–21; Ramanathan 2019: 98–111). In a parallel development, colonial documentation implied that artisanal communities in India conservatively stick to their hereditary profession for religious reasons and tend to show 'hostility to education' (McGowan 2009: 74). However, the common experience of migration – in terms of both geographical and occupational migration – was observed in artisans facing economic and societal changes during the colonial era, resulting in large-scale movements between occupational sectors irrespective of caste and community backgrounds (McGowan 2009: 14).[4] Border-crossing was certainly not a colonial phenomenon, as cultural exchanges and transference of skills were evident even in early modern and pre-colonial Deccan. Sharing commonality or, as Tim Ingold deftly delineates, 'walking along together' emerges as an effective framework to contextualize the painters' engagement with learning (Ingold 2013: 106). Under these circumstances, painters and their apprentices share the 'same visual field' which is 'experienced as a particularly companionable form of activity' (Ingold 2013: 106). Learning through companionship is much more expansive and diverts from the exclusive one-to-one conversational model. Ingold makes a clear distinction between shared participatory acts and one-to-one correspondence. In the latter case, correspondents engage with each other blocking other stimulants influencing this mode of communication. Building on Ingold, this has limited significance on sharing skills and experiences at the community level. In this regard, I propose that networking among temple painters in the city provides them a ground for sharing experiences, and companionship; this gradually turns out to be an equally, if not more, constructive form of learning for the painters than the hereditary paradigm.

Learning, for my interviewees, started with apprenticeship, which constitutes the base of their learning as well as their career. Most of them started learning painting after recognizing their interest in drawing and painting in general. Often, they reported initiating their training on completing their intermediate examination. Apprentices learn the techniques of temple painting by closely observing their masters. One of the painters received extra lessons outside their apprenticeship; thus, seeing and learning occur simultaneously in this profession. The eagerness and the ability of the learners determine whether they will become independent painters. Apprentices are trained between four and ten years before they start their journey as individual painters; some manage to earn recognition, whereas others remain under the shadow of their masters. Some even consider changing professions after struggling with an extended period of apprenticeship. Some of the painters started their journey by portraying deities and decorating the walls of function and marriage halls with ornamental motifs in their villages; for them, the next step usually is to paint the local gods and goddesses in their village temples before setting off for Hyderabad.

During their training, each painter develops a distinctive style under their master. Mathangi Mallesh, a Madiga painter from Kothaguda in Khammam, specialized in painting patterns to create the illusion of three-dimensionality, and the 'graph technique' – inspired by his brother-in-law and master M. Mukesh. The 'graph technique', to him, is the most accurate method to enlarge calendar and poster imagery: first, a parallel set of intersecting vertical and horizontal lines is drawn over a chosen image. Then, each square unit is multiplied while tracing it onto the temple walls. Another example is that of Sheikh Arsadulla, who developed his skills in depicting iconographical details as well as the portraiture of gods and goddesses from his master Ravi Kumar.

As I have stressed on the significance of apprenticeship, I must also mention that training is not confined to the temple sites alone; 'art' shops, where shop signs, commercial hoardings and posters are painted, double up as dedicated workshop spaces where many apprentices learn to paint. The master temple painters often employ their apprentices initially in these shops before taking them to the actual sites. Guru Shekhara Bondala from Kondampalli in Kurnool entered the profession by painting signboards and nameplates while pursuing his middle school education (Interview with Guru Shekhara Bondala, Hyderabad, March 2013). He sharpened his skills while working for painter Raju in his shop at Moosapet, Hyderabad. In his early thirties at the time of this interview, he had already acquired fourteen years of experience in the field and opened a shop of his own dedicated to creating stickers for the number plates of vehicles in the Kukatpally area of Hyderabad. Manda Ramakrishna, from Mettapalli in Mahbubnagar, recalled his training under painter Mayam Sagar, who was a member of the Housing Board Artist and Painters Association in Kukatpally and owned a shop named *Sagar Art* (Interview with Manda Ramakrishna, Hyderabad, March 2013). While an apprentice, Ramakrishna painted shop signs and advertisements on city walls. Orama Srinivas Reddy, another temple painter, received his training from his guru Mohan at his shop *Bindu Art*. *Karuna Art Shop*, which is owned by Nagendra and is managed by Perumala Madhu, an assistant to the owner. Vighneswara Chari and his shop, *Chitra Art*, played an important role in shaping the career of painter B. Srinivas.

The painters who started their training and career in the 1980s have extensive experience making painted advertisements for various organizations; with the advent of offset and digital printing, opportunities for painters to exercise their skills in these sectors became very limited. Painters such as Matangi Mallesh (fifty-two at the time of this interview) and Vittala Rao Gollu (also in his early fifties) confirmed that the demand for painted advertisements and signs was much higher until the 1980s.

A marginal fraction of the temple painters also received formal art school education. For instance, J. N. Raju completed his Bachelor's in Fine Arts from the Jawaharlal Nehru Technical University in Hyderabad (JNTU; presently, Jawaharlal Nehru Architecture and Fine Arts University) in 1992. Upon the completion of his degree, he moved to Bangalore (now Bengaluru) to work for an organization that designs greeting cards. He worked there for the next seven years. Eventually, he moved back to Hyderabad and is currently working as an auto rickshaw driver. Throughout his career, he painted three temples in the city. According to him, limited opportunities and benefits in the field of painting gradually made him disinterested in this profession; even though he still receives occasional commission jobs, it is not of interest to him.

Another practitioner, my colleague at the Department of Fine Arts at the University of Hyderabad, Jami Vera Venkat Rao, completed his Bachelor of Fine Arts degree from Andhra University in Vishakhapatnam before pursuing his master's degree in sculpture. Hailing from a Kapu family of Bhimavaram in West Godavari, he received his primary training in the workshop of Ponna Koti Ranga Rao. Under Ranga Rao's guidance, he painted a *Rāmālayam* (temple dedicated to Lord Rama) in Mahadevapatnam, West Godavari. Alongside, he also painted signboards and worked for commercial campaigns. By the time of his master's degree, he had fourteen years of experience in this field, which allowed him to balance the demands of his profession and the requirements of institutional education in fine arts.

Materiality of Paint and Painting

Learning temple painting usually begins by cleaning the surface (Figure 4.4) of the temple wall; the painters learn how to paint the first layer of white distemper evenly on the surface (Figure 4.5). In between this initial phase and the final one, blank walls are gradually transformed into the abodes of gods. Much of this transformation rests on the painters' abilities to evoke respect, awe and familiarity for the deities among devotees through their portrayal of the divine figures and narrative fragments from Hindu mythology. Images of gods and goddesses widely circulated in the public domain serve as reference material for the painters. The 'graph technique' mentioned earlier is often utilized by the painters to draw outlines of the forms and other necessary details.

The patrons and priests seldom interfere with the drawings, but the colour scheme is up to them; the painters pay keen attention to their colour-related demands. In the instructions they have to follow, two key rules are worth highlighting. First, they ought to follow widely accepted iconographic conventions and opt for a vibrant colour palette to hold the devotees' attention. Second, the colour of the bodies and clothes of the deities is usually predetermined. For instance, Yellamma, Peddamma, Durga and Kali would usually be painted in blue, red, yellow and green, respectively. A uniform and traditional colour scheme is followed to avoid confusion among viewers. Further, the use of gold paint – also prevalent in public statuary – is highly favoured by the patrons and priests for its glimmer and symbolic association with wealth. The demand by the priest Srinivas that the murals be brightened with gold paint led painter J. V. Satyanarayana to repaint the temple. Srinivas complained the initial painting job was improper, causing the walls to appear sombre (Interview with Orama Srinivas Reddy,

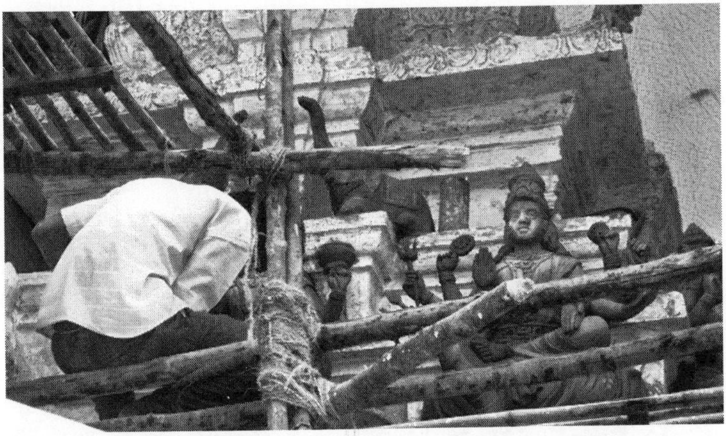

Figure 4.4 The Assistant Is Cleaning the Surface, Balaji Temple, Chandanagar, Hyderabad-Deccan. Courtesy: Bijay Nath, 2012.

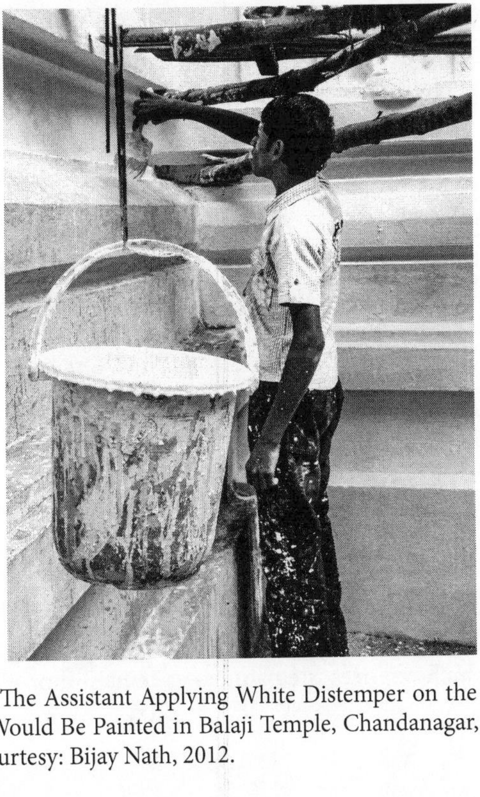

Figure 4.5 The Assistant Applying White Distemper on the Wall Where the Mural Would Be Painted in Balaji Temple, Chandanagar, Hyderabad-Deccan. Courtesy: Bijay Nath, 2012.

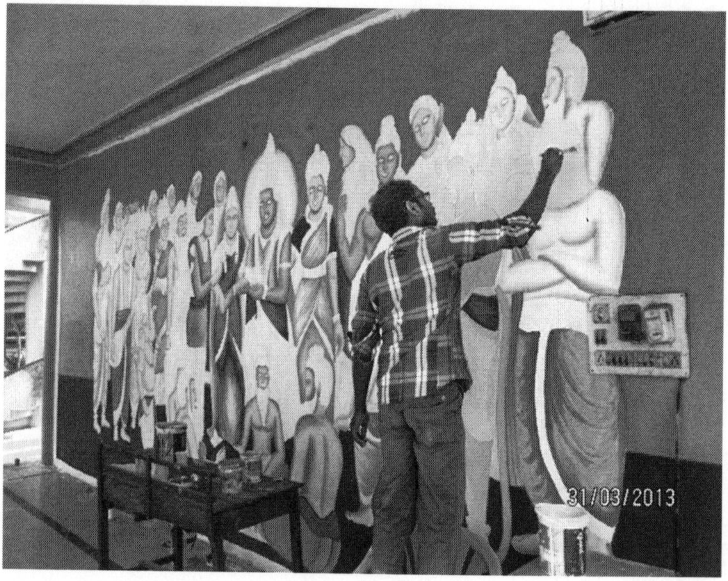

Figure 4.6 The Artisan Is Applying Middle Tone on the Mural, Sri Venkateswara Swamy Temple, Kukatpally, Hyderabad-Deccan. Courtesy: Bijay Nath, 2013.

Hyderabad, April 2013). During the application of paint, the middle tone is applied first, followed by darker tones to provide solidity to the figures. After that, light tones and highlights are overlaid according to the need. If, further, the protrusion of images is required, painters rework the areas painted in the middle tone (Figure 4.6). After completing the figures, the ornaments, borders and patterns are painted on. For repetitive ornamentation, many painters use templates, which accelerate the painting process. The strategy of colour application and the use of templates in the entire temple complex attribute uniformity to the painted visuals. The choice of colour palette, however, is also dependent on the funds available, which requires the painters to remain flexible with their choices as well as develop tactics to overcome constraints. Learning to paint thus unfolds not only as technical mastery but also as the ability to navigate facets of patronage and reception.

Primarily, the painters work with five industrially produced colours: red, yellow, blue, green and black. Therefore, learning entails a keen knowledge of mixing and creating a range of shades out of these colours. For example, J. V. Satyanarayana painted the Balaji temple in Chandanagar with his characteristic vibrant colour scheme and used metallic paints to enhance the brilliance of the images. J. V. Satyanarayana mentioned his knowledge about different sizes of the temple. He understands that there are many types of temples. The first kind is *yēkkaṇṭha vēdika*, which would be approximately fifteen-feet long. It takes ten days for an artist with four assistants to paint this type of temple. The second type of temple is *pānchakaṇṭha vēdika*, which would be around thirty-six-feet high. Two artists with six assistants would need twenty-five days to finish the work. The third type is *nāvakaṇṭha vēdika*, which would be twenty-two-feet high. Painting this type of temple in twenty days requires four artists and eight assistants. The fourth type, *kāramakuṇṭha vēdika, is* approximately seventeen-feet high. Two artists with six assistants need twelve days to finish the work. He avoids using black or mixing black to prepare any shade while painting. A short distance from Chandanagar, painter Orama Srinivas Reddy painted a Sivalayam (Figure 4.7) in Miyapur. Reddy's denser colour palette, in contrast with Satyanarayana's flamboyant one, is punctuated by the selective use of black paint. Learning colour mixing is crucial to reducing the budget allocated for buying paints; this is why the painters as well as the patrons stress on this specific skill. The different colour palettes and styles of mixing reflect the painter's training. When an apprentice learns techniques to apply and mix colours from their established masters, they follow the same style to situate themselves in the

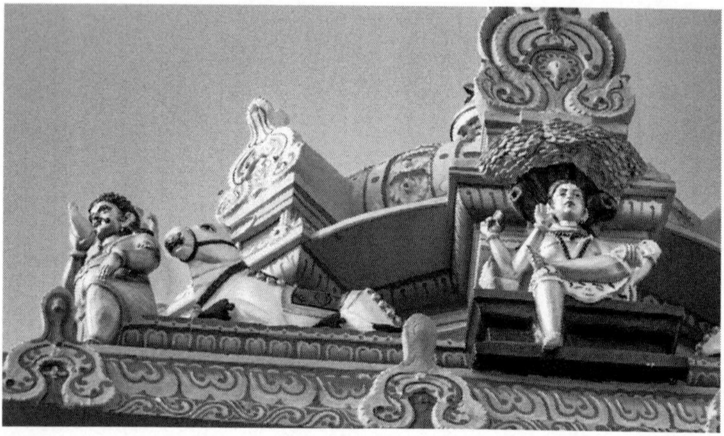

Figure 4.7 Oram Srinivas Reddy, the Artisan's Painted Temple Sivalayam, Chandanager, Hyderabad-Deccan. Courtesy: Bijay Nath, 2012.

lineage of their masters, which in turn also enables them to gain work and recognition.

Water-based emulsion, distemper and oil-based enamel paints are preferred for temple painting. The painters explain the quality, longevity and visual appearance of these materials to the patrons to decide. Oil-based paint being more expensive than water-based ones, the choice is often dependent on the budget. The affordable paint that dries up quickly after application is most preferred by the painters. Many of the painters I interviewed prefer the locally available Apex and Ace paints for affordability. They mentioned that painting done with these paints lasts up to five years. If the patrons are willing to pay more, then they switch to more established brands. Even though industrial colours are more popular among the present-day painters, the adviser at the Endowments Department, A. Velu, stated that herbal colours were in use until the 1980s. He himself always used herbal colours. He used to prepare shades of green from leaves, red from roses, black and grey from lamp black, and binder from the sap of *nāla tuṃmā* (vachellia nilotica). While recollecting his painting work on the ceiling of the *mandapa* (pavilion) in the Sri Ranganthaswami temple of Nellore, he mentioned that the outer walls of temples were not elaborately painted in those days. It is a widespread practice now. Herbal colours on lime-plastered surfaces are easily damaged after rains or in the scorching heat of summer. Thus, their painting jobs were mostly restricted to interiors. He also expressed his disappointment on finding that the ceiling at the Sri Ranganathaswamy temple had been painted over with enamel colours five years ago. According to him, a painter from Madras (now Chennai), L. Ramanatham Acharya, was responsible for introducing colours to the exterior walls, *gopuras* (the superstructure over the entrance-gate to the precinct of a temple in Southern India), and different kinds of temple gateways in Hyderabad in 1987. Before this, painters in Hyderabad would paint the *gopuras* and walls with lime plaster or white paint. The *gopura* of Laxminarayan temple near Manju Theatre in Secunderabad was perhaps the first one to be painted with multiple colours. This readily gained popularity, and within the next decade, the practice of using colour became standardized across this city and its suburbs.

Claims over Images

The painters claim their authorship by a simple act: writing their names and contact details on the walls. As noted earlier, the names and contacts often appear at the corners of walls or in less prominent parts of paintings. Within a group, however, only the master painter is allowed to write his name on the walls; the assistants' and apprentices' names do not find mention. For a viewer, it appears as an individual's name. For example, at the time of the interview, Jayaraman had ten members in his group, including three painters and seven assistants; Satyanarayana had thirty-three members working under his guidance, including ten artisans and twenty-three assistants. The assistants, who are unable to leave evidence of their participation on the temple walls, usually carry their photo albums to claim their share of ownership over a project instead. These photographs sometimes collected in the albums operate as the artisans' portfolios.

To those familiar with popular calendars, posters and other artworks, the practice of leaving traces of artisans/painters on their work does not appear unusual. However, the temple painters operate with more restrictions than their artisanal counterparts. There are instances where patrons and priests have resisted painters writing their names on the walls. During an interview, a painter recalled a similar event that took place while painting a temple within the My Home Hub, a luxurious gated community housing in Madhapur.

Even though it is the painters who transform a concrete building into a sacred space, their presence is welcomed only for the duration of their job. The painters at the Endowments Department, Jayaraman and Velu believe that the temple is a sacred space and the Brahmin priests rightfully have the authority to set rules and retain the sacredness of the temple premises. In a temple, only priests are allowed in the *garbhagriha* (the sanctum), and they hold on to their rights. The painters are required to finish the painting work before *kumbhābhiṣhekā* (the ceremonial evocation of the presiding deity of the temple). Once the *kumbhābhiṣhekā* is performed, no one except the priests is allowed to access the sanctum. After *kumbhābhiṣhekā*, if the painter is required to step in for some reason, the priests perform a special ritual named *bālālayam*[5] to accommodate this undesirable situation. In the ritual, the priests symbolically transfer the essence and presence of the god or goddess from the idol in the *garbhagriha* into a *kalaśha* (a terracotta pot with a bulbous base and narrow neck, usually used to carry water). The *kalaśha* is then worshipped by the priests and devotees until the painting is concluded. After the completion of painting, the priest ritually purifies the idol by performing another *abhiṣhekā* to re-invite the deity to reside within the sanctum. The painted deities within the temple complex are an essential part of the devotees' experience of visiting the site, but all traces of the painters, as well as the masons and other workers who created them, are suppressed. Though the insertions of the artisans' names and contacts at the margins of the paintings are primarily to attract prospective clients, I find that the practice is also a way for the painters to assert their identity.

Even though learning and sustaining temple painting, as I have delineated in this chapter, flourish as a dynamic practice, the hereditary- and community-based notion of the occupation, and the hierarchy between priests and painters, and between patrons and painters, are far from dissolving.

Conclusion

In this chapter, I have described the livelihood and artistry of the temple painters in Hyderabad with the hope of fostering further scholarship in the field. I have highlighted that the temple painters in Hyderabad often undertake other commercial works such as advertisement design and sign board painting. In short, though they are addressed as 'temple painters' in this chapter, they do not restrict their professional practice to temple painting alone. They explore other ventures, using their skills to enhance their livelihood options.

I have discussed the migrant temple painters in Hyderabad and their pattern of professional networking. Through my fieldwork across the city, I traced the suppressed accounts of the city temple painters to narrate their travel accounts as many of them have had to leave their ancestral homes and arrive in Hyderabad for work. I have shown that their profession demands a considerable commute (within Hyderabad and its suburbs), which in return offers an urban social life distinct from their villages or hometowns, and new ways of learning painting and acquiring knowledge about the new materials that are available to them to explore as they design their temple painting projects. The most lingering theme in my discussion is the transmission of skill between hereditary and non-hereditary painters, and the shift in the painters' practices as they navigate patrons' preferences and available materials such as paints. The sites of painting – the temples – therefore turn out to also be repositories of the painters' craftsmanship and identity. Hence, the vibrantly painted walls of the city temples, the painters' intra- and inter-community networks, as well as the networks of knowledge, are all enmeshed.

Notes

1 I thank my friends Nagajanu Surepally and Jami Veera Venkat Rao for their invaluable assistance during my field work and travelling with the temple painters. I also thank Sthapathi A.Velu, the Endowments Department of Telangana, Housing Board Artist and Painters Association, Jay Durga Artists & Painters Association, all artists and artists families who shared the memories, their personal records and diaries.

2 This fieldwork and my stint as a research assistant was part of a larger project on the religious structures in Hyderabad and its neighbourhood, supervised by Baishali Ghosh from University of Hyderabad.

3 The area under investigation fell under the Hyderabad Endowments Department (the then undivided) Andhra Pradesh, in 2012–13. The department looks after the temples, keeps an account of their annual income and supervises renovation works when necessary. See 'Telangana Endowments', Endowments Department, Government of Telangana, http://www.endowments.ts.nic.in/#carousel (accessed 25 April 2021).

4 In her analysis of craft making in colonial India, Abigail McGowan stresses that geo-political factors and rapid industrialization in Western Europe impacted craft communities across the nation. This enabled craft makers from diverse sectors to share similar experiences (McGowan 2009: 14).

5 To know more about *balalayam* may see BALALAYAM OF TEMPLES AT AVG, ANAIKATTI, https://arshavidya.in/balalayam/ (accessed 5 January 2024); Notermans (2016: 7–8).

References

Appadurai, Arjun (1974), 'Right and Left Hand Castes in South India', *Indian Economic and Social History Review* 11 (2–3): 216–59.

BALALAYAM OF TEMPLES AT AVG, ANAIKATTI, https://arshavidya.in/balalayam/, (accessed 5 January 2024).

Branfoot, Crispin (2013), 'Remaking the Past: Tamil Sacred Landscape and Temple Renovations'. *Bulletin of the School of Oriental and African Studies* 76 (1): 21–47.

Endowments Department, Government of Telangana, 'Telangana Endowments', http://www.endowments.ts.nic.in/#carousel (accessed 25 April 2021).

Ingold, Tim (2013), *Making: Anthropology, Archaeology, Art and Architecture*, London and New York: Routledge.

Leonard, Karen (2011), 'Hindu Temples in Hyderabad: State Patronage and Politics in South Asia'. *South Asian History and Culture*, 2 (3): 352–73.

McGowan, Abigail (2009), *Crafting the Nation in Colonial India*, New York: Palgrave Macmillan.

Notermans, Catrien, Albertina Nugteren and Suma Sunny (2016), 'The Changing Landscape of Sacred Groves in Kerala (India): A Critical View on the Role of Religion in Nature Conservation', *Religions*, 7 (4): 38. https://doi.org/10.3390/rel7040038 (accessed 5 January 2024).

Parker, Samuel K. (2003), 'Text and Practice in South Asian Art: An Ethnographic Perspective', *Artibus Asiae*, 63 (1): 5–34.

Parker, Samuel K. (2019), 'The Contemporary Political Economy of Traditional Aesthetics and Materiality', in Annapurna Garimella, Shriya Sridharan, and A. Srivathsan (eds), *The Contemporary Hindu Temple: Fragments for a History*, 114–21, Mumbai: Marg.

Ramanathan, Vaishnavi (2019), 'New Iconographies: Gods in the Age of Kali', in Annapurna Garimella, Shriya Sridharan and A. Srivathsan (eds), *The Contemporary Hindu Temple: Fragments for a History*, 98–111, Mumbai: Marg.

Sinha, Ajay J. (2000), *Imagining Architects: Creativity in the Religious Monuments of India*, Newark, NJ: University of Delaware Press.

Talbot, Cynthia (1991), 'Temples, Donors, and Gifts: Patterns of Patronage in Thirteenth-Century South India', *The Journal of Asian Studies*, 50 (2): 308–40.

5

Lives of the Family Photo Albums in Hyderabad

Keshawram

A family photo album is an embodiment of social relations. As a repository of the socio-economic history of family and kinship, it reconnects memories, places, time, happiness and sorrow with rolling stories, which are often oral. A family photo album (henceforth FPA) builds a sense of affinity between viewers and owners of the albums through an unfolding of oral narratives complemented by snapshots capturing various occasions and functions of the family, such as birthdays, weddings, ritual events, vacations and daily activities.

My research on FPAs constructs parallel readings between middle-class families living in Gopanpally Tanda (popularly known as Tanda), south of the University of Hyderabad (hereafter UoH), and migrant labourer families based in the construction sites around that area. During my fieldwork in 2017–18, the labourers were living near the construction sites at the University of Hyderabad. The Tanda settlement houses 250–60 families from Lambada, Madiga and Vaddera communities who have been living here for the last eighty to ninety years; they speak mainly Telugu and Hindi/Dakhani. The families that have migrated from northern and eastern India also constitute a significant section of the population there as well; mostly living in the rented apartments, some of them who migrated in 1990–2000s own newly built houses and apartments in Tanda. The middle-class people work in both government and non-governmental sectors, namely teachers, doctors, contractors, labourers and shopkeepers. On the contrary, the migrant labourer families living in the tents near the construction sites on the UoH campus are mostly on the move; they move when the construction is completed. As I started mapping Tanda and construction sites around UoH to understand the character of the settlement, residences, shops, markets and the locations of FPAs, I noticed people keep their photographs in various forms: conjoint displays in a cluster of framed photographs on a wall, table or desk, hidden away in a wallet, bag or box, or neatly arranged in plastic albums. Based on my interactions with the residents of Tanda and UoH construction sites, I suggest that the FPA is an embodiment of their growing and moving homes. The mapping allowed me to understand the process of making the FPA.

In this chapter,[1] I trace how an FPA reflects not only the family history but also the history of the materials used in making them. At the outset, I refer to Andrew L. Walker and Rosalind Kimball Moulton's compelling argument that establishes FPAs as a personal and private art form activated by the relationship between a presenter and viewer (Walker and Moulton 1989: 115). The sophistication and naivety of the FPAs reflect the intention, imagination and skill of the photographers (Walker and Moulton 1989: 160). Further, Mette Sandbye argues that the complex social and emotional communication facilitated by the FPA is rooted in their material community involvement (Sandby 2014: 1–5). Kodak and its impact on the Indian middle class and nuclear family albums, as discussed by Jennifer Orpana, delineated how Kodak, as a brand, promoted and preserved family stories through representational pictures (Orpana 2018: 3). While situating the FPAs within the history of the photographic archives of India, Suryanandini Narain established them as a mnemonic device (Narain 2019: 116). By flipping through the photographs of their family members, the viewer's sensory memories are rejuvenated; departed relatives are even momentarily brought back to life through this act. Christopher Pinney's seminal work *Camera Indica: The Social Life of Indian Photographs* traces the shifts in seeing and showing photographic portraiture from the colonial era to contemporary times in India (Pinney 1997). His contribution is especially essential to recognize how a photography tool initially imported to India for exercising the power control of the Empire was vernacularized through popular intervention and social relations. Drawing on this sustained scholarship on photographic albums, the chapter attempts to address the questions that are barely addressed in the existing scholarship: Are FPAs an inseparable part of homes? How does an FPA represent the family hierarchy? Is the storytelling process of FPAs an offshoot of the storytelling traditions of scroll paintings in different regions of India? How do people create and preserve FPAs?

Family Photos at the Construction Labourers' Camp, UoH

My exploration began at the temporary camps of the migrant labourers behind the boys' Hostel-H in the north campus of the UoH (Figure 5.1 – the left one); some of the labourers were from Mahbubnagar in Telangana, while others travelled from Madhya Pradesh, Chhattisgarh, Odisha, Rajasthan, Karnataka, Uttar Pradesh and West Bengal. They came to work with their family members, including their children. A very few were educated; they mostly studied up to the eighth and tenth standards. They lived in small huts, mainly made of tin shade, wood and roofing polythene sheets. The labourers living there used to get a daily wage of Rs 200–500 depending upon the work assigned and work hours. I mostly engaged in conversation with them in the evenings after their work hours; they avoided me while their overseers were around the construction sites. In the evening during my interaction with them, I observed a 40/60-watt bulb would move from their tent-like house to the cooking area when needed. Thus, my early sighting of the FPA of the construction labourers happened either in the light of these bulbs or my mobile phone's torch. They kept their photos in the pockets of their bags (Figure 5.1 – the right one) or in between the pages of bank and post office account passbooks.

Although initially reluctant, upon subsequent visits they started sharing stories of their travel, home, family and daily wages. I was particularly intrigued by the personal photo archive of these migrant labourers in an intangible form of keeping their belongings. As they started moving away from their homes to work, they held their family photos close to them and safeguarded those at utmost conditions. Jettam Anju, a seventeen-year-old girl from Mahbubnagar who was residing at the make-shift tent settlement of the construction labourers in the UoH campus, was depressed being separated from her family. Her father ran a *Paan* shop (a variety of small roadside shops primarily selling *paan* or betel leaf

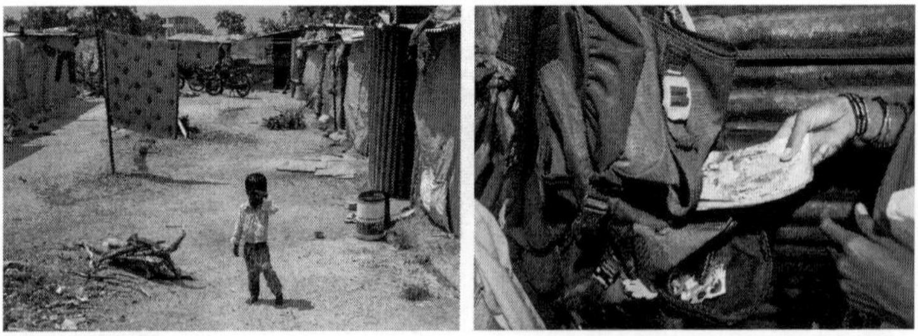

Figure 5.1 (Left) Temporary Camps of Migrant Labourers; **(Right)** Anju Placing the Photographs Together as a Bundle in Her Bag, Construction Site Near Hostel-H in the North Campus, University of Hyderabad. Courtesy: Keshawram, 2017.

and cigarettes) and her mother was a domestic worker in Mumbai. In her bag, she carried a bundle of photographs of her mother, uncle, aunt and grandparents, taken in Mahbubnagar and Mumbai between 2003 and 2004; in the evening she would often take out the photos from the bag and look at them while sitting in a corner of the tin-shed shelter. Away from home, the bundle of photographs operated as a fragment of Anju's family life (Interview with Jettam Anju, Hyderabad, September–November 2017).

One of Anju's photographs (Figure 5.2) shows her mother (left) and aunt (right) touching the feet of her grandmother. Her grandmother stands facing them and is captured with her hands on their heads, representing the affectionate bond as well as respect and hierarchy in the family. Anju's mother and aunt are dressed in new sarees, chains around their necks, colourful bangles adorning their wrists and *bindis*[2] on their foreheads; in contrast, her grandmother wears simple metallic bangles and a black thread around her neck; the absence of a *bindi* confirms her widowed status. Her grandmother is seen wearing a saree above the ankles, commonly found in rural areas. Anju's aunt has a garland of white flowers in her hair, indicating either that a special occasion was being photographed or that they were photographed to make the day memorable. Both the sisters sit on the ground, indicating the family's poor economic condition. Behind them, there is an incomplete brick wall. Anju noted that the photograph was captured in 2004 at Malad, Mumbai, where her family went to work. When Anju left her home (at Mahbubnagar) to work, she took the photographs from her mother's FPA to remember her family. This helps us to understand the function of a family photograph in establishing and maintaining intimate relations between relatives. It also reflects how the family photograph serves as a vehicle for transporting the memories and stories from place to place and person to person, and even generation to generation.

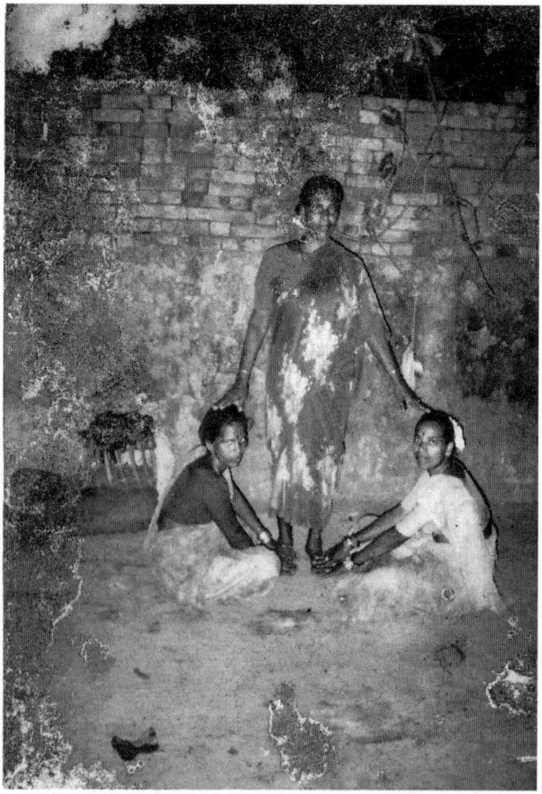

Figure 5.2 Jettam Anju's Mother (Left) and Aunt (Right Side) Touching the Feet of Anju's Grandmother (Middle). Malad, Mumbai, 2004, from the Family Photo Album in the Collection of Jettam Anju, Construction Site, University of Hyderabad. Courtesy: Keshawram, 2018.

The production and preservation of digital photographs trigger remembrance and forgetting differently from FPAs. The virtual photographs, in which memories, experiences and stories are embedded, may get suppressed in countless folders in computers or phones; they are also easily deleted with a single click. Whereas the tangibility associated with printed and mounted photographs strengthens the persistence of intangible memory. Nevertheless, due to the invention of new technologies such as mobile phone cameras and affordable digital cameras, visits to the photo studio have lessened over time. People now mostly keep their photos on mobile phones or in folders on computers, and on the internet. Thus, a soft copy of the FPA in mobile phones and computers is circulated during interactions over social media, inviting a virtual gathering of family members. However, social practice around the hard copy of the FPA continues.

Family Photo Albums of Tanda

In contrast to the migrant families' photos, the photo albums in Tanda's houses are mainly of two types: albums consisting of analogue photographs (Figure 5.3 – the left one) and digitally printed albums (Figure 5.3 – the right one). I closely examine a small-sized analogue photo album of approximately 7 × 5 × 1 inches, with around forty-three pockets, which belongs to Jarepati Swathi, the daughter of Eragadindla Srisailam; she made her family's album with the photos of family members, relatives and friends. Its cover page is made of a stiff polyethylene sheet tinted in blue and adorned with images of flowers. The pockets in the album are made of a transparent plastic, and the photos are kept back-to-back in each pocket. Thus, the family's old photos in Tanda are kept in the chosen album; it reflects the aesthetic preferences, material and images which also make the tangible property of the album as an object. The photos of this album are taken and processed at Santosh Digital Photo Studio in Tanda. These photos showcase the events and occasions of Jarepati Swathi's school and college life, birthdays and family rituals. Sometimes her family members pull out the photos to see them closely or tell stories, events or incidents related to the photos during gatherings of relatives or friends. The sequence of the photos in this album relates to the occurrence of family events and tours, attributing coherence.

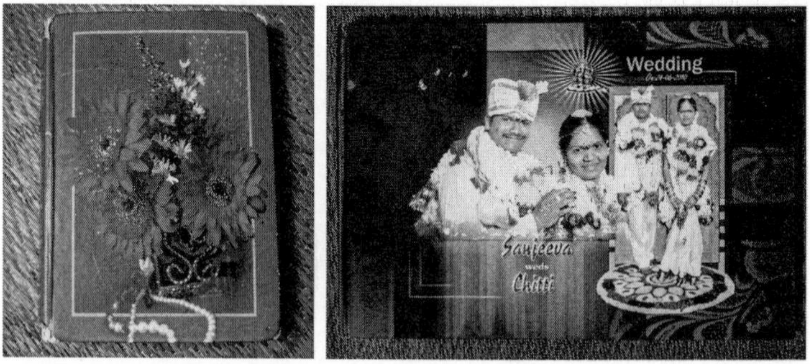

Figure 5.3 (Left) Jarepati Swathi's Photo Album; **(Right)** Eragadindla Sanjeeva Wedding Photo, 2010, from the Collection of Eragadindla Sanjeeva, Tanda, Gopanpally, Hyderabad-Deccan. Courtesy: Keshawram, 2018.

I was introduced to Jarepati Swathi through her uncle, Eragadindla Sanjeeva, a UoH outsourced office staff. During one of my initial visits, Sanjeeva pulled out a photograph (Figure 5.4 – top) to show Jarepati Swathi as a young girl in the backdrop of their old family home. He mentioned that the photograph is twenty-five to thirty years old and deeply associated with memories of Swathi's childhood and her family. The eagerness of photographing the family together comes through this photograph. On the left, Jarepati Swathi's father and mother (Srisailam and Jangamma) hold her brother Ramu and sister Raveli in their arms. Little Swathi, in a pink dress, stands next to her parents. Their home occupies a large section of the photograph, and perhaps the residents are shown as inseparable parts of this space. This is probably why the residents are grouped towards the left, leaving the rest of the photograph to the house. A glimpse of cattle fodder in the background establishes their connection to herding. Sanjeeva told me that they had cows and buffaloes at home a few years ago, which they sold while renovating the house. The cowshed was converted into rooms as the family expanded due to marriages; after that, Jarepati Swathi and her uncle Eragadindla Sanjeeva also got married, respectively.

At their present house, flipping through the album's pages, I tried to visualize the old house, as Sanjeeva and his family members continue to tell stories of it. A photograph (Figure 5.4 – below) from the sixth pocket of the album was shot to mark the occasion of the Dussehra festival in 2011. Here, Swathi sits on her father's new motor-bike adjacent to her bicycle. Many Hindus in this region clean their vehicles, draw auspicious marks on them and crush vermilion-smeared pumpkins as part of the Dussehra rituals. Both the motor-bike and bicycle in the photograph are thus decorated with garlands of fresh flowers. To enhance the festive mood, the photo studio has decorated this photograph by creating a border with white and blue outlines and four red flowers at the corners.

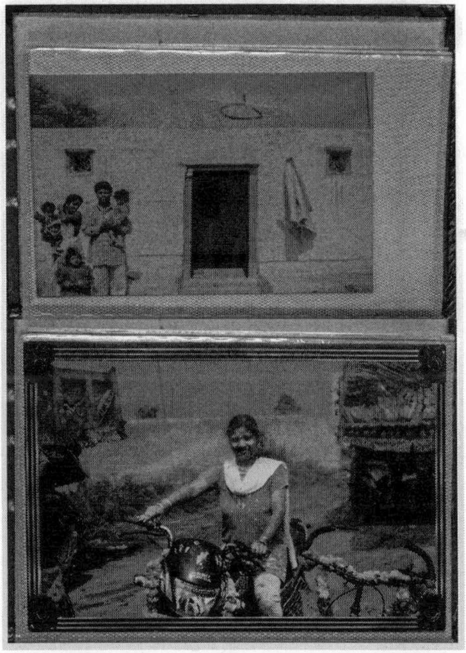

Figure 5.4 (Top) Old Home of Jarepati Swathi at Tanda; **(Below)** The Photo Is Related to Memory of the 'Dussehra' Festival in 2011 at Tanda, Gopanpally, from the Family Photo Album in the Collection of Eragadindla Sanjeeva, Tanda, Gopanpally, Hyderabad. Courtesy: Keshawram, 2018.

Showing FPAs to the visiting family members and guests almost turns into another family gathering celebration for them. With the arrival of a guest, the FPAs are enlivened to complement the act of storytelling about family, house and past events. The photos are often pulled out of the albums and brought to the viewers; the storyteller's finger often moves on the photos to draw the attention of the viewers to the specific events, persons and objects that appear in the photos, and also to help them follow the sequence and consequence of the narrative. Here, the storyteller is not fixed; anyone from the family or the guest who witnessed or heard the events with which that particular photo is associated becomes a storyteller. Other members also join to remind if any part of the story is dropped or not accurately told by the storyteller. The viewers enjoy, participate by questioning or enquiring more details of the attached story and simultaneously add to the existing stories; the narrator and audience sometimes disagree but mostly approve of each other, which keep the process moving forward. Sometimes the photograph moves from the hands of one kin to another from one room to another or courtyard and kitchen as a story grows and is recalled with laughter, giggles or tears. After mobile phone cameras became easily available, guests often began to click photos of the printed photographs during these sessions, with the intention of sharing them on social media. The viewers prefer taking pictures of the photographs after pulling them out of the albums, as the reflective plastic pockets affect the clarity of the images. Over time, the transparency of the pockets deteriorates; however, the memories are periodically rejuvenated. Jarepati Swathi informed that she calls her family to pull out a particular photo from the album and asks them to click a snap of that photo on their mobile phones and share it with her. She uses those to tell stories in her in-laws' house or in the social media groups. Thus, the photo in the shimmering plastic packets of the FPA moves physically, digitally and virtually by being produced (copied) several times on different occasions. It also generates and accumulates new stories and different ways of narrating. If the quality and clarity of the photo in the albums deteriorate, various apps available on the mobile phones are used to touch up and enhance the clarity of the picture. Jarepati Swathi stressed that the mobile phone apps make them appear brighter, fairer and a bit exotic which pleases all. Thus, along with the story, the visuality of the photo gets reconstructed in layers of the time.

Eragadindla Sanjeeva's wedding albums are digitally composed and printed FPAs. These are larger compared to the ones discussed above, and the photos are directly printed on the pages (Figure 5.5). Here, photos are arranged on a page through a digital graphic editing process and printed on the thick papers. In other words, the photos and the album are not two different objects any more. The photos are inseparable from the album. Thus, the digital photo's material quality collapses and merges with the printed pages of the album. The composer carefully chooses the photos from the camera roll and edits them according to the family's aesthetic choices. It is like curating a photo exhibition in the FPA. Often, the album-makers are not the photographers. The album-makers work from the photo studio or home, whereas the photographers work on-site.

Eragadindla Sanjeeva's wedding album depicts his wedding rituals and other related events that took place between 22 and 24 June 2010. This album is bulky in comparison to Jarepati Swathi's album. It is 17 × 11 × 1 inches with thirty-six photo-pages. A local photo studio in Tanda named Santosh Photo Studio made this album; it costed the family 4,000 rupees. The blue cover page of this album has two frontal photos of the groom and bride in their wedding costumes and smiling faces at the centre. 'Sanjeeva weds Chitti' (written in cursive English fonts) appears underneath the bride and groom's photo. On the right side of the cover page, another photo

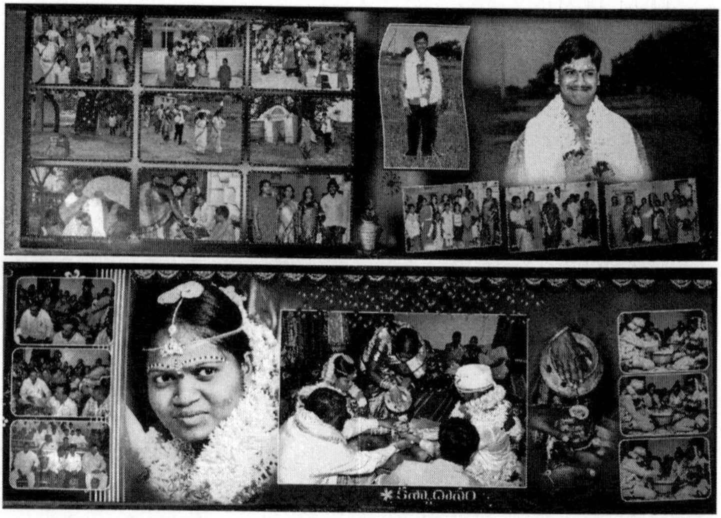

Figure 5.5 (Top) The Groom Is Going to Worship Pochamma Devi-Community Goddess with the Family Members; **(Below)** *Kanyādānam* Ritual, from the Family Photo Album Collection of Eragadindla Sanjeeva, Tanda, Gopanpally, Hyderabad-Deccan. Courtesy: Keshawram, 2018.

of the bride and groom standing on a colourful *rangoli* (ritualistic and ornamental floor design) marks a new beginning underneath an image of the Hindu god Ganesha. The album-maker has created an effect of showering rays all around the cover page to visualize the act of bestowing blessings and well wishes.

The album-maker has composed the photos capturing the bride and groom's marriage rituals and relatives, whose photos are important and have an emotional significance for the family. For example, the ritual on the second day of the marriage ceremony at the *Pochamma Devi* (a significant regional goddess in Telangana) temple was near their house.[3] On the third and fourth pages of Eragadindla Sanjeeva's wedding photo album (Figure 5.5 – top), the album-maker has arranged the nine photos in sequence so that the first seven photos are related to venerating rituals for

Pochamma. The first, second, third and fourth photos on the left (Figure 5.5 – top) depict the women, children and a few male members of the family walk along the temple trail. Eragadindla Sanjeeva's sister-in-law and two girls appear carrying white clothes on a *thal* (plate). The fourth photo shows a Hanuman shrine on the way. Even though he is not worshipped as part of the marriage rituals, the photographer and composer inserted the picture of Hanuman in the album with the family's consent. The sixth photo shows their arrival at the *Pochamma Devi* temple, a small lime-washed temple situated under a tree. In the seventh photograph in the sequence, the family members return home after the visit to the temple. However, the album-maker explores design possibilities to arrange photos. For example, on the fourth page's right side (Figure 5.5 – top), the album-maker uses two large photos of the groom, which are flanked by three slanted small-sized photos of the family members. For the backdrop, the album-maker has used a *kalash* (a metal vessel for ritualistic usage), pink flowers in the foreground and a green landscape as a symbolic representation of the wedding.

The relevance of the *kanyādānam* ritual, in which the bride's father presents her to the groom, is emphasized in the album (Figure 5.5 – below). The nineteenth and twentieth pages are merged to record the episode. The bride, groom and the priest, along with the family members of the bride and groom, are seated on the ground to perform the ritual. A group of observers, the relatives, encircle them. The album-maker has superimposed photos of the bride and the ritual[4] and complemented them with the word *kanyādānam* written in Telugu underneath. A prominent large portrait of the bride placed alongside the smaller narrative frames the relevance of this ritual in her married life. The sequential flow of narrative frames arranged by the digital composer evokes a sense of movement: as if a wedding video, popularly made during these occasions across

South Asia, is translated into a narrative image. A semi-circular hanging made of flowers and mango leaves is digitally added to the frame on top, apart from a showering of rose petals, to imbue a slice of festivity to the album.

This kind of storytelling process, I propose, is a continuation of the storytelling practices through narrative scroll, wall, and *phād* paintings (Figure 5.6) (Jain 1998; Mittal 2014). The compartmentalized page setup of the album to narrate the wedding sequences reminds me of the *Pabuji ka vivaah* (Pabuji's marriage) in the *phād* painting, practised in Mewar, Rajasthan (Smith 1991; Singh 2011). Painted on cloth, *phād* paintings depict narratives of Rajasthan's folk deities such as Pabuji and Devnarayan (Singh 1998: 100–15; Hiltebeitel 1999: 88). In these paintings, narrative scenes are compartmentalized and marked with yellow, white and black borders. The borders are decorated with motifs that are common in wedding rituals, such as banana and mango leaves in the marriage *toraṇa* (gateway), the way the album-maker composes such as leaves of banana, *toraṇa* of mango leaves and a wedding-kalash in the album. The prime characters of the narrative are usually shown in a larger scale compared to the narrative scenes, a trait that is noticed in the *kanyādānam* scene of Eragadindla Sanjeeva's wedding album. The *phād* paintings are brought to life when 'the *bhopā* (male performer-priest) and *bhopī* (female performer) stand in front of the painting and narrate stories through song and performance while pointing out the characters, places, and incidents with the bow of their fiddle (Smith 1991). This, I find, is similar to the presentation of wedding albums and FPAs in general in intimate gatherings. Drawing on these observations, I suggest narrativization and designing of wedding ceremonies through the FPA is a habitus of the storytelling tradition that prevails in the community's lives; Eragadindla Sanjeeva's wedding album is an example.

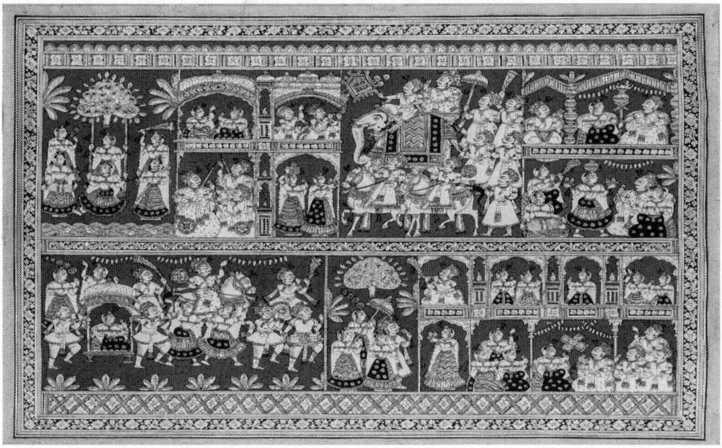

Figure 5.6 *Pabuji Ka Vivaah* (Pabuji's marriage). *Phād* Painting by Joshi Family from Bhilwara, Rajasthan, Natural Pigments on Cotton, 13 × 2.5 ft, 2020.

Layer, Care and Materials

The colours in Anju's photograph faded away over time, revealing the paper's white surface. This deterioration, caused by sunlight, humidity and weather conditions, bears the evidence of her travels and struggle to keep her memories safe within the clutter of their belongings. Sometimes photographs are folded to accommodate them in their pockets. More than keeping the photographs intact, holding them close to their bodies becomes a priority. Gradually, these pictures become their belongings to claim their existence in certain places and identity; hence, these bear the testimony of not only their family and home, but also uncertain travel, settlement and migration in the due course of time. Their album that holds the photos also contains other documents such as Aadhar card, voter ID card, ration card and bank account passbook.

In the case of Jarepati Swathi, she kept both new and old photos in her album, although the colours of the older photos had started fading when I interacted with her. Jarepati Swathi's album includes her photos with family members, friends from her school and college, and of special occasions, birthdays and family rituals. Each photo is associated with memories from her past. As Jarepati Swathi is married now and moved to her husband's home, her family members reminisce about Swathi's time at her parental home by referring back to the photos in the album. To preserve her memories, her family members have digitally photographed the printed, now fading ones from Jarepati Swathi's album and share them via social media, remembering her life before marriage. Swathi's album moves from the hands of one family member to another, whereas Eragadindla Sanjeeva's wedding album is usually carefully kept on a shelf. The wedding album is viewed occasionally when the couple reminisces about their wedding. On a regular basis, it would be touched for cleaning the dust on it.

The photos in the family albums of the Tanda residents and the migrant construction workers are produced under economic constraints: the quality of paper, printing and camera configuration are chosen so as to yield affordable images. The photographs of the economically challenged families, clicked by local photographers, differ materially from the artistic photographic practices of Henri Cartier-Bresson, Raghu Rai and Sohrab Hura, devoted to documenting commoners' lives, which include people like the communities of Jettam Anju, Jarepati Swathi and Eragadindla Sanjeeva discussed in the earlier part of this chapter. The patronage and reception of the photographs are the key: the Tanda photographers pay keen attention to the interests of the residents and respond to their needs rather than disseminating them to a larger metropolitan audience. Whereas protective measures such as using archival paper and ink are employed in artistic photographs to extend their longevity, the FPAs are simply kept under the protective care of the family members. If the lifestyle of the people being photographed emerges as the key theme in the artistic photographs, by contrast, the FPAs are an active part of the lifestyle of the residents of Tanda.

For the family members, the FPA is a part of their lives: life stories are documented, stored and shared with future generations through this mnemonic tool. Narain notes that the conversion of printed photographs into digital format for archiving purposes changes and loses their subjective meaning, and sometimes the memories associated with it also end (Narain 2019: 119–21). If we pay attention to Jarepati Swathi's family's small-sized albums, the photographs are arranged according to her activities and events. This is in contrast with institutional archives such as the Hiteshranjan Sanyal Memorial Archive in Kolkata, the American Institute of Indian Studies Photo Archive in Gurgaon where photographs once collected from an owner are grouped or separated by documentation, digitization and categorization. At archives, photos are usually preserved with extraordinary care, separating them carefully from the lives of the families where they originate. For example, in the archive of Alkazi Foundation for the Arts, New Delhi, hard copies of photographs have been kept carefully in acid-free sleeves in dehumidified rooms. The storage, care and sense of preservation of the FPA by the families of Jettam Anju, Jarepati Swathi, Eragadindla Sanjeeva is different from the care and preservation of the institutional archives. The way the FPA operates in a family charts a parallel path of the overlapping of individual-institutional preservation strategies. Thus, family as a social institution, and the making of private-public archive as an educational research institution have overlapping trajectories of the FPA albums' survival.

Conclusion

The FPA is an enduring presence of ancestors as well as the growing lives and memories of family members, revolving around the notion of home. At the construction site of UoH, the photographs of Jettam Anju were old and faded; scratches and folds on the surface of the photographs were visible. The scratches were perhaps Anju's addition to the stories of her family's migration. The temporary shelter of Anju's mother at Malad from the photograph was re-enacted in Anju's make-shift tent. Anju's photographs not only remain as evidence of her family's moving home but also as a memory aid that transports the notion of shelter across generations.

For Jarepati Swathi and Eragadindla Sanjeeva's albums, the idea of home translates into rituals and performances that occur around these sites. The printed analogue photographs showing Swathi's childhood and festivals, such as Dussehra, represent her ancestral home as the site of the unfolding of these events; the home has a silent yet unmistakable presence. The subsequent changes in the construction of their home run parallel to the gradual transformation of Jarepati Swathi's life; the photographs capture both these transitional processes. Further, the transitional process is activated through a gradual unfolding of the photographs showing family members, occasions and sites. The informal ritual of showing and sharing FPAs during the gatherings takes place at family homes; the act of showing photographs evokes the intangible memories of the home.

In Anju's photographs, 'home' always remains vulnerable to constant migrations and is thus unstable and fleeting. For Jarepati Swathi and Eragadindla Sanjeeva, their residences are unchanged. Nevertheless, the layers of transformations on site as well as in their lives are undeniable. For both cases, FPAs turn into a reserve of ephemeral memories associated with home. That is, FPA transmits the past to the present and future, thus always finding a way of artistic survival.

Notes

1 I thank the editors for their critical review that enabled me to bring the chapter to an appropriate form. I also thank Eragadindla Sanjeeva for introducing me to the families living in Gopanpally Tanda, Hyderabad.

2 *Bindi*s are circular stickers/powder on the foreheads of (Hindu) women, which are often used to indicate their marital status. Traditionally, *bindi*s are worn by unmarried or married women, but widowed women are not supposed to wear them.

3 The groom wraps the bride's wedding dress with white clothes, which also contains coconut, rice and other things for worship. After one or two weeks of marriage, the family offers a goat to the goddess *Pochamma*. Interview with Sanjeeva in Hyderabad, February 2018.

4 In the *kanyādānam* ritual for Sanjeeva's community, the bride keeps her right hand with a piece of coconut, betel leaf and nuts on the groom's right hand. Then the bride's father holds both the hands under his palms, and the bride's mother pours water on their hands.

References

Hiltebeitel, Alf (1999), *The Epic of Pabuji, Rethinking India's Oral and Classical Epics: Draupadi among Rajputs, Muslims, and Dalits*, Chicago, IL: University of Chicago Press.

Jain, Jyotindra (1998) *Picture Showmen: Insights into the Narrative Tradition in Indian Art*, Mumbai: Marg.

Mittal, Jagdish (2014), *Deccani Scroll Paintings in the Jagdish and Kamla Mittal Museum of Indian Art*, Hyderabad: Jagdish and Kamla Mittal Museum of Indian Art.

Narain, Suryanandini (2019), 'In the Family: Photographic Archives from India', in Julia Bärnighausen, Costanza Caraffa, Stefanie Klamm, Franka Schneider and Petra Wodtke (eds), *Photo-Objects: On the*

Materiality of Photographs and Photo Archives, 115–29, Max Planck Research Library for the History and Development of Knowledge: Studies 12, Berlin: Max-Planck-Gesellschaft zur Förderung der Wissenschaften. Available online: http://mprl-series.mpg.de/studies/12/ (accessed 14 December 2020).

Orpana, Jennifer (2018), 'Finding Family in The Times of India's Mid-Century Kodak Ads', *Trans Asia Photography*, 9 (1): 1–35. Available online: https://doi.org/10.1215/215820251_9-1-107 (accessed 14 December 2020).

Pinney, Christopher (1997), *Camera Indica: The Social Life of Indian Photographs*, Chicago, IL: University of Chicago Press.

Sandbye, Mette (2014), 'Looking at the Family Photo Album: A Resumed Theoretical Discussion of Why and How', *Journal of Aesthetics and Culture*, 6 (1). Available online: https://doi.org/10.3402/jac.v6.25419 (accessed 14 December 2020).

Singh, Kavita (1998), 'Fixed Image in a Changing World: The Phad Paintings of Rajasthan', in Jyotindra Jain (ed.), *Picture Showmen: Insights into the Narrative Tradition in Indian Art*, 100–15, Mumbai: Marg.

Singh, Kavita (2011), 'Transfixed by the Arrow of Time: Phad Paintings of Rajasthan', in Anna L. Dallapiccola (ed.), *Indian Painting: The Lesser-Known Traditions*, 115–18, New Delhi: Niyogi Books.

Smith, John D. (1991), *The Epic of Pābūjī: A Study, Transcription and Translation*, Cambridge: Cambridge University Press.

Walker, Andrew L. and Rosalind Kimball Moulton (1989), 'Photo Albums: Images of Time and Reflections of Self', *Qualitative Sociology*, 12 (2): 155–82.

6

The *Dargāh* Locale in Hyderabad: A Junction of the Architectural Past and Present

Sayan Gupta

Introduction

The 400-year-old Hazrat Syed Hussain Shah Wali Dargāh (Figure 6.1) at Raidurgam in Hyderabad is a nexus of local, devotional and social lives. It contributes to the aesthetics of contemporary architecture in its surrounding area, popularly known as the *dargāh*. The name '*dargāh*' for the area, in fact, has stemmed from the Hussain Shah[1] Wali Dargāh. Henceforth I refer to the area as the '*dargāh* locale' (Figure 6.2) in this chapter. Alongside the Hussain Shah Wali Dargāh, the tombs of other Sufis such as Hazrat Syed Shah Meeran Hussaini, Hazrat Syed Hyder Shah Quadri aka Zanjeer Peer, Hazrat Sayyid Muhammad Hasan Jeeli Kaleemi and the Naqshbandi Dargāh are also situated in the same locale (Figure 6.3). The first three *dargāh*s that are named after three Sufis were the kin of Hazrat Syed Hussain Shah. One of them Hazrat Syed Shah Meeran Hussaini was a cousin of Hazrat Syed Hussain Shah's grandfather (Siddiqi and Kugle 2009: 139). Hazrat Sayyid Muhammad Hasan Jeeli Kaleemi was a Sufi in the Chishti Kaleemi lineage and the *mureed* (pupil) of Hazrat Inayat Khan (Farida 2012; Kugle 2013). Hazrat Syed Hyder Shah Quadri Dargāh is known for a miracle that the local shopkeepers love to tell. The miracle narrates that a thief attempting to steal a gold chain from the shrine found himself tied to the shrine with an iron chain (*zanjīr*); and the thief died on the spot. Hence the residents of the *dargāh* locale call it the Zanjeer Peer Dargāh.

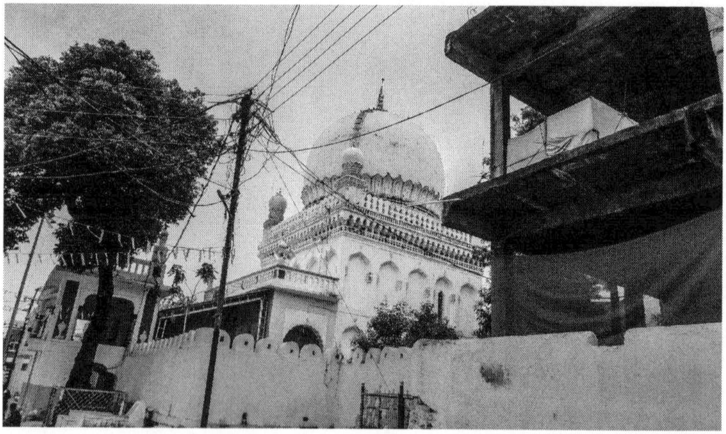

Figure 6.1 Hussain Shah Wali Dargāh, Hyderabad-Deccan. Courtesy: Baishali Ghosh, 2021.

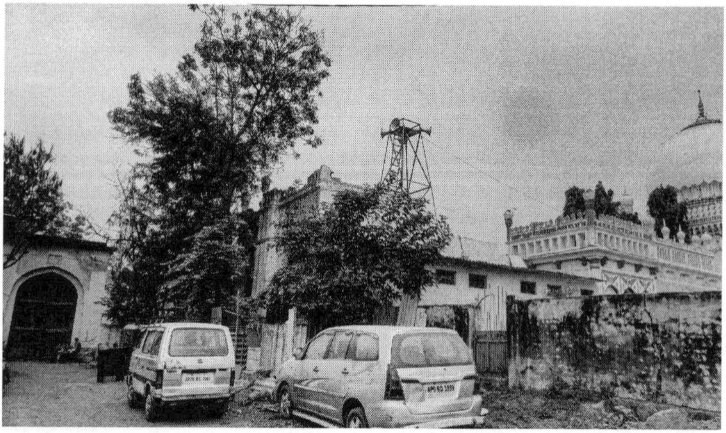

Figure 6.2 Hussain Shah Wali Dargāh Locale, Hyderabad-Deccan. Courtesy: Baishali Ghosh, 2021.

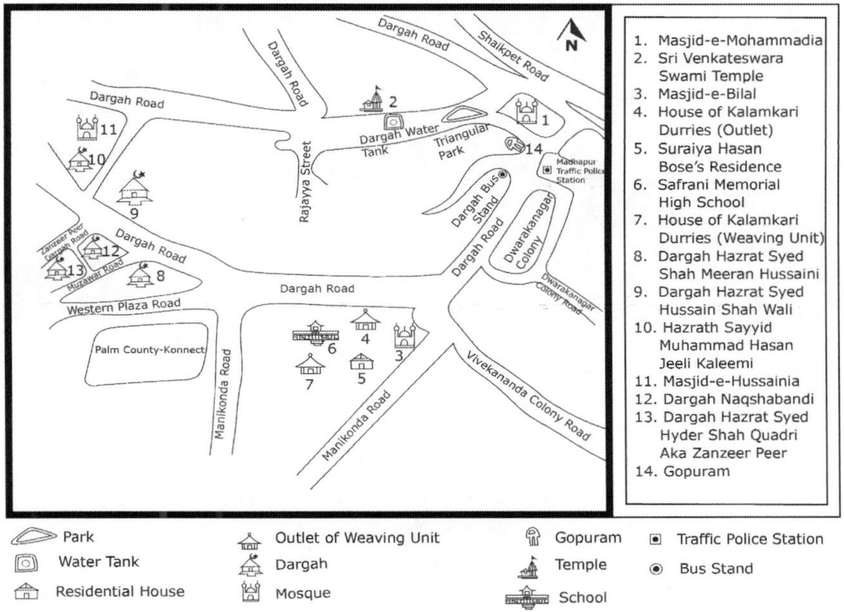

Figure 6.3 A Map of the Hussain Shah Wali Dargāh Locale. Credit: Sayan Gupta, Rajesh Lakkoju, Somedutta Mallik and Bijay Nath, 2024.

The architectural features of most buildings in the *dargāh* locale have close similarities with the Qutb Shahi tombs situated 4 km away. The Meeran Hussaini Dargāh and the Sayyid Muhammad Hasan Jeeli Kaleemi Dargāh were built many years after the Hussain Shah Wali Dargāh around the eighteenth century. The material evidence of Indo-Saracenic[2] architectural features in these *dargāh*s also bear stylistic expressions of the post-Golconda, Mughal Imperial and European neo-Gothic architecture. Though the Indo-Saracenic architectural style mostly flourished in the nineteenth century under the colonial regime, a chronicle of the nineteenth century about this architectural style reveals that it was explored in the architecture much earlier around the end of the seventeenth century. Chepauk Palace in present-day Chennai was built in the Indo-Saracenic architectural style in the mid-eighteenth century. The Hyderabad Nizam's architecture profoundly displays aesthetic choices similar to the Indo-Saracenic architectural style (Jayewardene-Pillai 2007: 2–6). However, Hussain Shah Wali Dargāh constitutes the nexus of all the Islamic shrines in the *dargāh* locale. My study of the Hussain Shah Wali Dargāh sheds light on the adaptation of the *dargāh*'s architectural features in the contemporary buildings of *dargāh* locale. I suggest that the aesthetic choice of using the *dargāh*'s architectural features in the contemporary buildings is determined by three factors – locally available materials, regional economy and widespread devotion centred on the Hussain Shah Wali Dargāh. The Hussain Shah Wali Dargāh was built under the Qutb Shahi patronage.

The Qutb Shahi patronage and its architectural styles can be traced in the predynastic period of the Deccan. It is possible to observe interesting shifts and synthesis in the buildings of the period. The governor of Deccan under the Delhi Sultanate in the fourteenth century, Muhammad Tughlaq, enjoyed the distinctive features of the buildings, which are an eclectic amalgamation of indigenous South

Indian Hindu temples and building techniques from Persia and Central Asia. The provincial Islamic architectural style continued to develop under Ala-ud-din Bahman Shah (also known as Hasan Gangu or Zafar Khan), who was initially a representative of Muhammad Tughlaq of the Delhi Sultanate and later established himself as the sovereign ruler of the Deccan from the capital city of Gulbarga (now known as Kalaburagi). The capital shifted to Bidar in the fifteenth century. The architectural style of this period saw the acculturation of Persian elements with the Delhi Sultanate style. It came to be reflected in the style and proportion of the domes. The domes were set above an octagonal drum. The Bidar style fully flourished under the Barid Shahi dynasty from the late fifteenth century to the early seventeenth century, then continued its development at Golconda under the Qutb Shahi dynasty (in the early sixteenth to late seventeenth century). The ornamentation of stucco works on the building walls and the bulbous or Tartar dome developed under the last phase of the Golconda style. A beautiful example of this style is the seven tombs at the Qutb Shahi necropolis. The style continued during the Nizam rule in Hyderabad (Troll 2003; Currim and Michell 2004; Green 2006; Sardar 2007; Juneja 2008). Thus, the royal architecture of Qutb Shahis is the visual marker of syncretic architectural practices which continued in the extended architectural practices after Qutb Shahi as well.

During fieldwork, the renovations that were carried out by the stakeholders of the *dargāh* on the 400-year-old structure between 2013 and 2016 have offered perspectives to the discussion of this chapter.[3] New architectural materials were introduced to the Hussain Shah Wali Dargāh, which somewhat altered its appearance. Yet, the connection with the Qutb Shahi past remains unbroken. The local association and affection for this *dargāh* come to be reflected in the contemporary buildings in its surrounding area. The replication of the Hussain Shah Wali Dargāh's architectural motifs on the contemporary architecture indicates that the classical

Qutb Shahi architectural style continues to live through the lives of inhabitants around the *dargāh*. The *dargāh* locale is a hub of the city migrants, and the co-existence of different ethno-religious and linguistic communities in the *dargāh* locale continues to enrich its distinctive character since the Qutb Shahi dynasty.

The period from the rule of the Qutb Shahi dynasty to the colonial era has seen an unprecedented permutation and combination of architectural styles, patronized by both the British and the Nizam princely state of Hyderabad, leading to the emergence of a distinct aesthetic preference in the architecture of the region. This new architecture is generally known as an Indo-Saracenic style (Jayewardene-Pillai 2007: 14). Shanti Jayewardene-Pillai writes, 'Indian (architectural) volumes and motifs were randomly mixed with largely classical themes. The classical frame was adorned with the Indian dripstone, domed pavilion, balconies, pierced screens and that unforgettable dome…' (Jayewardene-Pillai 2007: 14). Thus, the core concepts of Indo-Saracenic style, which are the acculturation, adaptation and absorption of architectural motifs and methods, have offered me a methodological framework to study Hussain Shah Wali Dargāh, a lesser-known devotional architecture made in the Qutb Shahi Style in the peripheral settlements of Golconda. Drawing on the cumulative style of Indo-Saracenic architecture, I propose that Hussain Shah Wali Dargāh is eclectic in nature – in that it allowed a flexible exchange of architectural elements with the neighbouring constructions through the process of renovation. I also suggest that this eclectic nature has helped to address and protect the vulnerability of lesser-known structures, including the Hussain Shah Wali Dargāh itself, amidst the radical urbanization of Hyderabad over the past decades, thus creating a way for these buildings to survive. This chapter unravels the layers of making and transforming the eclectic architectural practice of the Hussain Shah Wali Dargāh locale. It examines how the architectural style of Hussain Shah Wali Dargāh drew from its contemporary Qutb Shahi tombs at the necropolis, and how modification and alteration of this 400-year-old structure enabled the dissemination of its architectural style among contemporary buildings without a canonical bias towards its historical and architectural past.

Mapping the Monument

A close consideration of the Hussain Shah Wali Dargāh allows us to identify its Qutb Shahi features as well as later additions. The architectural features of the Hussain Shah Wali Dargāh, such as the central dome, parapet, finials, minarets, merlons, fluted lotus band surrounding the dome, blind arches on the wall and door of *hujrā* (an Islamic tomb chamber, surmounted by a dome with the cenotaph in the centre) and wind corridor, bear similarities with the tomb of Sultan Quli Qutb Shah. The *hujrā* is crowned by a big *gumbad* (dome), decorated with fluted lotus petals. Around the *hujrā*, the burials of Hussain Shah's son, daughter and daughter-in-law form three miniature tombs on the premises. The three outer walls of *the hujrā* (left, right and back sides) are decorated with the recess-point arches. All the arches are blind arches; five arches in every band appear on three sides. This one-storeyed structure creates a visual impression of a two-storeyed building because of the two bands of recess arches on the elevation wall. A broad rectangular entrance with the prodigious pointed arch of the *hujrā* provides clear visibility of the cenotaph and contributes to the devotees' experience of this space. The devotees can complete their prayers without compromising their visibility of the saint's cenotaph. The inside west wall of the *hujrā* has a small *mihrab* (alcove) on the *qibla* wall.[4] In the Islamic tradition, the west-*mihrab* indicates the direction of prayer and also Kaaba, the mosque of

Mecca (Tomory 2009: 501). A small rectangular niche over the *mihrab* looks like a Persianized wind corridor and echoes another one over the door's head.

The central *gumbad* is almost round and slightly tapered towards the top, crowned with a finial, and set on a fluted lotus base. It is decorated with a band of projected lance-shaped lotus petals and set on a high drum. This drum is not visible from outside because of the parapet covering the drum outside the *dargāh*. All four sides of the parapet have four small *gumbad*s with the fluted lotus bands and finials over the domes. These small domes are set on the small rectangular minarets with a rounded base below the *gumbad*. The body of the minarets is decorated with an eight-angled star. The top of the parapet is adorned with two layers of decorated *kangurās* (battlements). The small domes are also decorated with two bands of lotus petals, and each of them has finials. A rectangular two-storeyed *darvāzā* (main gateway of the *dargāh*) with a towering pointed arch has a parapet at the top. The four sides of the parapet have four towers with four domes and finials over the *gumbad*. These *gumbad*s are decorated with two-storeyed bands of fluted lotus petals. These *gumbad*s are pumpkin-like in shape and slightly tapering at the bottom.

The *darvāzā* is flanked by two bands of *chājjā*s (eaves), crowned with the Bengal dome[5] and supported by four pillars, which hold three *mihrab*s like arches on three sides – front, left and right. The pillars with fillet and fluting on their body are bulbous at the bottom, just above their bases. The lower bands of the doorway have six *candraśālā*s (half-crescent moon-like arches). These arches provide passages for entering the small galleries on both sides. The left and the right sides of the doorway are designed with four large opening arches. A staircase inside the doorway leads to the upper gallery. The upper gallery is possibly a *minbar* (pulpit) used to deliver the sermon on Fridays. This mausoleum is embraced by a *sher hajji* (a defensive fortified wall) with a band of *kangurās*, similar to Golconda Fort and the Qutb Shahi tombs. A *vazū khānā* (water tank) is situated in front of the doorway for visitors' and worshippers' ablutions. This trabeated structure has a fountain marking the centre of the water tank. Beside the water tank is a two-storeyed structure known as the *nahāvaṭ khānā*, an arched and pillared gallery made for musicians. The roof has a parapet; the four sides have four pinnacles, each crowned with a cupola. The lower part of this structure has an open-pillared structure, and the upper part is the arched structure divided into three parts. The middle part has a *chājjā*s (eave), shaded by the Bengal dome. The descendants of Hussain Shah, known as *jagirdar*s, live in a two-storeyed house on the Hussain Shah Wali Dargāh premises, separated from the *dargāh* by a small fence. Next to the *dargāh* is the *k̲h̲ānaqah*, a small pillared hall for meditation and fest. The Dargāh Post Office is also set on the *chabutra* (plinth) of the Hussain Shah Wali Dargāh.

The dome of Sultan Quli Qutb Shah's tomb, with a finial, looks like a big drum, slightly tilted at the top, decorated with a band of upward-facing lotus petals at the bottom. It is set on the drum but is not visible from the outside. It is hidden by a parapet band divided into two layers and four cardinal minarets, crowned by small domes with finials. The minarets are decorated with the pattern of eight-angled stars. The upper layer of this parapet is a band of merlons. The tomb is open from three sides. The *hujrā* is made over the basement and decorated with arabesque and foliage in stucco and fresco. Quli Qutb Shah's actual grave is in the basement, while a suggestive cenotaph has been made inside the *hujrā*. The enclosure wall is decorated with merlons similar to the Golconda Fort. Despite the striking similarities between the Quli Qutb Shah tomb and the *dargāh*, there are subtle differences in the design of the parapets and the cardinal points of the minarets at both tombs. Hussain Shah's parapets are decorated with open arches, while Quli

Qutb Shah's tomb has blind arches. The minarets of Quli Qutb Shah's tomb start from the base, unlike the ones at the *dargāh* set at the upper layer of the parapet. The minarets of Quli Qutb Shah's tomb are more prominent in size than those of the *dargāh*. Both the mausoleums have enclosure walls decorated with the merlons. The striking architectural similarities and subtle differences between these two structures cannot account for why the Hussain Shah Wali Dargāh looks mundane and blends in with the locale, whereas the Quli Qutb Shah's tomb appears astonishingly regal.

The Qutb Shahi tombs complex is recognized by UNESCO as a heritage site.[6] The recent renovations (made in between 2013 and 2020) at Quli Qutb Shah's tomb, conducted by the Aga Khan Trust and Tata Trust, attempted to reconstruct the early-seventeenth-century structure and return the accuracy of the architectural expression of the Qutb Shahi legacy.[7] However, the renovations carried out at the *dargāh* beheld the continued veneration of the believers. The renovation and alteration works undertaken by the Hussain Shah Wali Dargāh Waqf Board and local people contributed to its distinctive nature. The Waqf Board and the locals cannot afford or have access to the craftsmen hired to renovate the Qutb Shahi tombs. Usually, the renovation of this *dargāh* happens on the basis of need and/or priority of a certain portion of the building, devotees' donations, and the availability of materials used for renovation. For example, in October 2014, the commissioned agency used cement, bricks and white marble slabs instead of the original building materials.[8] Locally available stones and other architectural materials very similar to Quli Qutb Shah's tomb were employed. The renovation workers were local masons, skilful but not well-acquainted with the techniques, materials and architectural details of the Qutb Shahi era. As part of the renovation, they are usually told to mend parts of the Dargāh that display visible marks of deterioration. The building is usually painted (Figure 6.4) during

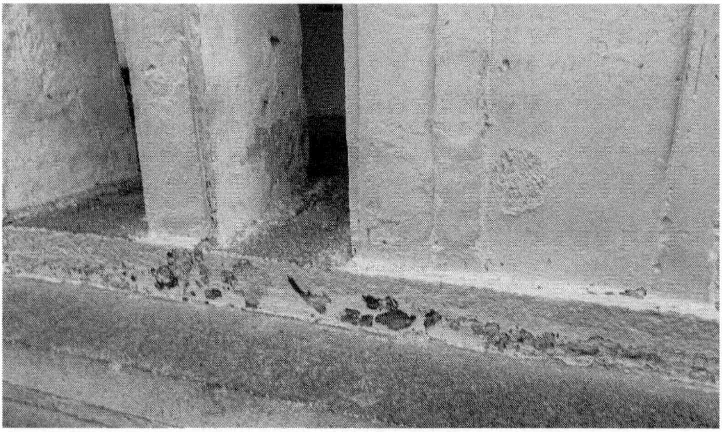

Figure 6.4 Layers of Synthetic Industrial Paints on Hussain Shah Wali Dargāh, Hyderabad-Deccan. Courtesy: Baishali Ghosh, 2021.

the *Urs* (the death anniversary of the Sufi saint). Every year, the Hussain Shah Wali Dargāh performs two *Urs* rituals. One is the *baḍā Urs* (big *Urs*) of Sufi saint Hussain Shah Wali, and the other is the *chotā Urs* (small Urs) of Hazrat Khwaja Banda Nawaz Gesu Daraz. In the *dargāh* locale, the *chotā Urs* is called *Urs-e-Shareef* or simply Urs by the residents. The *baḍā Urs* falls on the thirteenth and fourteenth of Jumada al-Thani. The *chotā Urs* falls on the sixteenth and seventeenth of Zilqad (Abhilash 2014: 31). The *Urs* brings devotion and donation, care and conservation, share and exchange of earned and surplus materials of devotees, and local business closer. This is the time people share their long association, and observation on the *dargāh* and its changing and growing surroundings. The *Urs* also brings new materials for the purposes of decoration and devotion. The local *pankha* (hand fan used for devotional offerings) makers introduce new motif, and sizes on the occasion of the *Urs*. Thus, during the *Urs* the Hussain Shah Wali Dargāh building receives special inspection from the Waqf Board, daily caretakers and devotees. The older architectural features of the *dargāh* alter with every bit of repair work done. However, the aspect that remains unchanged is the utmost care the locals take to keep the building sturdy and sustainable; they prefer to do this rather than to research, revive and refabricate its antiquarian appearance.

Dargāh Locale

The boundaries of the residential, commercial and public areas are often blurred in the *dargāh* locale, thus creating an overlapping settlement with various ethno-religious and ethnolinguistic communities, such as Telugu- and Dakhani-speaking Hindus and Muslims, and migrants from Uttar Pradesh, Bihar, Rajasthan, Punjab, Madhya Pradesh, West Bengal and Gujarat. This area mainly belongs to the middle and lower classes and is apparently dominated by Mudiraj (agrarian), and Yadav (pastoral) communities. Other groups residing in this area are Kumharis (potters), Kamsalis (goldsmiths), Vadrangis (carpenters) and Saakalis (washermen) (Abhilash 2014: 6–8). Since the 1980s, the *dargāh* locale has become a hub of skilled migrant craftsmen and professionals as well as unskilled migrant labourers who work in the film, IT and real estate industries. They are mostly Hindi, Bengali, Odia, Bhojpuri and Punjabi speakers belonging to different sectarian denominations. For example, parallel to the *dargāh galī* (narrow lane) has a stretch of *zardosi* fabric workers, who mostly migrated from the northern and eastern parts of India. Small traders from west and north-west India have been living here for not less than sixty or seventy years (Sheela 2014). Since the 1990s, the *dargāh* locale has witnessed the settlement of young graduates working in the animation and different IT industries. It is in the foothills of the Jubilee and Banjara Hills, which are the hub of wealthy communities and industries.

In the 1990s, the economic rent of the residential arrangement in the *dargāh* locale attracted the migrant workers working in the various industries and real estate businesses as skilled and unskilled employees. At present, the living expenses in this locale have considerably increased, and it has become an area of city migrants' network and settlement. Thus, the co-existence of different ethno-religious and linguistic communities in the *dargāh* locale has enriched its distinctive character.

This makes the *dargāh* locale complex and plural in its organization of business, markets and living on an everyday basis. However, the settlement grew beside the three routes that directly lead to the *dargāh*: (i) a lane adjacent to the Masjid-e-Mohammadia, a Qutb Shahi Mosque opposite the *dargāh* bus stop of the Old Mumbai Road; (ii) a road through the *gopura* of Sri Venkateswara Swamy Temple, opposite the Dargāh Traffic Police Station; and (iii) a lane beside Masjid-e-Bilal. The residential quarters of this area are primarily centred on the Hussain Shah Wali Dargāh and the Sri Venkateswara Swamy Temple. Residents in this area are mostly self-employed and work by selling milk, farm produce and pottery. There are also artisanal groups, such as goldsmiths, carpenters and leatherworkers, as well as occupational groups like butchers, barbers and launderers. In recent times, there has been a rapid growth of software companies around the *dargāh* locale, in areas such as Dabha, Gachibowli and Manikonda. As a consequence, the local people of the *dargāh* locale – primarily young people – have begun to work in these new office spaces as office attendants, cleaners and security guards.

Most commercial structures, like grocery shops, beauty parlours, medical stores and nursing home, are built adjacent to and along with residential houses. Often the shops are on the ground floor, while their owners live on the upper floors. Government offices and public structures, like water tanks and schools, also exist beside residential areas. Some of the buildings have been used for multiple purposes and physically overlap with each other. Some of them are divided by enclosed walls to enable privacy. These divisions create clusters of wealthy and upper-middle-class bungalows and housing complexes on one side, flats and two-storeyed buildings of the middle class on another side, and congested slums of small mud houses belonging to the lower middle class on the corner. Networks of small alleys and lanes connect the divided clusters of habitations of various classes. Mostly bungalows, flats and two-storeyed buildings of the upper-middle-class and middle-class families are built near the local main road, whereas the slums of lower-middle-class families (both Muslim and Hindu) are seen near the Hussain Shah Wali Dargāh. The inhabitants have built their residential and commercial buildings both in front and behind the *dargāh*. The old monuments and the contemporary buildings contribute to an ambiance where the seventeenth and the twenty-first centuries co-exist in the '*dargāh*' locale.

The contemporary buildings often have architectural elements like pillars, arches and parapets very similar to those of the Hussain Shah Wali Dargāh. These buildings are at the most forty or fifty years old, and a majority of them have been built in the past two decades. The newer buildings are built with bricks, ferro concrete and cement, unlike the Hussain Shah Wali Dargāh that was initially built in stone, stucco-plaster and lime mortar. Nevertheless, the architectural elements, like the arch (Figures 6.5 and 6.6) vault, of these contemporary residential as well as public buildings are resonant with the *dargāh* architecture. The half-rounded arches of residential buildings, commonly seen in the *dargāh* locale, have close affinities with the elliptical *candraśālā* that we find on the upper band of the *darvāzā* of Hussain Shah Wali Dargāh.

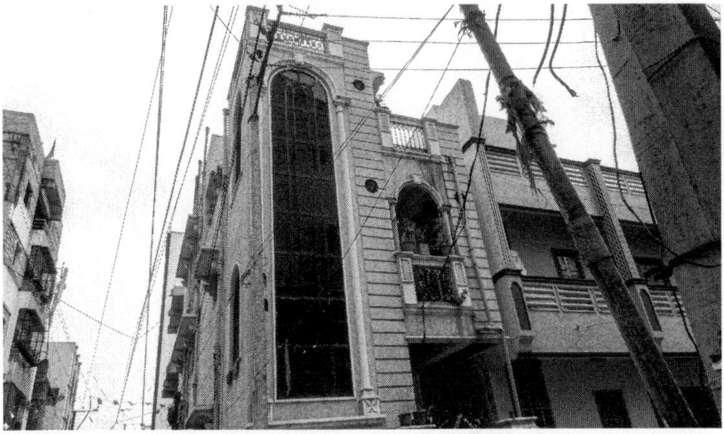

Figure 6.5 Hussain Shah Wali Dargāh like Angular Archways in the Residential House in *Dargāh* Locale, Hyderabad-Deccan. Courtesy: Baishali Ghosh, 2021.

These examples show that the Hussain Shah Wali Dargāh has some influence on contemporary buildings, yet not directly because of the materials. The architectural forms of the Hussain Shah Wali Dargāh appear to be replicated – in fragments – in metal, glass, wood, plaster of paris, plastic sheets as add-on décor on the walls, false ceilings, doors and gates. I suggest that the formal affinities with the architectural motifs of the Hussain Shah Wali Dargāh are not a one-way track, but lie at the crossroads of a naïve exchange of workers, devotees, materials and aesthetic preferences that enable the fluid mobilization of architectural knowledge between the historical tomb and contemporary buildings. For instance, though the Hussain Shah Wali Dargāh was made of stone and stucco, it is renovated with the materials generally used to build the houses and shops in the *dargāh* locale. I have found that devotees often make donations to the *dargāh* when they build new houses for themselves; donations often include the offering of raw materials, such as cement and

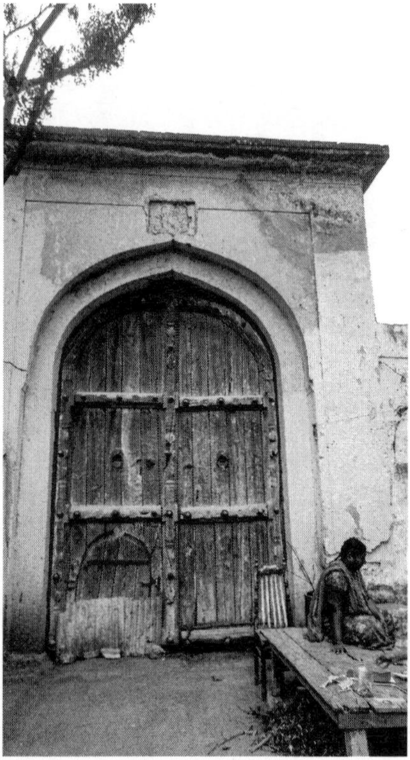

Figure 6.6 Hussain Shah Wali Dargāh like Angular Archways in the Old Residential Building in *Dargāh* Locale, Hyderabad-Deccan. Courtesy: Baishali Ghosh, 2021.

paints. It is the lives of the devotees, expressions of their devotion and their domesticity (here house-making) that are entangled with the settlement around the *dargāh*. Apart from cash, the devotees also donate their agricultural produce and other goods. They donate what they can afford, cultivate, earn and/or trade. Sometimes donors also sponsor workers who do repair and renovation work for the *dargāh*. It is important to note that these workers also work on the various real estate construction sites in the *dargāh* surroundings.[9] Thus, the sharing of labour, skills (masonry) and devotion turns out to be the crossroads through which architectural motifs and knowledge travel.

A comparison between the arches on the pillars of the veranda or corridor of the Nagarjuna High School and the cusped arched openings at the *darvāzā* or main entrance of the *dargāh* further illustrates this issue. The masterfully executed cusped archways, a Mughal addition to the Deccani architectural vocabulary, in the Hussain Shah Wali Dargāh were achieved by the use of thin bricks plastered with lime mortar. Since the use of thin bricks has fallen out of practice, the contemporary masons and architects employ available bricks to replicate the cusped arch-like appearance. The delicate cusp, which emerged as a result of selected materials and fine craftsmanship, has been replaced with angular archways in the school corridor and residential houses (Figure 6.5). The repetition of these geometric arches also accentuates the presence of the *darvāzā* in the old residential building (Figure 6.6). Furthermore, in both architectures (Hussain Shah Wali Dargāh and the Nagarjuna High School), the arched openings are employed to welcome visitors to the interior spaces. During festivals, performers and individuals from the shrine committee are often seen at these arched openings welcoming the flocks of devotees inside the tomb. The arched openings at the school extend the welcome of school authorities to existing and prospective students. Thus, the replication of the cusped arches from the *dargāh* to the school and other buildings is not only visual but also functional.

While tracing the spread of the Qutb Shahi style in the suburbs and neighbouring villages, Robert Alan Simpkins found that a number of monuments have been forgotten and lost. Rapid urban encroachments in recent Hyderabad left lesser-known monuments of the Golconda style and period endangered and unprotected. He indicates that the lack of proper archival records and study of these lesser-known monuments that were built in connection with and in the pattern of the Golconda architectural style suggest the erasure of complex historicity and the expansion of the Golconda kingdom (Simpkins 2014: 31–4). Drawing on Robert Alan Simpkins's argument, here I suggest that the Hussain Shah Wali Dargāh stands at the junction of the architectural history of the Golconda style and contemporary adaptations of architectural materials. Though the contemporary stakeholders' attempts to renovate the *dargāh* do not impose newer architectural materials and elements onto the historical ones, the priority of the management, the devotees and differences in craftsmanship of the masons' eventually effect, alterations and transformations of the architecture. Thus, the *dargāh* gets accommodated and adopted in the growing Hyderabad radical urbanization of recent decades by means of its architectural elements, which sets up a conversation of its fragmentary historical past with the contemporary.

The historical architectural motifs of the Hussain Shah Wali Dargāh survive under the layers of glossy synthetic industrial paint annually applied before the festival of the *Urs*. Presently, the structure is painted in industrially produced synthetic white paint, with an ornamental distribution of red, yellow and green to highlight individual sections. The significance of white in Islamic belief and philosophy is a tangible presence in the Hussain Shah Wali Dargāh where the durability of the synthetic colour adds to the pertinence of this belief. The synthetic industrial paints replaced the elaborate application of lime-stucco on the building (Figure 6.4). The preparation of lime-stucco increases the expenses and requires specialized craftsmanship; for both these reasons, lime-stucco is not affordable for the stakeholders of the Hussain Shah Wali Dargāh. The treatment (here lime-stucco), which was once common and preferred, was therefore gradually replaced with materials readily available in the market. The consumers' or devotees' hands-on experience of using these materials also affects their choice for the Hussain Shah Wali Dargāh. As many consumers opt to paint their residential spaces with synthetic paint, given its shine and durability, they perhaps prefer to use the same to paint the shrine of their venerated one. This intrinsic relationship between the mundane material world and devotion is the core of Sufi practice. I would like to stress here that the Hussain Shah Wali Dargāh architecture and the recent buildings in its surroundings resonate with this *silsilā* (chain/continuation) of the built environment, which is the culture of the Sufi shrines across South Asia. As I perceive it, the architectural deviation and continuity in the case of the Hussain Shah Wali Dargāh is a descendant of the popular devotional practice of Sufism rather than an extension of the provincial, classical Qutb Shahi architectural style, which is being overshadowed in recent times by the rapidly urbanizing landscape of Hyderabad.

Conclusion

The *dargāh* locale is a fascinating settlement where the medieval and contemporaneity reside together. The contemporary and historical buildings are brought close to each other through the practices of devotion, as well as masonry and craftsmanship. Many of the contemporary architecture in the area are influenced by the 400-year-old Hussain Shah Wali Dargāh. The *dargāh* survives and thrives through its close relationship with the courtly Qutb Shahi style and the subsequent fluid architectural additions over centuries. As I have stressed, additions made to the *dargāh* architecture by the locals are rooted in their everyday practices that bring materiality, care, conservation and devotion together. This resulted in the palpable intertwining and overlapping of architectural styles observed across the residential and public buildings of this neighbourhood.

Notes

1 Hussain Shah was a Sufi saint of the Chishti sect. He belongs to lineage of Hazrat Syed Mohammad Ali Hussaini, elder son of Khwaja Banda Nawaz Gesu Daraz, the most venerated Sufi saint of the Deccan. He was also a well-known architect and engineer responsible for constructing the Hussain Sagar Lake in Hyderabad in 1562. His patronymic name is Abdullah and his full title is Nasir Uddinan; he belongs to the Sadat family of the Hussaini chain. Hussain Shah was married to Khairat-un-Nissa Begum, the daughter of Muhammad Qutb Shah VI. There are some differences among historians compiling his genealogy records but all of them have agreed and confirmed that he belongs to the lineage of Hazrat Khwaja Banda Nawaz Gesu Daraz of Gulbarga (now known as Kalaburgi). According to the book titled *Tazkirat-al-Awliya Deccan*, his genealogy record is as follows: (i) Hazrat Hussain Shah Wali, (ii) Syed Saqir Ullah alias Safi Ullah Thani, (iii) Asad Ullah Amin, (iv) Askar Ullah alias Safi Ullah and (v) Shah Mohammed Akbar Hussaini (Abhilash 2014: 33–4).

2 Indo-Saracenic architecture is a syncretic visual vocabulary of architecture that emerged with the establishment of colonial governance. Thomas Metcalf writes, 'Central to its conception was always a combination of "European science" and "native art," of "traditional" forms and "modern" functions' (Metcalf 1989: 77–8).

3 I also thank Shimhachalam Abhilash and Sai Sheela, my cohorts during fieldwork, and I got new insights from their research. I thank Sita Reddy and Baishali Ghosh for their suggestions; Rajesh Kumar, Somedutta Mallik and Bijay Nath for helping me in digitizing the hand drawn maps; and Anoop Daniel for photography.

4 The '*qibla*' is the direction towards the Masjid al-Haram or the Sacred Mosque in Mecca, which is used by Muslims in various religious contexts, particularly the direction of prayer for *namaz*. The *qibla* wall in a mosque faces Mecca.

5 A carved roof whose two sides meet at a single spine or ridge, this architectural element has been derived from the shape of the Bengal

hut's roof. Interestingly, the Bengal dome is a Mughal prototype. The architectural motif probably travelled to the Deccan from North India when Golconda came under Mughal suzerainty in the seventeenth century during the reign of Emperor Shah Jahan (Asher 1992: XXV).

6 See 'The Qutb Shahi Monuments of Hyderabad Golconda Fort, Qutb Shahi Tombs, Charminar', *UNESCO*, https://whc.unesco.org/en/tentativelists/5573/ (accessed May 2021).

7 'India | Restoration in Hyderabad', *AKDN*, https://www.akdn.org/where-we-work/south-asia/india/cultural-development/restoration-hyderabad (accessed 8 May 2021).

8 Excerpts from fieldwork conducted in Hyderabad from 2014 to 2016. I thank Mhd Mehbub Kureshi, Mh Latif Kureshi, Yusuf, Khaja, Chayej, Syed Chanda Hussaini, Syed Md Yusuf Mirallah Hussaini, Syed Mhd Qubullah Hussaini, Md Dilawar Faizullah, Md Dilawar Qair Uddin, Shabir Khan, Khaja Babu, Yusuf Khan, Mhd Munir Uddin, Khaja Moinuddin and Amjad Ahmed.

9 For the escalation of land issues around the *dargāh*, see Safoora (2017), 'Waqf Loot: Dargah Hussain Shah Wali Property Is Worth 81,614 Crores'. Moin (2019), 'Hyderabad: Dargah Head Accused of Selling Wakf Lands'.

References

Abhilash, S. (2014), 'Ganesh Chaturthi and Urs in Dargah', MA diss., University of Hyderabad, Hyderabad.

Asher, Catherine B. (1992), *Architecture of Mughal India*, Cambridge: Cambridge University Press.

Currim, Mumtaz and George Michell, eds (2004), *Dargahs Abodes of the Saints*, Mumbai: Marg Publication.

Farida, Syeda (2012), 'Remembering Sufi Mystic Hazrat Inayat Khan', *The Hindu*, 29 January. Available online: https://www.thehindu.com/features/friday-review/music/remembering-sufi-mystic-hazrat-inayat-khan/article2840803.ece (accessed 21 May 2021).

Green, Nile (2006), *Indian Sufism since the Seventeenth Century: Saints, Books and Empires in the Muslim Deccan*, New York: Routledge.

Jayewardene-Pillai, Shanti (2007), *Imperial Conversations: Indo-Britons and the Architecture of South India*, New Delhi: Yoda Press.

Juneja, Monica, ed. (2008), *Architecture in Medieval India: Forms, Contexts, Histories*, New Delhi: Permanent Black.

Kugle, Scott (2013), 'Memories of Pir Rasheed (Syed Mohammad Rasheed-ul-Hasan Jeeli Kaleemi)', 30 December. https://pirzia.org/memories-of-pir-rasheed/ (accessed 23 May 2021).

Metcalf, Thomas (1989), R. *An Imperial Vision: Indian Architecture and Britain's Raj*, Berkeley: University of California Press.

Moin, Ather (2019), 'Hyderabad: Dargah Head Accused of Selling Wakf Lands', *Deccan Chronicle*, 21 February. Available online: https://www.deccanchronicle.com/nation/current-affairs/210219/hyderabad-dargah-head-accused-of-selling-wakf-lands.html (accessed 5 June 2021).

Safoora (2017), 'Waqf Loot: Dargah Hussain Shah Wali Property Is Worth 81,614 Crores', *The Siasat Daily*, 23 May. Available online: https://archive.siasat.com/news/waqf-loot-dargah-hussain-shah-wali-property-worth-81614-crores-1188200/ (accessed 21 May 2021).

Sardar, Marika (2007), 'Golconda through Time: A Mirror of the Evolving Deccan', PhD diss., New York University, New York.

Sheela, Sai (2014), 'Zardozi Craft Traditions around Hazrat Hussain Shah Wali Dargah in Hyderabad', MA diss., University of Hyderabad, Hyderabad.

Siddiqi, Mohammad Suleman and Scott Kugle (2009), 'Special Issue on Sufism in Deccan', *Deccan Studies*, VII (2): 133–9.

Simpkins, Robert Alan (2014), 'Golconda's Mosques and Tombs: Distribution, Chronology, and Meaning', in Laura E Parodi (ed.), *The Visual World of Muslim India: The Art, Culture and Society of the Deccan in the Early Modern Era*, 31–52, New York: I.B. Tauris.

The Aga Khan Development Network, 'India | Restoration in Hyderabad', *AKDN*, https://www.akdn.org/where-we-work/south-asia/india/cultural-development/restoration-hyderabad (accessed 8 May 2021).

Tomory, Edith (2009), *A History of Fine Arts in India and the West*, Chennai: Orient Blackswan.

Troll, Christian W., ed. (2003), *Muslim Shrines in India: Their Character, History and Significance*, Delhi: Oxford University Press.

UNESCO,'The Qutb Shahi Monuments of Hyderabad Golconda Fort, Qutb Shahi Tombs, Charminar', *World Heritage Convention*, https://whc.unesco.org/en/tentativelists/5573/ (accessed 8 May 2021).

7

Reclaiming Multiplicity in Deccani Craft Making: Case Study of a Transitional Artisan

Rajarshi Sengupta

Upon my first visit to artisan Bhikshamayya Chary's[1] workshop in June 2017 in Uppuguda, Hyderabad, I was confounded by an assortment of tools, books, objects and machinery, which are not usual in a block makers' workshop. Over the course of our conversations that afternoon and beyond, I came to terms with my disquiet at not finding scattered woodblocks and tools in Chary's workshop. The problem had less to do with Chary and more with my approach towards Deccani craft making. Transition, adaptability and co-existence have always been integral aspects of artisanal practice, and yet institutional and disciplinary practices stress on equating a specific craft with its maker. Chary's multifaceted exercises allow us to assess interconnections between craft practices and the fluidity of community occupation. More importantly, it sheds light on the role of woodworkers in shaping several Deccani crafts, including carving, and loom and machinery making, while reflecting on the possibilities of writing artisanal histories.

Multiplicity and the Myth of Specialization

During a month-long training programme on natural dyeing at the Weavers Service Centre (WSC) as part of my doctoral research on making kalamkari textiles, I happened to meet the retired master woodblock carver at WSC, Bhikshamayya Chary.[2] Owing to the colonial legacy of craft specialization and its subsequent validation by the craft scholarship, I thought of Chary primarily in terms of his institutional designation as a block maker. The division between craft and fine arts, and the emergence of further specialized categories within these divisions, goes back to nineteenth-century Europe (Mathur 2007; McGowan 2009; Cardoso 2010: 321–32). The curriculum of the colonial art institutions in the subcontinent and the major expositions during the colonial era, such as *The Great Exhibition* 1851, promoted these categorizations. Emphasis on hereditary artisans and community bound occupations was established in the 1961 *Census of India* (McGowan 2009: 12). Various initiatives to revitalize craft making in the 1950s by the newly formed Indian government, including the establishment of the All India Handicrafts Board (AIHB) in 1952 and the WSC in 1956, fuelled the demand for an extensive documentation of the maker communities (Chandra Sekhar 1964; Chisti 2011: 6). Understandably for documentation purposes, the reports highlighted the master artisans with specialized skill sets. Then, during the preparation of the *Visvakarmā* exhibitions (1981–1991) to showcase the master textile makers of India[3] – initiated by textile scholar, activist and conservationist, Martand Singh and supervised by Pupul Jayakar—Jayakar visited WSC Hyderabad in the early 1980s.[4] After interacting with Chary, a contractual worker at WSC upon his arrival in the city from the neighbouring district of Nalgonda, Jayakar created a post for block carver to accommodate him in the Centre.[5] For the next twenty-five years or so, Chary remained there as the master block carver. After my visit to Chary's residence-cum-workshop, it was certain that his institutional affiliation is not synonymous with his artisanal subject position. Framing craftspeople from a 'traditionalist' point of view in the governmental ventures since the 1950s resulted in equating craft practice with generational, homogeneous and single occupational groups, making inadequate room for fluidity (Greenough 1995: 235–43).[6] The fixation on a site and authority to punctuate authenticity, as delineated by the Geographical Indication (GI), tend to overlook craft makers' innate relationship with localized knowledge structure and 'affective ties' to other producer communities (Bose 2016: 134). In recent scholarship, many aspects of the colonial divisions and specializations are challenged and countered. However, artisans are still recognized in the scholarship by their specialised skills more than their problem-solving abilities (Varadarajan 1982; Frater 2002; Cohen 2016; Greru and Kalkreuter 2017). Therefore, theorizing Chary's subject position manifests into a twofold exploration: reclaiming artisanal ability to transcend specialized occupational categories, while altering the structure of art historical writing to accommodate these nuances.

Chary's exercise within and outside the institutional space indicates the simultaneity of specialized and diverse craft practices. Within the folds of the institution, surplus knowledge of the craftspeople is removed to give prominence to specialized modes of production. This fails to acknowledge craft practice as part of the social lives of the practitioners, which are continuously evolving (Bhattacharya 2002). Since the 1980s, with changes in economic patterns and large-scale migration of rural craftspeople like Chary to India's urban centres, craftspeople have come to represent a certain region and, at the same time, their experiences in urban spaces (Sethi 2013: 49–55). Assessing the multifaceted craft practices thus calls attention to account for fluidity and mobility within the structure of art historical writing. In South Asia, colonial rule imposed a tradition of history writing that was imperialist in design and employed for serving the administration of the state, which often entails a failure to recognize underrepresented groups, such as craft makers (Spivak 1987: 199). To reclaim the unearthed facets of the past as well as the subject position of the oppressed, a critical take on the simultaneity of disciplinary and 'minority histories' is essential (Chakrabarty 2000: 105–6). Addressing the simultaneity of the two kinds of practices used by Chary runs parallel to the simultaneity of institutional and marginalized narratives. The knowledge system of Chary and similar versatile craft practitioners was neglected and denied by the institutional accounts; whereas in their intangible memory, a diversity of craft making persisted. This intangible knowledge is activated through the sensorial engagement of practitioners with materials, tools, and surroundings (Marchand 2010).

As noted in the Introduction, moving beyond the scope of tangible evidence-based investigations is also raised by the advocates of ephemeral histories of the Deccan. With the turn to intangible histories, multiplicity has manifested as perceiving histories through different sensory perceptions; for this, Chary's accounts of material handling specifically hold significance. His craft practice has evolved from listening to elders and master craft makers, sensing the surface as well as the internal structure of wood and iron, studying existing objects and tools, and employing physical actions to materialize his lessons; the process entails different kinds of *knowing* which cannot be obtained from a single knowledge base. His ease at traversing through varied materials also demonstrates the dynamism of carving wood is perhaps not distinct from moulding metals. It gives considerable attention to investigate the interrelations between multiplicity, simultaneity, adaptability and transition. My emphasis on these notions surfaces as an attempt to better accommodate the transition and adaptability of practices in the field of Deccani crafts. Through this enquiry, the consideration of discrete boundaries of community, occupation and skill has been challenged and reinvented.

The Transitional Artisan

Hailing from Ghattuppal – some 5 km away from Puttapaka, famed for ikat weaving and *telia rumal* – Bhikshamayya Chary is an artisan with many interests, including woodwork, metalwork and medicine, among others. His interests and multi-layered practice present an alternative account of the more recognized narratives on craft making. Chary's father Kammari Brahmayya was well known for woodworks and iron works. *Kammari* (కమ్మరి) indicates blacksmiths in Telugu. His ancestors were also dedicated practitioners of Ayurvedic medicine, which Chary inherited and sustained. Contrary to what his community identity suggests, Chary introduces himself primarily as a woodworker. He stated:

> We work with wood of all kinds and make a range of objects. Woodwork or *karrapani* (కర్రపని, where *karra* indicates carving) has been practised in our family for generations. My ancestors made carved doors, window frames, statues, *vigrahamu* (విగ్రహము) or icons, *ratham* (రథం) or temple chariots, tools for agricultural usage including wooden wheels and plough, and woodblocks. They also simultaneously practised ironwork. I heard they made large wooden doorways [for forts] and iron joinery for them. As you urban folks understand the term 'technical engineer', that is the closest to what we do.
>
> (Interview with Bhikshamayya Chary in Hyderabad, June 2017)

While equating himself with a technical engineer, Chary intended to draw attention to problem-solving methods. Far from bolstering the traditionalist point of view, he considers craft making an intervention or a problem-solving method – an innovative process to overcome an existing problem (Sennett 2008: 151–2). For Chary, finding a solution is independent of a specific material practice, which allows him to move between wood carving, metal craft, machinery making and indigenous medicine practice. This makes it particularly difficult to identify him with one kind of craft making. As I noted earlier, the problem figures from the long-standing institutional and scholarly practices of craft documentation. To contextualize Chary's endeavours, I perceive him as a transitional artisan; his transitional skills are sustained and flourish underneath his institutional identity as a block maker at the Weavers Centre.

Chary joined the Weavers Centre in 1980 under a renewable contract. The Hyderabad Centre provided support and training in the field of fabric and *dhurrie* weaving, kalamkari painting and block printing (both natural and industrial). Here, he remained responsible for the construction of printing tables, a variety of looms and building up a rich repository of carved woodblocks. Chary learned making looms from his ancestors. I would like to remind us of Ghattuppal's close proximity to Puttapaka where master ikat weaver Gajam Govardhana set up ikat weaving units in the 1970s (Interview with Gajam Govardhana in Hyderabad, June 2017). Setting up ikat looms on a large scale in the Nalgonda district must have relied on woodworkers such as Chary and his family. Among other kinds, Chary specifically recalled his experience of making drawlooms, which feature extra heddles for executing patterns and are comparatively more complex than floor or pit looms. Understanding the functionality of different types of looms requires a sound knowledge of regional weaving techniques. While Chary implemented this knowledge in making the looms for the Centre, he simultaneously responded to the needs of carpentry. The large tables at the Centre are primarily used for block printing but are also used for kalamkari and wax drawing. Across India, printing, painting and resist drawing were usually done on small wooden *chowkis* in artisanal workshops. However, this started changing since the 1950s to facilitate faster production. The large rectangular tables at the Centre reflect this design strategy, which allows trainees and trainers to stand around the table during demonstrations. As the maker of the looms and furniture at the Centre, Chary had to internalize the loom mechanism of the regional weavers as well as the design principles put forward by the officials and implement them.

Intrigued by his ease at handling a range of woodworks, I wanted to hear his approach towards the material. He responded:

> It starts from understanding different kinds of woods. Developing an intimate relationship with wood has enabled our ancestors to decide which wood is fitting for what purpose. Smell, visual presence, hardness, softness and annual growth rings – one needs to account for all these aspects of the wood under observation. Only then, we begin to comprehend the character of every kind of wood and how they can serve our purpose. Old and hardwoods are the best for making doors, window frames, and structures of houses. If the wood is more than 100 years old, they are seasoned, and they do not bend. Even iron can decay and bend with passing time, but seasoned wood would not. The forest range close to my hometown was a great resource for this kind of wood. However, in the last forty years or so, deforestation has heavily affected the availability of such wood. I have seen wood that is around 500 years old. Such old wood can be so strong that iron chisels are damaged while working on them. Wood that is aged twenty-five to thirty years are considered new, and are easily bent, fragile, and unable to bear weight. As you see, this should not be used for making structures to support buildings or door frames … Relatively softer and lightweight wood is required for woodblock making. While printing, woodblocks are continuously pressed against a printing pad and then pressed on the fabric surface; a heavy block would tire the printer easily. When we understand the [salient] features of wood then purposing them to serve our needs becomes effortless.
>
> (Interview with Bhikshamayya Chary in Hyderabad, May 2020)

In his delineation, establishing an affective relationship between material and artisans was foregrounded. Interactions or entanglements between materials and human beings, according to archaeologist Uzma Rizvi, are constitutive of subjectivities (2015: 256). Chary's multisensory perception of the 'different kinds' of wood assists him in efficiently moving between carpentry, loom making and block making; this sensory perception also allows him to extend his knowledge beyond the scope of woodworks. In his statement, he also implied the need to be cognizant of the capacity of iron tools, which perhaps surfaces from his training in iron smelting and tool making by his ancestors. I will suggest, a deep knowledge of the smell, weight, softness and texture alongside visual features of materials enhances artisanal ability to intervene in the depth of problems relating to material handling, crafting techniques, as well as their livelihood.

Among many projects he has undertaken at the Centre, a humble wood and iron block caught my attention (Figure 7.1). Ranging from intricate geometric to complex figurative motifs, the varied range of woodblocks is evidence of Chary's excellence in carving. However, the simplicity and ingenuity of the wood and iron block are quite striking. In this block, a series of blunt iron nails are hammered in rows on a rectangular thick wooden base. The nails are levelled carefully to ensure evenness in print. The four corners of the base are smoothened to avoid sharp angles. Two corners feature a set of two nails with their diagonally cut upper ends, specially made for registration during printing. A thin metal strip is nailed to a corner of the base, possibly for lengthening the life span of this block. Further, the back of the wooden base is carved into a handle. For this, a lengthwise strip is left at the centre of the base with the sides scooped off. The center is cut diagonally to provide a better grip during printing. Primarily, this block is used for resist printing. For resist printing, both wooden and metal blocks are used; however, the images on the blocks

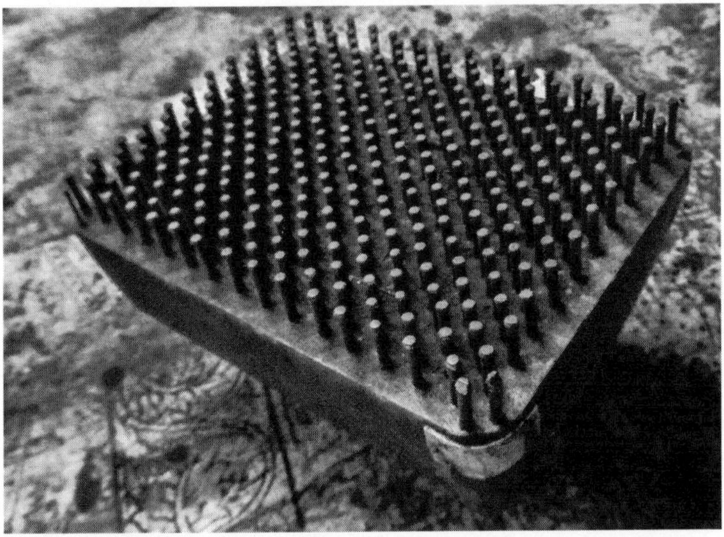

Figure 7.1 V. Bhikshamayya Chary, a Woodblock with Iron Nails, Weavers Service Centre, Hyderabad-Deccan. Courtesy: Rajarshi Sengupta, 2017.

need to be deeply cut, which is not a requirement for dye printing. Molten wax tends to penetrate the sunken area of woodblocks. For that, the image area is required to be raised. It would require painstaking work to carve this block entirely in wood. The present structure of the block allows both resist and dye printing in a much more efficient way.

For Chary, his ancestors and similar artisans in the Deccan, wood and iron works grow simultaneously; knowledge derived from one kind of work transforms into another. This case study draws special attention, I must stress, to the fact that interconnectivity between craft communities has been practised in the Deccan at least since the early modern period. Contextualizing Chary's practice against the backdrop of the Deccani past widens the scope for assessing transitional craft practices.

Visvakarmā and *Joinery* between Communities and Materials

To illustrate the intra- and intercommunal interactions between artisans in southern India, I will refer to the concept of *Visvakarmā*. *Visvakarmā* is considered the Hindu god of crafts, machinery and technologies; moreover, *Visvakarmā* is also synonymous with the five artisanal groups, including ironsmiths, wood workers, sculptors, goldsmiths and brass smiths in South India. Often the figure of *Visvakarmā*, tools and associated rituals are situated within caste-bound and hereditary artisanal practices (Narayan and George 2017); however, it is equally important to explore the larger implications of this layered notion. Vijaya Ramaswamy argues that the notion of *Visvakarmā* suggests the collective identity of the five artisanal groups without defining them as homogeneous units (2004: 551). Ramaswamy foregrounds interconnectivity and migration among these artisanal groups and supports her argument with inscriptional records and activities of *Visvakarmā* craftspeople.[7] Ramaswamy's argument about economic factors being a crucial aspect of craft production and migration of craftspeople also indicates how craft production and economic networks had been integrally connected. She notes that urbanization and the emergence of port cities in the south resulted in the migration of weaver communities (2016: 171). This also resonates with David Washbrook's argument on the intra-local movement of agrarian workers and craftspeople in early modern South India (2007: 94). As noted in the Introduction, internal migrations and cultural exchanges between the Deccani kingdoms enabled considerable mobility of the elites, simultaneous to the movement of the producer communities (Eaton 2005: 78–9). Against the backdrop of socio-cultural and economic exchanges in the pre-colonial Deccan,

Visvakarmā emerged as a network of exchanges within the maker communities united by their use of tools.

These interconnections are evoked during the annual worship of *Visvakarmā* in southern India. I happened to be present on one such occasion in Machilipatnam in 2015. *Visvakarmā* Jayanti (an annual festival for *Visvakarmā*) was celebrated by *Bandaru [Bandar] Pattana Svarnakāra Sangham* (Association of goldsmiths in the town of Bandar) and *Bandaru Pattana Visvabrāhmana Sangham* (Association of Visvabrahmanas or goldsmiths in the town of Bandar) near the city centre of Machilipatnam (Figure 7.2). An invitation to one of the associations listed the communities who consider *Visvakarmā* as their patron deity.[8] The communities include ironsmiths, woodworkers, sculptors, goldsmiths and *padrangam*.[9] Even though the goldsmith community living in the coastal belt is more privileged than the rest, all these craftspeople are united as worshippers of *Visvakarmā*. The worship of *Visvakarmā* by craft makers at present implies the continued veneration of this

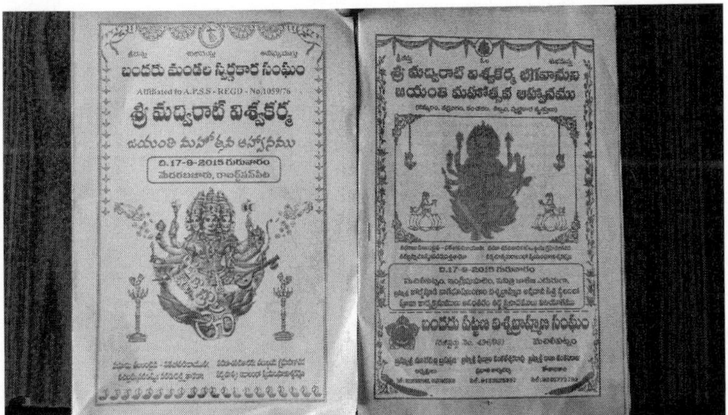

Figure 7.2 Invitation for *Visvakarmā* Jayanti by *Bandaru [Bandar] Pattana Svarnakāra Sangham* and *Bandaru Pattana Visvabrāhmana Sangham*, Machilipatnam. Courtesy: Rajarshi Sengupta, 2015.

deity and the relevance of intercommunal exchanges from historical times. I read the annual invocation of *Visvakarmā* as a formalized social practice of reclaiming the collective coexistence between artisanal groups of Naveen Kanalu's rendering of *Pirla Panduga* (Kanalu 2016).

Situating Chary's transitional practice in the context of cultural, linguistic and artisanal syncretism of the Deccan yields further queries rather than a conclusion. Did the Deccani spirit of socio-cultural intermingling foster border crossings in the occupational sectors as well? As Chary stated, his ancestors were equally invested in producing weapons before the colonial rule banned wood and metalworkers from manufacturing them (Interview with Bhikshamayya Chary in Hyderabad, May 2020). Did artisans such as Chary silently resist the colonial subjugation by nurturing their multiple interests?

In the context of exercising multiple modes of crafting, Chary's statement on 'joinery' [for wooden gateways] appears to be a metaphor of assimilating knowledge. While reflecting on his ancestral workmanship and their ease at constructing both massive wooden doors and steady iron joinery, he implied that there was a bodily *knowing* of how to strike a balance between materials of different nature. Possibly, the embodied knowledge was intensified through exchanges between neighbouring maker communities; for example, close contact between ikat weavers of Puttapaka and loom makers of Ghattuppal enabled artisans like Chary to envision the dependence of highly skilled weaving on an unfailing loom structure. Utilization of the dependence between wood and iron, seen in the case of the gateways, suggests assimilation is strategic and indispensable. Chary's cognitive understanding of the applicability of iron tools and the character of materials activates the methods of assimilation: letting one idea flow into another and one material guide the path to another. His ancestral knowledge of Ayurveda perhaps enriched his empathetic understanding of the human body's interaction with plants, animals and minerals, towards creating an effective response. The simultaneity of woodworking, blacksmithing, and Ayurvedic practice in Chary's workshop is far from being coincidental; both Ayurveda and craft making involving wood and metals draw the practitioners' attention to the minutest material qualities of organic and inorganic elements from the surroundings. Whereas this sound knowledge is responsible for Chary being able to distinguish between various kinds of woods, it also provides him with hints in relation to approaching a new material, thus contributing to his subject position as a transitional artisan. This consideration demands further exploration of the layered notion of *Visvakarmā*: did the spirit of intercommunal exchanges also result in shaping artisans who transcend occupational divisions or artisans like Chary who act as joinery between the descendants of the god of tools?

From Transition to Innovation

How does the co-existence of multiple material practices impact practitioners' approaches to adaptation and innovation? For Chary, the flexibility and command over materials and techniques have expanded his problem-solving skill beyond the limitation of a focused practice. Chary's use of the term 'technical engineer' to introduce himself also adheres to his multimedia approach. In his late sixties, Chary is never tired of experimenting with tool-making or loom mechanisms. Retired from his post from the Centre, Chary continues to practise his many interests at his workshop in the old city of Hyderabad. His urge to experiment comes from a careful understanding of past conditions and contingencies of the present. At the Centre, he familiarized himself with the historical dyed and resist-dyed kalamkari textiles from the Coromandel and

Deccan. The evidence of wax resist in historical kalamkari urged Bhikshamayya Chary to make a tool for fluid wax drawing (Figures 7.3 and 7.4).

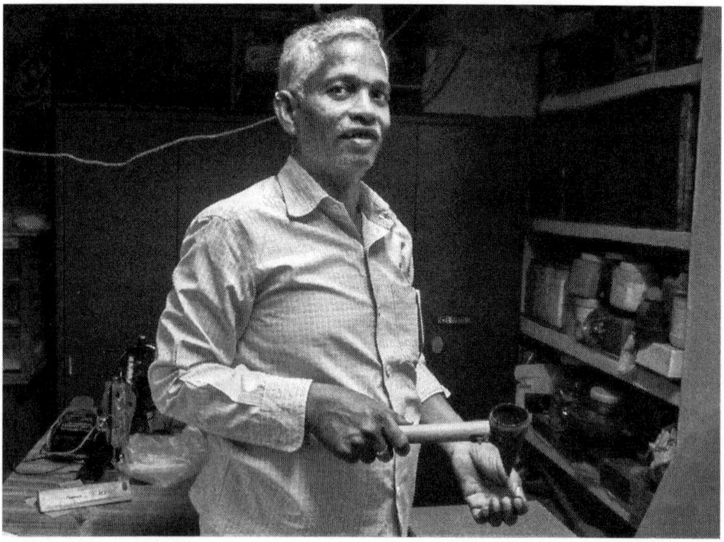

Figure 7.3 V. Bhikshamayya Chary with a Tool of His Own Making for Wax Drawing, Hyderabad-Deccan. Courtesy: Rajarshi Sengupta, 2017.

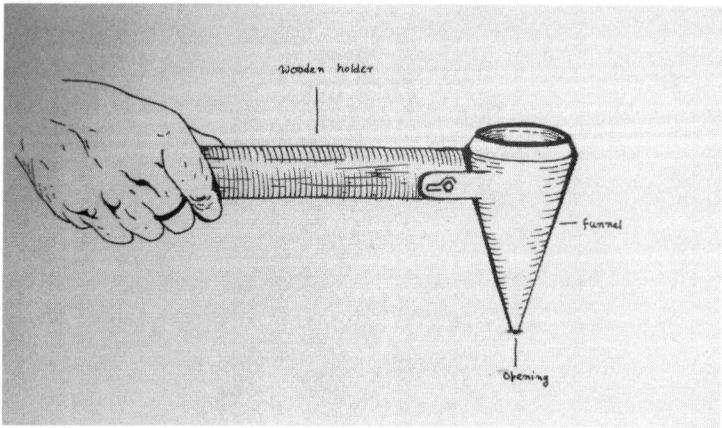

Figure 7.4 Drawing of Chary's Tool for Wax Drawing, Ink on Paper. Courtesy: Rajarshi Sengupta, 2018.

For wax drawing, usually a bamboo pen or *kalam* with an iron wire tip wrapped with a thick layer of human hair is used. Chary was aware of such tools used for wax resist at the Centre but was dissatisfied with its performance as it failed to deliver consistent drawing as seen in the historical ones. He mentioned that the flow of wax from the *kalam* is discontinuous, which negatively affects the quality of the drawing. The tool he made is less than 30 cm in length and constructed of a cylindrical wooden shaft joined to an iron funnel. The funnel has a minute opening at the bottom for allowing molten wax to flow. The funnel could be dipped in molten wax and used for making resist drawing. Wood, being a poor conductor of heat, prevents the high temperature of molten wax from affecting the worker's hand. The basic working principle of Chary's tool has some resemblance to Sri Lankan and Indonesian resist drawing tools (Clark 2013; Hitchcock and Nuryanti 2016). The Indonesian tools are finer and smaller in shape; however, the construction follows a similar logic using a metal repository and wooden/bamboo holder. It was not clear how Chary decided to make this tool. He is an avid reader, especially of books on astrology, traditional medicine and machinery making. However, he did not mention any specific source as a reference for his redesigned tool. Chary thought through materials and tools to envision past practices. His tool does not resemble the historical kalam for wax drawing in the south, but his intentions and material engagement help us to envision how the historical wax resist drawers thought about the applicability of their tools. Chary's decision to implement a design change also indicates how the artisans' disagreement with the existing practice can prompt innovations.

Chary's transitional and innovative practice perhaps conveys a crucial implication to us researchers. His questioning of medium-specificity and reclaiming ancestral knowledge by overturning the colonial occupational categories compel us to perhaps do the same;

that is, to question the established criteria defining the parameters of a craft practice. More importantly, this presents us with methods for reclaiming the underrepresented artisanal pasts. The narrative fragments collected from Chary and his empathetic engagement with materials and tools – which constitute a rich reserve of bodily knowledge – put together a version of Deccani craft history prioritizing the makers. The interweaving of the rich scholarly accounts of the Deccan and Chary's lifelong involvement in transitional practices enhances the reciprocity of institutional and sensorial histories. In turn, the simultaneous versions of histories, co-existence of wood and iron working, syncretic cultural flow and cross-media approach of Chary enrich the notion of multiplicity in the context of Deccan. Whereas I find Chary's lifelong dedication to transitional practice a silent but firm refusal of the institutional legacy, he smilingly puts it as his humble responsibility to sustain and pass on this knowledge: 'Jo bhi main janta hun, zameen ke upar rehna chahiye', which translates to 'Whatever I know should stay on earth; it should not die like humans' (Interview with Bhikshamayya Chary in Hyderabad, May 2020).

Notes

1 Bhikshamayya Chary is responsible for carving the majority of the woodblocks that are part of the collection of the Weavers Service Centre (WSC) in the city.

2 I enrolled myself in the training programme to have a better hands-on understanding of the natural dyeing techniques. My programme fees and stay in Hyderabad were enabled by the IARTS Textiles of India Fellowship, Royal Ontario Museum, Toronto. I am thankful to the staff at WSC, B. M. Kamtikar, M. C. Murali Krishna and Tapas K. for their overall support.

3 The Festival of India in Britain (1982) and America (1985–6) were parts of the decade-long *Visvakarmā* series which prompted another

wave of governmental and scholarly intervention into craft sectors, especially textiles after the 1961 Census. The exhibitions were held in Britain, France, Sweden, Russia and the United States, alongside India (Sengupta 2019: 230–1).

4 Weavers Service Centres in the major cities in India set up a platform for textile makers to interact with designers, educators and government institutions in India during this time, and played a pivotal role in the collaborative endeavours.

5 Interview with Bhikshamayya Chary in Hyderabad, May 2020. I have taken the liberty of transliterating the interviews to convey the prime aspects of our conversations to the readers. I acknowledge my role as a mediator between Chary and the readers and strongly believe that all ethnographic narratives rest on the mediation of the ethnographer.

6 Greenough reflects that the Congress Government in India promoted the 'traditionalist' viewpoint on crafts, which left a deep impression on their policies on craft development, including the establishment of a national museum dedicated to crafts in New Delhi. The Congress party in India was the dominant political power until the 1970s.

7 This view is also shared by anthropologist Jan Brouwer. Brouwer focuses on blacksmithy, carpentryer, braziery, foundry, sculpture and goldsmithy in Karnataka, and the interconnections between the artisanal groups involved in these practices. See Brouwer (1995).

8 The invite was sent to G. Suresh, an artisan trained in weaving and rolled gold works, who owns a jewellery shop near Koneru Centre, Machilipatnam. I am grateful to him for his support during my fieldwork in 2015.

9 పడ్రంగం is possibly a community name similar to the woodworkers.

References

Bhattacharya, Malini (2002), 'The Rural Artist and Secular Culture in the Era of Globalization', in K. N. Panikkar, Terence J. Byres and Utsa

Patnaik (eds), *The Making of History: Essays Presented to Irfan Habib*, 515–29, London: Anthem.

Bose, Chandan (2016), 'Geographical Fixity or Affective Ties: How Do Artists Respond to Geographical Indications?' *The Journal of Modern Craft*, 9 (2): 117–37.

Brouwer, Jan (1995), *The Makers of the World: Caste, Craft and Mind of South Indian Artisans*, Delhi: Oxford University Press.

Cardoso, Rafael (2010), 'Craft Versus Design: Moving beyond a Tired Dichotomy', in Glenn Adamson (ed.) *The Craft Reader*, 321–32, Oxford and New York: Berg.

Chakrabarty, Dipesh (2000), *Provincializing Europe: Postcolonial Thought and Historical Difference*, Princeton and Oxford: Princeton University Press.

Chakravorty Spivak, Gayatri (1987), *In Other Worlds: Essays in Cultural Politics*, New York: Methuen.

Chandra Sekhar, A. (1964), *Census of India 1961, Volume II, Andhra Pradesh, Part VII-A (1), Selected Crafts of Andhra Pradesh*, New Delhi: Manager of Publications, Govt. of India.

Chisti, Rita Kapur (2011), 'Tradition and Beyond', in Martand Singh (ed.), *Handcrafted Indian Textiles: Tradition and Beyond*, 6, New Delhi: Lustre Press.

Clark, Marshall (2013), 'The Politics of Heritage', *Indonesia and the Malay World*, 41 (121): 396–417.

Cohen, Steven (2016), 'Materials and Making: Indonesia-Malaysia cultural contestations', in Rosemary Crill (ed.), *The Fabric of India*, 16–77, London: Victoria & Albert Museum.

Eaton, Richard M. (2005), *Social History of the Deccan, 1300–1761: Eight Indian Lives*, Delhi: Cambridge University Press.

Frater, Judy (2002), 'This Is Ours': Rabari Tradition and Identity in a Changing World', *Nomadic Peoples*, 6 (2): 156–69.

Greenough, Paul (1995), 'Nation, Economy, and Tradition Displayed: The Indian Crafts Museum, New Delhi', in Carol A Breckenridge (ed.), *Consuming Modernity: Public Culture in a South Asian World*, 216–48, London and Minneapolis: University of Minnesota Press.

Greru, Chamithri and Britta Kalkreuter (2017), 'Design and the Evolving Tradition of Sanganer Hand Block Printing: Formation and Negotiation of Artisanal Knowledge and Identities against the Backdrop of Intangible Cultural Heritage', *The Journal of Modern Craft*, 10 (2): 137–56.

Hitchcock, Michael and Wiendu Nuryanti (2016), *Building on Batik: The Globalization of a Craft Community*, London and New York: Routledge.

Kanalu, Naveen (2016), 'Pirla Panduga: Muharram Practices of the Deccan Weavers, Their Migrations, Songs and Memories', in Vijaya Ramaswamy (ed.), *Migrations in Medieval and Early Colonial India*, 129–64, London and New York: Routledge.

Marchand, Trevor H. J. (2010), 'Making knowledge: Explorations of the Indissoluble Relation between Minds, Bodies, and Environment', *The Journal of the Royal Anthropological Institute*, 16 (s1): S1– S21.

Mathur, Saloni (2007), *India by Design: Colonial History and Cultural Display*, Berkeley, Los Angeles and London: University of California Press.

McGowan, Abigail (2009), *Crafting the Nation in Colonial India*, New York: Palgrave Macmillan.

Narayan, Kirin and Kenneth M. George (2017), 'Tools and World-Making in the Worship of Vishwakarma', *South Asian History and Culture*, 8 (4): 478–92.

Ramaswamy, Vijaya (2004), 'Vishwakarma Craftsmen in Early Medieval Peninsular India', *Journal of the Economic and Social History of the Orient*, 47 (4): 548–82.

Ramaswamy, Vijaya (2016), 'Migrations of the Weaver Communities in Medieval Peninsular India, Thirteenth to the Eighteenth Centuries,' in Vijaya Ramaswamy (ed.), *Migrations in Medieval and Early Colonial India*, 165–92, London and New York: Routledge.

Rizvi, Uzma Z. (2015), 'Crafting Resonance: Empathy and Belonging in Ancient Rajasthan', *Journal of Social Archaeology*, 15 (2): 254–73.

Sengupta, Rajarshi (2019), 'Ruptures, Continuations, and Innovations: On Contemporary Kalamkari Making in the Coromandel and Deccan', in Sarah Fee (ed.), *Cloth That Changed the World: The Art and Fashion of Indian Chintz*, 228–39, New Haven, CT: Yale University Press.

Sennett, Richard (2008), *The Craftsman*, New Haven, CT: Yale University Press.

Sethi, Cristin McKnight (2013), 'Mapping Craft in Contemporary India: Dilli Haat and Dastkari Haat Samiti's Crafts Maps', *The Journal of Modern Craft*, 6 (1): 49–78.

Varadarajan, Lotika (1982), *South Indian Traditions of Kalamkari*, Bombay: The Perennial Press.

Washbrook, David (2007), 'India in the Early Modern World Economy: Modes of Production, Reproduction, and Exchange', *Journal of Global History*, 2 (1): 87–111.

8

Becoming a Master: Discourses on Weaving and Its Transmission

Somedutta Mallik

Introduction

My fieldwork from 2016 to 2021[1] was at the weaving workshop of Suraiya Hasan Bose[2] who is fondly known as Suraiya apa (hereafter Suraiya apa). Suraiya apa's weaving workshop, called the *Loom* by the weavers in their conversation, is officially named *Suraiya's workshop*, although the old paint on the wall outside still bears the centre's previous name, *House of Kalamkari and Durries.* The land where the house and the workshop stand today was purchased by her uncle Abid Hasan Safrani in 1971. A shop-cum-office, a weaving unit, a residence and the Safrani Memorial High School all share the premises. The weaving unit is situated behind the shop and consists of a spacious rectangular hall with approximately 1,480 cm × 850 cm in size. Ten looms were installed in two rows and one next to the entrance of the hall. On several occasions, I heard stories about the atypical behaviour of Syed Omer (fondly called Omer sahab; hereafter Omer sahab), the master weaver. One such peculiarity I heard about was his utter dislike of taking leave from work, even on Sundays, despite his advanced age (he was in his mid-70s) and poor health conditions. Commuting for hours on a motorbike from Bagh Amberpet to reach the workshop at Raidurg Khalsa had never bothered him. At the workshop, I mostly found Omer sahab sitting on the floor, bending over the loom or the *jālā* (the wooden graph of the design in *ḥimrū* weaving) frame, invariably engrossed in either making, repairing, adjusting or fitting parts of the loom, *jālā* or threads (Figure 8.1). He would greet whoever would pass by with an *adab* and quickly return to the loom or the stuff of the loom. My repeated encounters with this humble man kindled a few questions in me: what made Omer sahab take on this hardship every day? What do looms mean to him? Why was staying close to the loom so important to him?

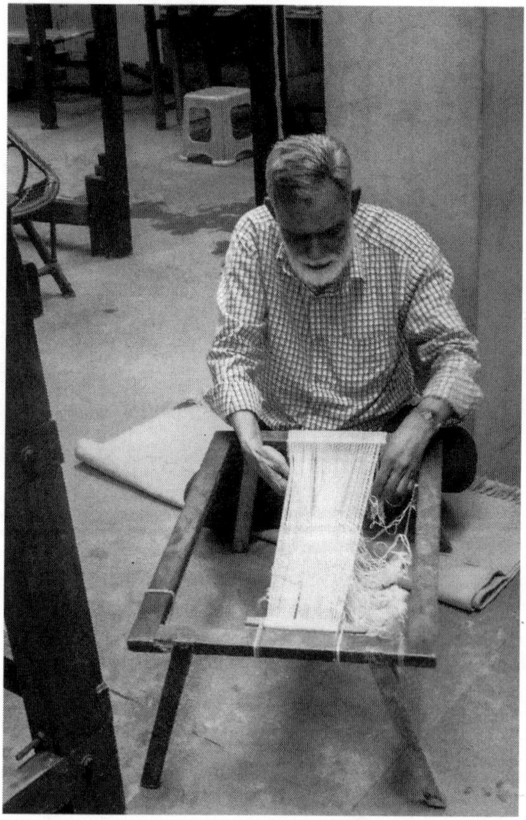

Figure 8.1 Omer Sahab Is Engrossed in Making a *Jālā*, Hyderabad-Deccan. Courtesy: Somedutta Mallik, 2017.

To contextualize Omer sahab's deep engagement with the loom, I refer to the fictitious character of Madan *tanti* (weaver in Bengali) in Manik Bandyopadhyay's celebrated Bengali short story '*Shilpi*' (artisan) (2016: 323–8). Madan, the protagonist of the story, faces hurdles when a middleman forces the weavers to weave in poor-quality yarn to cut costs. Albeit burdened with financial crisis and family responsibilities, Madan's commitment to his ancestral profession prevents him from compromising the quality of yarn; hence, his loom sits idle. But his aching body craves for its habitual practice. His physical yearning for the loom pushes him to sit at the empty loom and run the shuttle through the darkness of the night, leaving his neighbours baffled. To me, Madan's longing to work with the loom is the key to understanding Omer sahab's involvement. Noting a similar account of how emotion plays a key role in the knowledge-making process in craft, Kristina Niedderer and Katherine Townsend write that crafts' real strength 'seems to rest in the intimacy of handling, and their multisensory appeal including the visual, sound, touch, smell and taste' (2014: 624–47). In my analysis, I will adhere to Omer sahab's intimate sensorial relationship with his lifelong practice of weaving.

In existing scholarship, Omer sahab's representation remains at the periphery. Radhika Singh's book *Suraiya Hasan Bose: Weaving a Legacy* (2019) establishes Suraiya apa first as a textile connoisseur and then as an entrepreneur and revivalist of *paiṭhāni, ḥimrū* and *mashrū* textiles. Singh suggests that her workshop became a melting pot of new ideas for many accomplished revivalists and designers in decolonized India, including the founder of Fabindia, John Bissell, designer and entrepreneur Terence Conran, and master kalamkari printer Mukkantieswarudu Rao (2019: 26). Master weaver Abdul Qadir and Omer sahab exchanged thoughts, shared knowledge and collaborated on several occasions. Over time, some of these collaborations came to an end, but Omer sahab continued to work at Suraiya apa's workshop until his last days in October 2019. In a section of Singh's book (2019), Mayank Mansingh Kaul prioritizes the legacy of Suraiya apa's family business, highlighting empowering narratives of non-hereditary women weavers who were trained by Omer sahab, while Omer sahab and his immense contribution remain in the shadow. Kaul states,

> In a country where family-run businesses dominate the economy, it is worth considering how legacies of such revival efforts are passed down the generations within a family: her own father's lead in starting a handloom emporia in Hyderabad, her own adventures in the textile field, consolidating itself in a focused workshop for the revival of sophisticated handlooms, and Simbul's partnership in Hasan's work, for which, often, she has remained a face. With Sayed Bhai, the master *jālā* maker who has been a part of her workshop for almost twenty years, and Zeenat Panah, who has managed Hassan's store and workshop for almost as much time, this circle of inheritors of her legacy extends to a network beyond the family.
>
> (2019: 166)

Singh's identification of Omer sahab as a 'master *jālā* maker' fails to recognize Omer sahab's intellectual and structural contribution in building the weaving workshop not only as a production house but also as a means of survival with integrity and passionate bondage on what the workshop stood for. The methodological approach of Singh's book (2019) shows how narratives of subaltern people are further marginalized by the burden of a constructed legacy of entrepreneurship. Following Deepali Dewan's argument that the body of the craftspeople transformed into a site of contesting ideologies by the colonial officials, I see the legacy of colonial scholarship continuing in Singh's portrayal of the artisans. The artisans are portrayed as mere spectators of socio-political changes, and their ability is reduced to being mere keepers or deterioration of tradition (Dewan 2004: 118–34). The reason I stress on Omer sahab's enduring legacy is that his death resulted in the closing Suraiya apa's workshop in late 2019. The management asked the existing weavers to leave, even after the weavers pointed to sufficient resources to continue weaving for at least a year and vowed to ask for no monetary benefits until sales took off again. This firmly attests to Omer sahab's capability not only as a master weaver but also as a dedicated organizer who mediated between the workers and management.

This chapter studies into Omer sahab's five-decade-long journey, from being a naïve apprentice to growing into a skilled master weaver. It unfolds his lifelong relationship with the loom and his role as a 'master', a teacher and an accomplished weaver in the process of disseminating knowledge through training women weavers and constituting artisanal identity. I propose that Omer sahab speaks through the loom like a ventriloquist; the loom translates his weaving-life beyond the scope of craft revival of post-independent India. Furthermore, in this chapter, I argue that the historiography of craft revivalism primarily focuses on the process and success of various agencies in hierarchical tier, relocation of crafts and their makers, materials of production and market management, while pushing craftspeople like Omer sahab to the margins. Whereas entrepreneurs deploy the image of the craftsman at work as an icon of craft revival, my investigation presents the artisan's perspective on their intimate relationship with materials, tools and mechanisms as a process of belonging in the craft world and becoming an embodied craftsman.

The Path He Chose

Syed Omer was born into a farmer's family to father Syed Ahmed and mother Jilanibi nearly seventy-four years ago.[3] He was the only son, with one elder and three younger sisters. His father owned agricultural land in Patel Nagar, Hyderabad, where he grew rice and vegetables. As a school-going kid, Omer sahab spent the summer holidays visiting a weaving workshop in Quadri Bagh, set up by the weavers who had migrated from Aurangabad. Amir Khan, the master weaver there, introduced him to *ḥimrū*.

Himrū, an exquisite Indo-Persian fabric, was popular amongst the royalties of Hyderabad. Aurangabad weavers were the chief practitioners of this craft. With the support and encouragement of the Nizams, Hyderabad was gradually setting up looms and creating a small production unit on its own; on the other hand, the jacquard loom was introduced in Aurangabad, which caused degradation in the quality of their fabric. In 1953–4, a group of skilled *ḥimrū* weavers from Aurangabad were brought to Hyderabad to increase the *ḥimrū* production in the city. Slowly, there grew to be a significant demand for *ḥimrū* products, which encouraged the state government to establish the Furnishing and Allied Fabrics Industrial Co-operative Work Centre Ltd. (henceforth Centre) in Amberpet in 1955. This was done under the guidance and supervision of the State Directorate of Industries and Commerce. The age group of workers ranged from less than ten years to sixty-five years, and they were categorized into skilled (weavers) and unskilled (helpers and winders) workers (Gowd 1964: 50).

In the 1950s, at the age of eleven, Omer sahab had to leave his formal education and search for a job owing to his father's ill health, followed by a financial crisis in the family. Weaving *ḥimrū* struck him as a profitable job, prompting him to join the weaving unit in Quadri Bagh as an apprentice at the time. Coming from a non-weaving community, the young boy learnt the complex techniques of weaving *ḥimrū* on pit looms. Weaving as a physical performance involves harmonious coordination between eyes, hands, feet and mind. While throwing the shuttle, the weaver has to be careful about pulling the reed, pressing the pedal and lifting the wooden plough (*ākhattā*) to pass the weft through the warp. In the initial days of learning, the tedious hours of work at the loom caused Omer sahab muscle cramps and body ache, a common phenomenon for whoever learns weaving on the loom. Like other embodied skills, weaving brings changes to the corporeal condition, which over a period becomes habitus. Greg Downey argues, '[S]kill is not simply the "embodiment" of "knowledge," but rather physical, neurological, perceptual, and behavioural change of the individual subject so that he or she can accomplish tasks that, prior to enskilment, were impossible' (2010: 21–38). Omer sahab's multisensory engagement and willingness to learn made him a confident weaver at the age of fifteen. He left this weaving unit only to join the Centre as a *ḥimrū* weaver since *ḥimrū* shawls were in high demand. Here he worked under Rasool Khan, a master weaver and designer from Aurangabad. Khan, along with his wife, daughter and son, was employed in the Centre. Though the craft economy was in perennial crisis, he was hopeful about the revival of the lost fame of *ḥimrū* (Gowd 1964: 50). Khan's passion for his craft must have made a lasting impression on young Omer sahab, which will become evident as we advance towards the later part of his career.

A few years later, the Centre was relocated to Goshamahal. There, Omer sahab was elected to be the General Secretary of the Centre and served in this position for fourteen years. Alongside working here, he taught weaving to students of Anjuman-e-Khadimul Musleeman, a school for orphans in Kachiguda. It was during the 1970s when Omer sahab met Suraiya apa during her visits to the Centre for production sale purposes. In the late 1970s, when the Centre was shut down, Omer sahab took up a supervisory job at the Charminar Cigarette Company and continued working there for eight years. These eight long years were crucial for him to realize his passion for weaving in this specialized form of Indo-Persian textile. Amit Kumar delineates that factors of the production system and sustenance of specialized crafts, in this case, *ḥimrū* should not be compared to the 'quotidian' crafts since the skillset and artisan-patron relationship in the specialized artisanal forms remain somewhat unchanged over time despite socio-political changes (2022: 81). Drawing on Kumar, it is essential to consider that Omer sahab's love for weaving cannot be generalized and applied to all revivalist projects in post-independence India. When Suraiya apa finally set up her weaving unit, Omer sahab was delighted and relieved to be reunited with his beloved profession.

Rediscovering Self

The experience at the Centre allowed Omer sahab to learn the craft of *ḥimrū* in all its complexities, including making the *jālā* from the existing designs, setting up looms and working closely with carpenters to build a loom. As the General Secretary, he was responsible for managing orders and supply. When he joined Suraiya apa's workshop, he brought with him not only in-depth knowledge about the craft but also ancillary activities essential to run a weaving unit. On several occasions, Kamaladevi Chattopadhyay, in her book *India's Craft Tradition* (1980), mentioned how the post-independence revivalist movement revisited the connection between the craftspeople and their pre-industrial modes of knowledge-making. Omer sahab too emphasized this holistic knowledge about the craft, '*weaver bhi hona aur weaver jankar bhi hona*' (to be a weaver, you must have the complete knowledge of the craft).

As soon as they started setting up the looms, Abdul Qadir from Benaras and Munaf and Ajmal from Paithan, Maharashtra, joined Omer sahab. From them, Omer sahab learnt *paiṭhānī* weaving techniques. Before introducing *mashrū* to the workshop, Suraiya apa and Omer sahab travelled to Ahmedabad and other parts of Gujarat to obtain first-hand knowledge about this historical fabric. Upon their return to Hyderabad, Omer sahab gave the designs of the looms to Darga Satyanarayan, a neighbourhood carpenter with no previous experience of making looms. From his earlier experience, Omer sahab knew that pit looms will cost them less than frame looms. Hence, Omer sahab and Abdul Qadir verbally conveyed the structural requirements of a pit loom and specified the requisite measurements to Satyanarayan, who then made a mindful choice of woods: teak wood was used to build the stronger parts of the loom such as the frame, *bhem* (warp beam) and *amboda* (tool used by the weaver's assistant to lift the threads of the *jālā*), whereas *neem* and *babool* wood were used for making the less strong parts like *hatta* (sley), *rach* (reed) and *dam* (top arm connected to treadle). *Neem* and *babool* also helped to cut down the production cost of the looms.

Once the looms were ready, considerable attention was devoted to developing new designs as well as to making *jālā* or graphs based on the old designs. Omer sahab already had a small collection of old fabrics from the historical bazaars of the city, such as the old textile shops at Gulzar Houz near Mitti Ka Sher, Hyderabad. Suraiya apa, hailing from an aristocratic family herself, had connections with families in Hyderabad who were happy to generously hand over their century-old *ḥimrū* and *paiṭhāni* pieces to a textile connoisseur like her. A handful of designs were also collected from the rich collection of the Salar Jung Museum, Hyderabad. The museum authority lent them a few *sherwanis*, which were later returned after the designs were copied and *jālās* were made accordingly. Omer sahab knew the city like the back of his hand as far as it concerned identifying what to source from where. They used to collect cotton ropes *kadia* (usually used for tying buffaloes) from Pan Bazaar and silk threads from the bazaars near Puranapool, which they would then send to Md. Sukur of Goshamahal, a *raṅgrez* (dyer) from Jaipur, Rajasthan. Md. Sukur had the dyeing unit at his home, where his other family members were also engaged in the business.

Describing the expertise of a craftsperson and what makes a person—a *shilpi* (an artisan), Kamaladevi Chattopadhyay writes,

> [Y]outh learnt more than technique, he also learnt the true value of things, metaphysics, aesthetics and in short, culture. In the Indian tradition it is said that a craftsman is considered accomplished only when his repertoire of creation covers ten different materials which include earth, wood, stone, plaster, metal, ivory etc. In fact, even the title 'shilpi' was not applied to craftsman until he became an expert in his line.
>
> (1980: 11)

Omer sahab, in his six-decade-long career, learnt the techniques of *ḥimrū, paiṭhāni* and *mashrū*. He was proficient in making *jālā* from the old designs of *ḥimrū* and thus recreated some of the designs popular in the Nizams' time (1724–1948). During the long conversations I had with Omer sahab, he frequently mentioned the master weaver from the Centre and Rasool Khan, the master weaver from Benaras who worked at the *Loom* (the workshop) the initial years, Abdul Khader, and Munaf and Ajmal, who taught him *paiṭhāni* weaving. He used to reminisce about the activities of Pandit Nehru[4] and Padmaja Naidu[5] that he felt during the revivalist movement.

Being a Master

Soon after the weaving workshop began its journey with male weavers, Suraiya apa decided to engage the underprivileged women of the Hazrat Syed Hussain Shah Wali Dargāh locale in weaving to offer them some financial stability. Her women empowerment mission included widows, single mothers, girls and women from economically challenged families. All of them except Sheshamma belonged to non-weaving communities. Thus, Omer sahab had to put much time and effort into communicating the technique of specialized *ḥimrū* weaving to them. Starting from scratch, with his intrinsic patience and ability to teach, he taught the women the intricacies of weaving. The first group consisted of Parveen, Kausar, Balamani and Manju. Nasrin Begum, aka Nasrin apa, joined the workshop in 1993 and continued to work there until 2018. She provided me with detailed accounts of Omer sahab's teaching methods. The training began with understanding the knots of *jālā* and handling it with the weaver sitting at the *Loom* (the workshop) (Figure 8.2). At the very beginning of her training, Nasrin apa used to lift the *jālā* sitting on the table, with Omer sahab on the weaver's seat. Observing him, Nasrin apa slowly learnt the movements of the hands, though working on the loom on her own was altogether a different challenge. Omer sahab, being an experienced weaver himself, suggested that she should concentrate on the weft as it would reduce the chances of them tearing off. Initially, Omer sahab gave them small and simple designs to weave. However, the apprentices, including Nasrin apa, made frequent mistakes while learning; these accounts were kept secret from Suraiya apa's watchful eyes. Sheshamma was an exception as she hailed from the Padmashali weavers' community from Yemmiganur village in Kurnool district. She had a fundamental understanding of weaving and learnt to weave *pattu* (silk, in Telugu) sarees. After joining the workshop in 1998, she assisted the existing weavers by lifting the threads of the *jālā* for a month or so before working as a weaver in the workshop. During this month, she carefully observed the hand movements of the weaver throwing off the shuttle and the operation of pedals at regular intervals. Recognizing her ability, Omer sahab asked her to try her hand at the bigger and more intricate designs much sooner than the others. The contrast between Omer sahab's teaching strategies for Sheshamma and other apprentices shows the attention he paid to the needs of individuals.

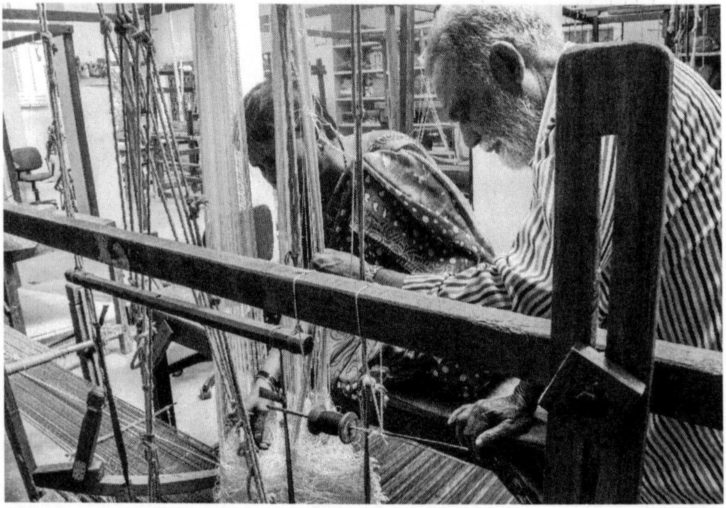

Figure 8.2 Omer Sahab examines a *Jālā* set on a *Himrū* loom, Hyderabad-Deccan. Courtesy: Somedutta Mallik, 2016.

Omer sahab, now a teacher and fondly called 'Master sahab', was patient with his students. It was the continuous practice of the craft that he emphasized (Figure 8.3). During my fieldwork, a weaver in the workshop, Hashmat Begum, told me about the difficulties of weaving *ḥimrū*: the fabric on the loom tore if she unmindfully put her elbows on it, creating tension in the threads and making the fabric flawed. Omer sahab was always available to intervene and rectify the mistake by skilfully stitching the torn portion of the fabric. His hands became an extension of the tool, i.e. the loom; in Kamaladevi Chattopadhyay's words, 'Tools are after all only extensions of the hands, to reach beyond the range of human limitations' (1980: 11). Years later, when I asked Omer sahab about the achievements of his students, I could see the pride and elation of a successful teacher in him. He particularly praised Nasrin apa at length, whom he described as smart, intelligent and sincere enough to learn the craft very fast. He considered her '*hośiyār*' (smart). A

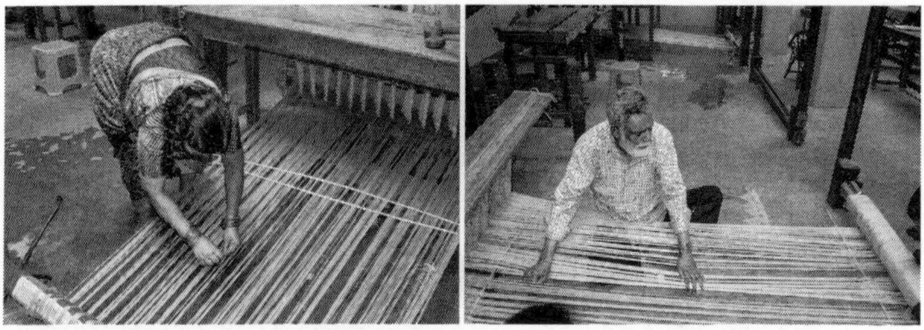

Figure 8.3 (Left) Sheshamma Ties the Yarns of the Warp. **(Right)** Omer Sahab Adjusts the Warp Threads before the Weaver Starts Working on a New Piece of *Himrū* Fabric (Right), Hyderabad-Deccan. Courtesy: Somedutta Mallik, 2017.

non-hereditary weaver himself, Omer sahab was empathetic to the efforts of his students trying to learn and master the techniques of weaving: '*aaj ke zamane mein itna sikhna bole to bohaut hay*', which means learning this much of the craft in today's time is a huge achievement for someone (Interview with Omer sahab, Hyderabad, August 2017).

Clinging to the Looms

Omer sahab's affectionate ties to the loom, his fellow weavers and Suraiya apa were not compromised for financial well-being. The Government of Andhra Pradesh (undivided Andhra) offered him a lucrative job as a weaver in the famed textile town of Chirala, but he chose to work at Suraiya's workshop for a significantly lower salary. For him, the reasons were many. Firstly, he could not let go of his long association with the *Loom* (the workshop) as well as the people who worked there; secondly, he enjoyed teaching the newcomers and cherished his status of a 'master'; most importantly, he was aware of Suraiya apa's trust and dependence on him. The workshop was Suraiya apa's brainchild, but Omer sahab invested nearly three decades for the workshop to flourish. In his words, '*hamare bhi bohot badi mehnat hay iske andar*', which translates as 'I too have put immense effort into it' (Interview with Omer sahab in Hyderabad, March 2017). Like Suraiya apa and the weavers, Omer sahab too was aware of the fact that his presence in the workshop was essential for developing new designs and *jālā*s, supervising the weavers and guiding them whenever they faced any challenge in the process of weaving (Figure 8.4). This, to him, was a greater reward than financial gains.

During my long chats with Omer sahab, he would enthusiastically show me the *ḥimrū* pieces he prepared for *jālā*, the final products, or his renewed take on historical pieces from the collection. He would run his fingers across the motifs and explain their intricacies and material qualities, such as the yarn and warp count (Figure 8.5). His fingers recognized the quality of each stage of yarn

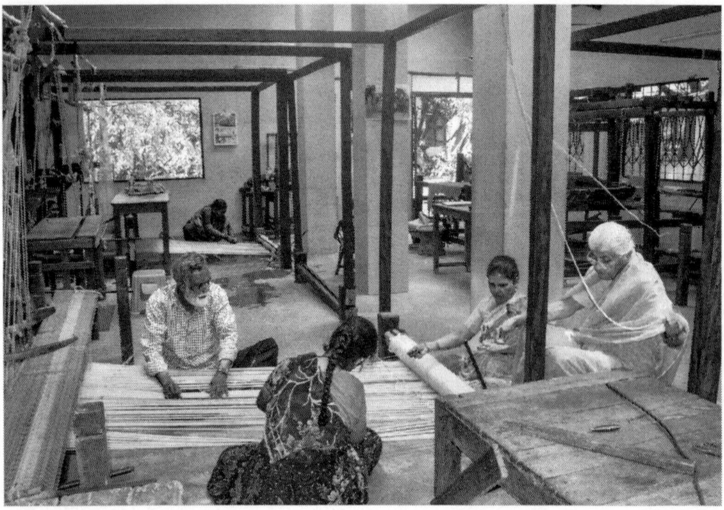

Figure 8.4 Omer Sahab, along with Other Weavers, Sets the Warp Threads while Suraiya Apa Quietly Observes Them, Hyderabad-Deccan. Courtesy: Somedutta Mallik, 2017.

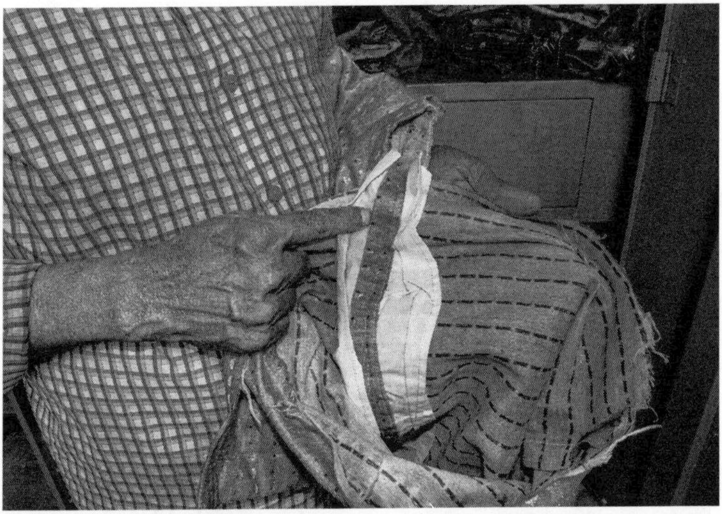

Figure 8.5 Omer Sahab Shows the Design of an Old Piece of Fabric from the '*Loom*' (Workshop) Collection, Hyderabad-Deccan. Courtesy: Somedutta Mallik, 2017.

preparation: from cultivation to processing, and finally weaving. His knowledge of weaving rested on the correspondence between his fingers and the hair-thin yarns transforming into woven fabric. The accounts of these intricate details and intimate knowledge of weaving and weavers are often missing in the historical studies of South Asian textiles, which often end up posing Omer sahab as a mere '*jālā* maker' as a result (Kaul 2019: 166). Challenging the dominant trend, Chandan Shafiqul Kabir argues how the yarn makers, who create the count in yarn from cotton, signify the whole process of weaving (Kabir 2020). Paradoxically, they are almost absent in the scholarship on textile. Another instance of this kind comes to the fore when we turn to the story of the recent revival project of muslin in Bangladesh, which informs us about the story of three fingers in making count for muslin. It delineates how the *phūṭī karpā*s (a type of Gossypium arboreum), climate and sensitivity of the fingers are responsible for making yarn with high counts. Even though up to 500 thread counts were noted in the historical records, the present-day *sūtā kāṭani* (yarn maker) could make yarn with a maximum of 150 counts (Azad 2020). Here I propose that the skill of defining the count of the yarn depends upon the artisans' (here *sūtā kāṭani*, yarn makers) knowledge that is formed through the correspondence between their fingers and the raw cotton. Failing to recognize this made the *sūtā kāṭani* (yarn maker) endangered. Similarly, the sudden demise of Omer sahab and the collapse of the workshop bury this kind of knowledge and bring an end to a revived and cultivated craftsmanship.

In 2013, Omer sahab survived a heart attack and underwent a bypass surgery. His family was thereafter reluctant to let him travel to the workshop every day, but Omer sahab insisted on continuing his work as he could foresee the critical state of the workshop without him. Considering Suraiya apa's age (she was in her late 80s at the time) and her impairing memory, he knew his absence would bring an end to the weaving centre and consequently, all the weavers would lose their jobs. He could not let this happen. He highly valued the love for and the relationship with the *Loom* (the workshop), as well as the people associated with it. After the major surgery he underwent, his health did not allow him to sit at the loom and weave. But to stay close to the looms, he chose his place next to an idle *mashrū* loom, where, surrounded by old *ḥimrū* pieces, he would make the jālās and supervise the weavers at regular intervals.

Omer sahab was 'infamous' for his punctuality and discipline. Women weavers often complained that Omer sahab insisted that they work even on holidays. They used to get upset, but little could they realize his yearning to visit the workshop and stay near the looms. Now that the *Loom* (the workshop) has closed down, unemployed weavers express their yearning to return to the looms and their habitual practice of weaving. Sitting idle at home causes them terrible body aches. They continue to remember the empty workshop (Figure 8.6). Thus, the phantasmagoria of Madan *tanti* from Manik Bandyopadhyay's story '*Shilpi*' comes alive in the dejected weavers even today.

Omer sahab's command and camaraderie formed a community in the workshop, and his sense of pride was transmitted to others. His presence in the workshop assured the weavers about the functionality of the *Loom*. He motivated them. For instance, Hashmat Begum continued her job with pride against all the odds. Other well-paid jobs tempted her, yet she chose to continue her work at the workshop because this was a respectable job and a prized skill she had acquired over the years. Even now, like other weavers, she is not ready to take up any other job. Gradually, she has developed the pride of being a weaver and can relate to the identity of an artisan. None of Omer sahab's six children learnt weaving.

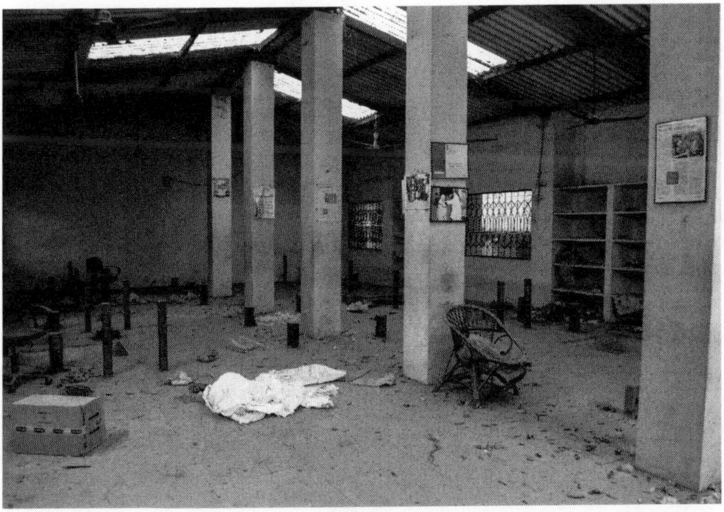

Figure 8.6 The Empty '*Loom*' (the Workshop) after It Got Shut Down in November 2019, Hyderabad-Deccan. Courtesy: Somedutta Mallik, 2021.

Suraya apa's kin are also not interested in running the workshop after Omer sahab's demise. The learners in the workshop were Omer sahab's last hope, to whom he could impart what he learned from his masters, Amir Khan and Rasool Khan. He was also the last hope of the group of women weavers, with whom he had shared his knowledge and lifelong experiences. They, in return, elevated his status to 'Master sahab' with much respect and gratitude. This love, respect and acknowledgement that resonated around him in the workshop made him content until his last days. He once mentioned that it was not money, but '*mohabbat*' (love in Urdu) for the yarn and the loom, and the special bond he shared with Suraiya apa that kept the workshop alive. The group of weavers is now scattered, pushing themselves to make do with various odd jobs, looking for appointments related to weaving, and craving to hold the shuttle to run on the loom.

Conclusion

Omer sahab's journey of becoming a 'master'– as a skilled weaver, teacher and supervisor– unravels a few important aspects of how an artisanal identity can be embraced by a craftsperson who does not possess the baggage of generational occupation and yet develops this belongingness through years of practice. Tracing his journey also enables me to understand how his body and mind were associated with the looms and other instruments in the workshop. Further, it emphasizes the significance of considering the individual histories of artisans against the grand narratives of revivalism. How immense his contribution was can be understood from the present condition of the *Loom*, which has been shut ever since Omer sahab's demise. Suraiya apa could not run the workshop without Omer sahab. In her words, 'when the "master" is not there, who else can take care of things?' (Interview with Suraiya apa, Hyderabad, January 2021).

Notes

1 I owe this chapter to Omer sahab and Suraiya apa who taught me the meaning of passion and diligence. I thank Akhter bhai, Zeenath apa, D. Ramesh, Nasrin apa, Hashmat apa, Shobha aunty, Sheshamma garu and all the weavers whom I met during my fieldwork at Suraiya apa's workshop for sharing their personal experiences of learning and the editors for their critical inputs.

2 Suraiya Hasan Bose, fondly called Suraiya apa (elder sister), is a textile revivalist and entrepreneur, based in Hyderabad. In 1982, she started entrepreneurship of dhurries and kalamkari fabrics. Her association with the textile industry began and her love for weaving flourished under the guidance of textile activist Pupul Jayakar. Jayakar inspired her to bring back the glorious past of Indo-Persian textile in Hyderabad. Suraiya apa's passion for textiles and weaving was more like a family heirloom passed on to her from her nationalist father, Syed Badrul Hasan. Once she was able to make her fortune in this business, she stepped forward to accomplish her dreams of entrepreneurship in weaving.

3 Omer sahab mentioned his age seventy when I interviewed him in 2016–17.

4 During the seventeen years (1947–64) of his service as the first prime minister of independent India, Pandit Jawaharlal Nehru focused on the empowerment of the handloom and handicraft sectors of rural India. To give shape to his revivalist project in the 1950s, Nehru invited activist scholar Pupul Jayakar to hold the chair of the All India Handloom Board and Handicrafts and Handlooms Export Corporation (Clifford 2018: 44–56; Divya 2020; Sackley 2023: 236–58).

5 Padmaja Naidu, mostly recognized as a daughter of Sarojini Naidu, participated in India's struggle for independence in 1940s. Later she served as the governor of West Bengal. Amongst her many social activities, she is remembered for her association with the All India Handicrafts Board (Jha 2017; Paranjape 2012: 164–90).

References

Azad, Abul Kalam Muhammad (2020), 'Dhakai Musliner Punorjanmo', *Prothom Alo*, 31 December. Available online: https://www.prothomalo.com/bangladesh/ঢাকাই-মসলিনের-পুনর্জন্ম (accessed 10 February 2021).

Bandyopadhyay, Manik (2016), *Manik Bandyopadhyay Rachanasamagra* 5, Kolkata: Pashchimbanga Bangla Academy.

Chattopadhyay, Kamaladevi (1980), *India's Craft Tradition*, New Delhi: The Director Publications Division.

Clifford, Ruth (2018), 'Challenging Hierarchies, Enhancing Capabilities: Innovations in Design and Business Education for Handloom Weavers in India', PhD Thesis, Nottingham Trent University, Nottingham.

Dewan, Deepali (2004), 'The Body at Work: Art Education and the Figure of the 'Native Craftsman', in James H. Mills and Satadru Sen (eds), *Confronting the Body: The Politics of Physicality in Colonial and Post-colonial India*, 118–34, London: Anthem Press.

Divya, A. (2020), 'What Does the Dissolution of the All India Handloom Board Mean for the Industry?' *Indian Express*, 8 August. Available online:https://indianexpress.com/article/lifestyle/art-and-culture/what-does-the-dissolution-of-the-all-india-handloom-board-mean-for-the-industry-ministry-of-textiles-6545819/ (accessed 10 February 2021).

Downey, Greg (2010), 'Practice without Theory: A Neuroanthropological Perspective on Embodied Learning', in Trevor H.J. Marchand (ed.), *Making Knowledge: Explorations of the Indissoluble Relation Between Mind, Body and Environment*, 21–38, London: Royal Anthropological Institute of Great Britain & Ireland.

Gowd, K. V. N. (1964), *Census of India 1961, Vol-II, Selected Crafts of Andhra Pradesh, Part VII-A (3)*, New Delhi: Office of the Registrar General India and Superintendent of Census Operations, Andhra Pradesh.

Jha, Rakesh (2017), 'Remembering Padmaja Naidu: From freedom fighter to Governor of West Bengal', *INUTH*, 13 August. Available online: https://www.inuth.com/india/women-freedom-fighters-of-india/

remembering-padmaja-naidu-from-freedom-struggle-to-governor-of-west-bengal/ (accessed 10 February 2021).

Kabir, Chandan Shafiqul (2020), 'Muslin-er dabi ebong ek sachetan bismriti-sutakatunir golpo', *DW Studios* [Facebook video] 8 December. Available online: https://www.facebook.com/sutairabydwstudios/videos/2867466263508866/ (accessed 10 December 2020).

Kaul, Mayank Mansingh (2019), 'Suraiya in Context to the History of Textiles in India', in Radhika Singh (ed.), *Suraiya Hasan Bose: Weaving a Legacy*, 157–75, New Delhi: Tara Press.

Kumar, Amit (2022), *Precious Threads and Precarious Lives: Histories of Shawl and Silk Industries of Kashmir, 1846–1950*, London and New York: Routledge.

Niedderer, Kristina and Katherine Townsend (2014), 'Designing Craft Research: Joining emotion and knowledge', *Design Journal*, 17 (4): 624–48.

Paranjape, Makarand R. (2012), *Making India: Colonialism, National Culture, and the Afterlife of Indian English Authority*, London: Springe.

Sackley, Nicole (2023), 'The Bankura Horse as Development Object: Women's Work, Indo-American Exchanges, and the Global Handicraft Trade', in Harald Fischer-Tiné and Nico Slate (eds), *The United States and South Asia from the Age of Empire to Decolonization*, 235–66, Amsterdam: Leiden University Press.

Singh, Radhika (2019), *Suraiya Hasan Bose: Weaving a Legacy*, New Delhi: Tara Press.

9

What Is Natural about Natural Dyeing?

Tanaya Pashankar

Introduction

Natural indigo has re-emerged as a potent tool for producers and consumers who recognize the need for the revival of a simpler, kinder, and sustainable future. Presently, the anxiety over the dwindling traditional knowledge base[1] and ecological concerns about mindless production and consumption are rejuvenating the cause of natural indigo dyeing.[2] By excavating the story of natural indigo dyeing from Hyderabad-based dye practitioners at the end of a decade that has seen the heavily marketed revival of natural indigo, I recontextualize the process of natural indigo dyeing by drawing out the challenges and concerns faced by practitioners. I also critically examine the notion of 'natural', which is largely missing in the rich scholarship on indigo dyeing that traces the history of this dyestuff and its revival.

I draw inspiration from the unique nature of indigo that transforms the inanimate to the animate, from plant to colour, in a complex series of chemical reactions driven by human interventions. Ian Hodder attributes agency to inanimate 'things' (here, natural indigo) by establishing their interaction with other things and humans within chains of entanglements characterized by dependence and constraints (Hodder 2012: 14, 17–18). Following Hodder, the complex chain of indigo dyeing can be understood to consist of interlinked ingredients, tools, locations, expertise, processes, markets and mechanisms. The elements involved in this entangled chain are susceptible to being broken while creating a need to repair and restart. Any attempts to repair or 'revive' natural indigo that prize only the pursuit of colour do not adequately account for their impact on ecology and producers, which limits the scope of innovations (Hodder 2012: 111–12). Particularly vulnerable are *natural* and *traditional* practices, which struggle to compete with the innovations in synthetic dyeing. More successful practices indicate that natural and 'non-natural' dyeing practices exist not as binary opposites but as ones that converge and diverge within the trajectories of one another. In this context, I observe that the terms 'adulterated' or 'cheating', used for 'non-natural' indigo dyeing practices, when supported by artisanal perspectives, refer to negotiations and not negligence in the face of the changing markets and environment and must therefore be appropriately recalibrated.

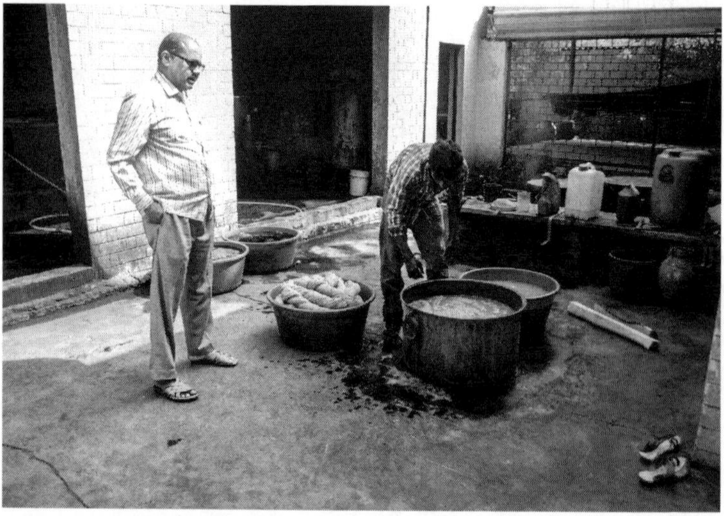

Figure 9.1 Salim Pasha, the Master Dyer Supervising the *hāṛdā* Treatment Carried Out by Habeeb Anna, A Dye-Artisan. NIRD Dyehouse, Hyderabad-Deccan. Courtesy: Tanaya Pashankar, 2019.

The archival research and my fieldwork[3] at the indigo-making workshops of the institutions, engaging in conversations with workshop artisans, and the intangible and empirical knowledge of the dye-experts – Mohammed Salim Pasha (hereafter Salimji),[4] a master dyer who worked at the dye-house of the National Institute of Rural Development (henceforth NIRD) and Panchayati Raj, Hyderabad (Figure 9.1); Keshav Rao,[5] the co-founder and master dyer at the Creative Bee textile design studio; and Jagada Rajappa, an independent dye specialist who has been involved in training artisans in India and abroad in traditional weaving and dyeing practices[6] – have contributed to shaping my argument.

The Natural Indigo Dyeing Process

At NIRD, the traditional natural indigo dyeing process involves numerous activities, each performed parallelly yet dependent on one another (Figure 9.2 Above and Below). In the initial phase, the dyers prepare the dyeing vat, which takes around forty-eight hours (Figure 9.3 Above). Simultaneously, they prepare the yarn by washing and boiling it. The dyers at NIRD use three-foot-tall terracotta *maṭkā* (pots) buried into the ground for indigo fermentation and dyeing.[7] A group of dyers dye indigo twice a day – first thing in the morning and last thing before they leave.[8] The dyeing technique is as follows: the dyer dips *kōrā* (undyed) yarns into the indigo vat so that a small section of the yarn is exposed out of the vat while the rest remains submerged. The yarn is rotated away from the dyer's body, anticlockwise, for a pre-determined count. The dyer's hands work in tandem, picking up yarn and transferring it from one hand to the other, turning the hank, and squeezing the excess liquid out (Figure 9.2 Above). They finally pull-out yarn, green in colour which transforms into

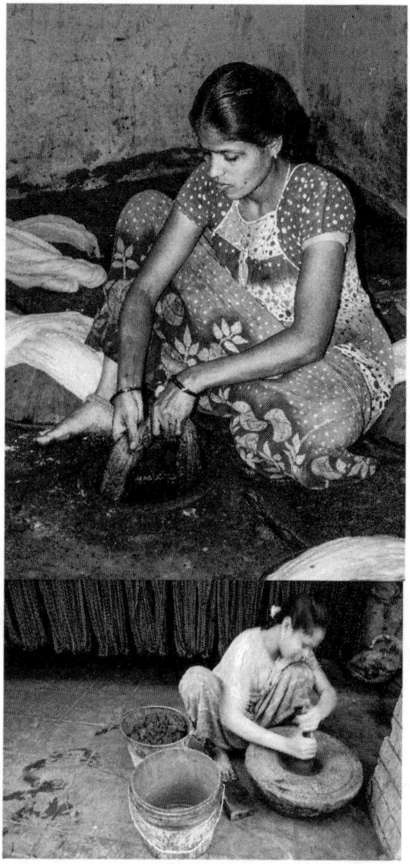

Figure 9.2 (Above) Govindamma a Dye-Artisan Rotating the Cotton Hank in the Indigo Vat. **(Below)** Ankita, a Dye-Artisan Crushing the Indigo Using a Mortar and Pestle. Courtesy: Tanaya Pashankar, 2019.

blue by oxidation. The depth of indigo is built on the surface of the yarn through multiple dipping (Figure 9.3 Below). With use, the dyeing vat slowly loses its potency, finally transforming from green to blue, indicating that it is no longer viable. The vat must be revived by feeding in more dyestuff. Every day, the dyers attend to several vats in different stages of their life cycle.

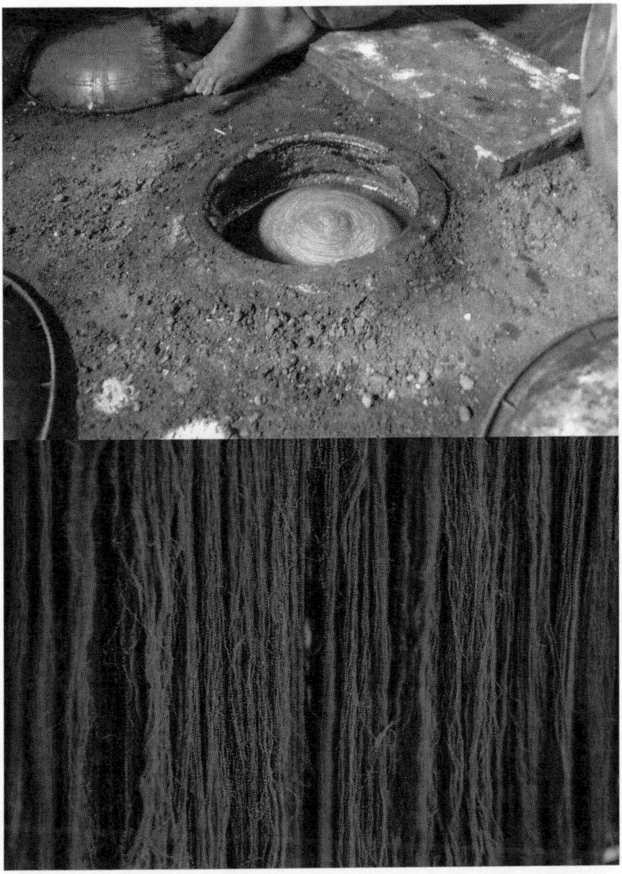

Figure 9.3 (Above) Newly Fed and Stirred Indigo Vat with Foam on Top. **(Below)** Indigo Dyed Yarn, NIRD Dyehouse, Hyderabad-Deccan. Courtesy: Tanaya Pashankar, 2019.

The revival of natural indigo and traditional practices has emphasized its being 'handmade'. The process is labour-intensive and time-consuming. Due to an injury in his spine, Salimji faces enormous difficulty in regular activities such as squatting while dyeing, bending to wash the yarn, picking up water, transporting wet heavy yarn and carrying other materials across the dyehouse. Back pain, he states, is a common complaint of traditional indigo dyers and most of them turn to alcohol for relief from the stress. While tracing the 'redemption' of natural indigo, Michael Taussig recognizes the contradiction between the lure of the (natural) colour and the exoticization of the 'hideous and extreme' labour in the colonial context (Taussig 2008: 5).[9] On the one hand, the toiling body of the artisan was considered a source of high profit; on the other, the laborious and lengthy dyeing process was rejected to popularize synthetic dyestuff in the early twentieth century.[10] The idea of 'natural' dye, thus is associated with the idea of labour-intensiveness; the mechanisms of synthetic dye offer the reduction of labour-intensity, and is hence perceived as unnatural.

At NIRD, a series of interventions of machines in labour-centred work was spearheaded by Dastkar Andhra to make 'natural' dye. One example is the introduction of a washing machine and hydro extractor in 2011 to reduce the dyers' workload (Figure 9.4 left and right). This also ensures better results, as hand-washed and dried yarn may lead to patchiness and banding. Most importantly, this machinery is the same as the ones used in synthetic dyeing factories (Interview with Mohammed Salim Pasha, Hyderabad, December 2019). Therefore, the adoption of machine-based work in certain steps of the dyeing process indicates the convergence of the natural, labour and machinery. This also resonates with Ananda Coomaraswamy's measured support for the use of mechanization to reduce the labour of the artisan (Coomaraswamy 1912: 34–5).

Measured mechanization in the natural dyeing sector is efficient as it promises cost-effectiveness for the final products. Unlike other dyes, the subtle and delicate chemistry of indigo requires careful management by skilled practitioners with alert senses. This creates what Coomaraswamy refers to as a protected space, both physical and intellectual, where machinery does not encroach upon artisanal expertise (Coomaraswamy 1912: 35). But the biggest challenge according to producers is the scarcity of skilled labour, leading to

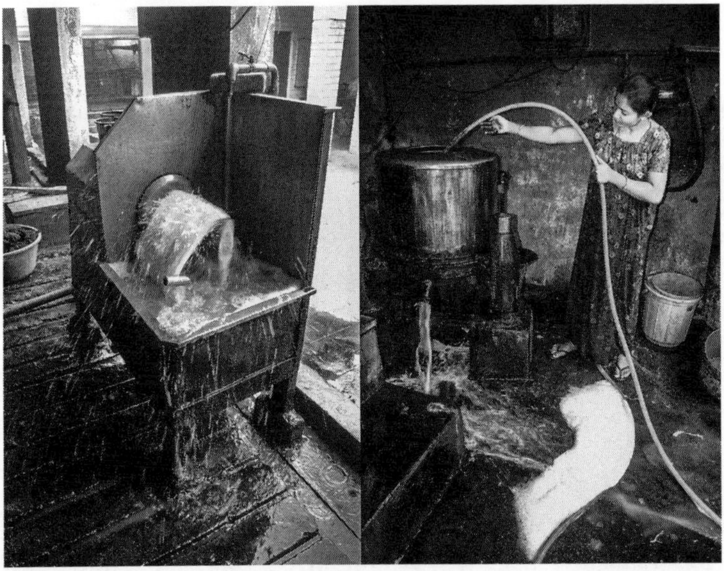

Figure 9.4 (Left) Washing Machine with Un-Dyed Yarn. **(Right)** Bhanupriya, a Dye-Artisan, Adds Water to the Hydro Extractor with a Water Pipe. NIRD Dyehouse, Hyderabad-Deccan. Courtesy: Tanaya Pashankar, 2019.

inevitably high costs in the search and training of skilled artisans.[11] Synthetic dyeing adapts easily to mechanization and therefore seems more attractive. Producers are thus faced with a tough alternative; to repair with the aid of the non-natural seems inevitable, but the fear that it may usurp the place of the natural is palpable.

Adulteration or Alternative?

Even when dyers utilize natural indigo, their practice might not be considered 'natural' because of the dyeing process they follow. Natural indigo dyeing utilizes a chemical reduction agent, caustic hydros (caustic soda and hydrosulphite), which sits uneasily in the category of natural dyestuff. Using this classification system, Salimji and Rao observe that a large portion of contemporary artisanal indigo dyeing falls under chemical dyeing. Other 'cheating' techniques include pre-treating the yarn with *hāṛdā* (myrobalan) and then dipping it in a solution of ferrous sulphate prior to natural indigo dyeing (Figure 9.1); ferrous sulphate dulls the white yarn to grey, which, when dipped twice in the indigo vat, will yield a dark blue shade (Interview with Mohammed Salim Pasha, Hyderabad, December 2019). Alternatively, the yarn or cloth dyed with synthetic indigo will be given a final bath in *hāṛdā* to achieve a 'natural' look and a 'vegetable' smell (Interview with Keshav Rao in Hyderabad, November 2020). These techniques are preferred by artisans as they are cost-effective and time-saving. Often, difficulty in the procurement of natural dyestuff and transportation costs make it unsustainable for practitioners – especially for those in semi-urban areas, such as Salimji – to strictly stick to the 'natural' dyeing protocols. Besides, almost all natural indigo (*Indigoferra Tinctoria*) is sourced from a single production site at Tindivanam, Tamil Nadu, adding to the exclusivity of this material. Further, the lack of governmental support for indigo farmers led to the abundance of cheap synthetic dyeing materials like German indigo in the market (Interview with Jagada Rajappa, Hyderabad, March 2020; Uzramma 2002). Ghulam Ahmed Nadri notes that adulteration of indigo led to a decline in the reputation of Sarkhej indigo in the seventeenth century, leading to the collapse of the indigo industry in the area. The producers might resort to adulteration of indigo as it gets harder to justify cultivation and manufacturing efforts (Nadri 1994: 339–40). These urgent concerns demand a critical consideration of the relationship between adulteration and adaptation.

The artisans and producers have long responded to these challenges by creating their own innovative solutions in the face of artistic, financial and environmental concerns. Jenny Balfour-Paul writes that just as in medieval Europe woad dyers would add natural Indian indigo to their vats to strengthen the colour, indigo dyers responded to the onset of synthetic dyeing by adding a small amount of synthetic dye to their fermentation vats (Balfour-Paul 1998: 122–3). Even within natural indigo dyeing, manipulating material and process to save effort and money has long been the practice. In the nineteenth-century Mysore province, the *Niligārū* (indigo dyers) used natural indigo, *Indigoferra Tinctoria,* to dye all shades of blue. However, the *Dēvāṇgā* weavers used the bark of the *Swāmi* [Indian Redwood] to obtain a dark blue shade which was substandard to the *Indigoferra* (Buchanan 1907: 216). The material and technique (multiple dipping) used by the *Niligārū* ensured that the colour was durable but expensive. The *Dēvāṇgās,* therefore, bought less-expensive indigo-dyed yarn of a lighter shade from the dyers and sprinkled it with a decoction of the *Swāmi* bark (Buchanan 1907: 216). Throughout the history of natural indigo dyeing, materials have replaced others to adapt to newer and better technologies.

Both adulteration and the extreme variations in natural indigo cause issues such as a lack of standardization and reproducibility, which are key metrics for achieving textile production at scale. Natural dye producers, however, reject the indiscriminate imitation of chemical standardization in natural dyeing and advocate consistency of colour as a hallmark of natural dyeing.[12] Nevertheless, without resources to scientifically assess the quality of natural indigo, the dyer must stay alert and ready to make improvisations.[13] Alongside dyestuff, human methods and modules of measurement are uniquely susceptible to error and produce variable results. For example, at the NIRD dyehouse, a plastic mug (of 1.5 litres) is used both as a measuring tool and a measuring unit, contributing to the unique variability of shades. Annapurna Mamidipudi underscores that *veesa* or pots were used as a unit of measurement by dyers as per material (2016: 134). However, this very lack of consistency makes it viable for many producers. Keshav Rao notes that the success of synthetic dyeing relies on accurate measurement and grading of dye materials; further, most discussions on natural and synthetic indigo overlook the process of preparing the chemical dye and only address the prepared chemical dye in its standardized value in comparison to the raw material for the natural dye. A fair comparison between the two would require both natural and synthetic dyestuff to be analysed, graded and adjusted.

To overcome these problems, the NIRD dyehouse created a dye-laboratory that is currently equipped to handle colour, wash and light fastness tests; however, its presence in the dyehouse indicates a bridge between the natural and synthetic practices towards fruitful results. Furthermore, it rejects the romanticization of the 'traditional' and instead accounts for the urgent challenges faced by artisans and the unpredictability of natural dyestuff. In a similar vein, Keshav Rao has prioritized innovation in the dyeing apparatus, which allows him to dye faster and in larger quantities. He identified three drawbacks to the traditional vat: firstly, the traditional vat works in cycles; as the vats vary in potency and strength, many are unavailable to dye at the same time; secondly, the size of the earthen vat restricts the amount to be dyed; and third, vats are usually buried in the ground, tying the dyer down to one place.[14] Rao prefers the 'concentrate' system, which is quicker and suitable for dyeing larger quantities on a regular basis.[15] In Rao's workshop, dyeing vats are placed above ground, allowing the dyers to stand and dye easily. The innovations observed here emerged from a deep association with practice. This diverts from the traditionalist viewpoint and linear narrative of continuing generational knowledge; they represent rather underrepresented facets of 'natural' dyeing, which interweaves through a broad range of issues, including standardization, adaptation and craft knowledge.

Sustainability

An integral aspect of practising natural dyeing is the commitment to sustainability, which could be interpreted in different ways from different artisanal perspectives. Natural indigo, as a low-energy and cold-vat dye, is an attractive proposition for environmentally conscious producers and consumers.[16] Synthetic colours, on the other hand, have long been derided as inferior to the vitality and aesthetic of natural colours as well as for distancing both the producer and consumer from nature.[17] All dyeing requires freshwater. The most urgent and disastrous drawback of the use of synthetic dyes is the water pollution associated with it, as the untreated chemical runoff goes back to water bodies. Thus, it results in disastrous health implications for the entire ecosystem.[18] Simultaneously, the growing difficulty of accessing freshwater in both urban and rural areas is forcing artisans to give up their traditional practices. While natural indigo runoff can safely be sent back to water bodies, natural dyeing consumes copious amounts of water. At the NIRD workshop, yarn is washed four to five times during the indigo dyeing process (Figure 9.4 Left). Given that water scarcity is a common plight in the summer season in Hyderabad, arranging freshwater tankers (a common sight in Hyderabad during the summer) for the dyehouse causes a massive financial strain on Salimji. Both the NIRD dyehouse and Creative Bee primarily use groundwater, which differs in aesthetic quality due to soil and weather conditions. The variations in water quality translate into variations in dyed fabric, which is often unacceptable to corporate buyers. Adding a water purification/treatment system might bring back the water of yore, but will the dyer or consumer be able to bear the expense?

The role of water within the natural indigo dyeing chain is not without its concerns even before it reaches the workshops.

For example, indigo farming is land and water intensive. Farms dependent on regular rainfall patterns are increasingly finding cultivation harder to sustain.[19] As fewer farmers are involved in production, it creates a market monopoly, as in the case of Tindivanam in Tamil Nadu, which supplies natural indigo to almost the entire country. A large demand and low supply ensure that natural indigo is sold today at a whopping price of 2,800 INR/kg.[20] All these factors prove a burden to many who wish to work with natural dyes but either cannot access or afford it, or are getting substandard quality. It is against this background that I review the adoption of synthetic dyeing in Rajasthan. According to Salimji, dyers have adapted to synthetic dyeing due to the extreme shortage of water. Natural dyeing, with its water entanglements, is shunned to save the community precious water in the short term and the artisan money and time in the long term.

Sustainability, as understood today, encompasses not only environmental concerns but also responsibilities towards producer communities. Jagada Rajappa says that when master dyer Kattubadi Yellappa began teaching the artisans natural indigo dyeing in the late 1990s, the goal at the time was to spread natural indigo dyeing knowledge, dissuade the artisans from using caustic hydros in the dyeing process, encourage collaborations, and activate allied sites.[21] But Yellappa, she points out, had concerns about the integrity of the practice and was worried about misappropriation.[22] While the recipe for indigo natural dyeing is readily available today, traditional processes of indigo dyeing have been heavily guarded and kept within traditional dyeing communities. Keshav Rao posits that both factors may have been the reason for the preference of synthetic over natural indigo.

Sustainability also translates into continuing efforts to empower artisanal communities. Rao argues that while safeguarding artisanal knowledge is pivotal, steps must be taken to ensure the transference of knowledge between masters and disciples is not restricted to familial bonds. Most of Rao's own knowledge has been obtained through practice and experimentation with recipes from archival research, besides sharing and collaborating with dyers at meetings held by the World Crafts Council.[23] Artisans on the ground level, however, largely do not have access to any archival research or international support. It is a rightful matter of concern that knowledge which belongs to artisanal communities may be appropriated by others for their gain and to the detriment of the artisanal stakeholders.

Finally, both Salimji and Rao, through their respective organizations cater to urban consumers. The rural audience and producer communities cannot afford natural dyed prooducts because of their high pricing. This widens the distance between producers and urban consumers, reducing the artisans to mere labourers. Increasingly, indigo and natural indigo-dyed products are being feted and coveted by the luxury fashion market chasing 'sustainability' and 'conscious consumerism' goals.[24] Urban wealthy consumers, seduced by fast fashion, have imbibed the polarity between synthetic and natural colours as a tussle between fast and slow, bright and subdued, modern and traditional, Western and Indian. Natural dyeing is often classified as slow, dull, and traditional, and its success depends on the marketing of the product. Throughout my fieldwork, Salimji himself was dressed in a simple shirt and trousers tailored from mill-made fabric (Figure 9.1). The women dye-artisans would always be clothed in mass-produced printed cotton nightgowns (Figure 9.2 Above and Below; Figure 9.4 Right). My final visit to the NIRD dyehouse was on a day when a group of indigo enthusiasts were gathered to learn about the dyehouse and indigo dyeing techniques. That day, I learnt that the women dye-artisans had been gifted natural-dyed sarees, and Salimji was dressed for this visit in a natural-dyed kurta. However, it would be hard to imagine these sarees or kurtas being a part of the daily or working wardrobe of the dyers. More likely, the prohibitive cost of naturally dyed items makes them novelty garments to be worn for 'special' occasions.

Blue Hands

While a normal rinse of indigo-stained hands with soap and water is enough before a meal – women dyers' families refuse to eat food prepared by blue hands (Figure 9.5). Salimji despairs of this attitude towards natural indigo within the dyeing community itself. Historically, both colour and the dye process contributed to the *Niligārū* occupying an ambiguous status in society. Indian notions of purity and pollution define social order, and menial work is especially looked down upon in the Hindu caste system.[25] The work of the indigo dyer, while much in demand, was also shrouded in secrecy and seclusion due to the smell and raw materials associated with their work (Sarkar 2014: 109–21). C. A. Bayly implied that cloth was indicative of the transformation of individuals, apart from being an identifier of the life stages of the wearer (consumer) (Bayly 1986: 285–7). Indigo was considered a 'polluting dye' in northern India, where a Rajput woman on her way to commit *sāti* would be made to don an indigo veil or be forced to drink indigo on her way to the funeral pyre, thereby diminishing her *sāt* or internal fire. Similarly, in north India, an indigo saree was worn only by lower caste women; 'other than a "*sūḍrā*" (lower caste), a married woman would never wear blue sarees while her husband is alive' (Hiltebeitel 1999: 318).[26] However, this association may have been regional and was not uniform across India. Bharati Govindraj elaborates on the significance of the deep blue-black *Chānḍrākāli* saree made in Ilkal, Karnataka: a newlywed bride wears an indigo saree when entering her marital home for the first time, thereby channelling virtue and the goodness of Goddess *Bhāṇaśāṅkarī* (Govindraj 2014: 228).[27]

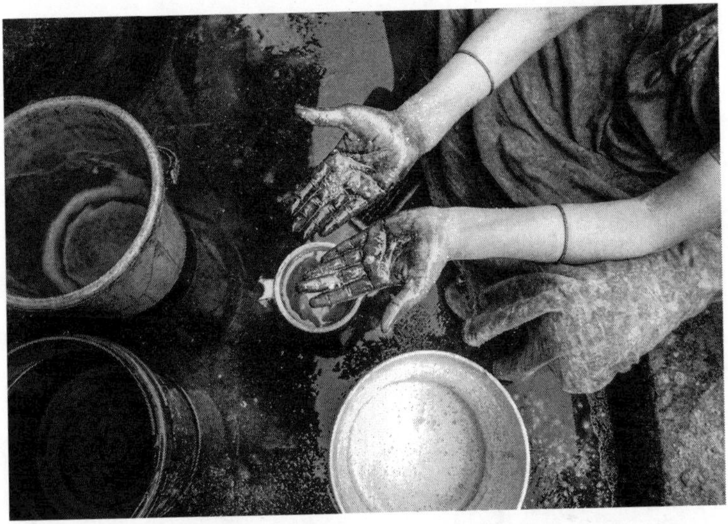

Figure 9.5 Ankita, a Dye-Artisan Cleaning Her Hands Post Indigo-Dyeing with Bleaching Powder, NIRD Dyehouse, Hyderabad-Deccan. Courtesy: Tanaya Pashankar, 2019.

Indigo is often likened to the whimsical nature of a young woman but demands nothing less than reverence akin to a goddess.[28] The physical presence of women in the dyeing spaces is complicated. At NIRD, Salimji prefers the assistance of women artisans as he finds men to be distinctly unreliable when it comes to dyeing. In his experience, men find the work of dyeing too hard and the remuneration too little.[29] Salimji's socio-political identity, as a Muslim man who is unencumbered by the space of generational and community-based practice, means that he has been able to shed ritual and superstition, hiring only women. But the women dyers at NIRD are seen as itinerant. With demanding husbands and children, the women artisans are not empowered to carry the craft forward, reducing their years of training and expertise to mere labour. This follows Jenny Balfour-Paul's observation that women were considered domestic practitioners, while men were the 'experts' (Balfour-Paul 1998: 142–4). Typically, the craft is not passed on to unmarried daughters, who may take the secrets of the craft out of their natal home after marriage. Women were also barred from the dyehouse either temporarily (due to menstruation) or longer (their fertility posed a threat to the fertility of the vat). Bharati Govindraj notes that the preparation of indigo preparation involved the ritual invocation of Goddess Neelambari in the '*Kalemane*', the dyehouse built by *Neelagaras* of north Karnataka. Being a sacred space, menstruating women were forbidden from entering the dyehouse, and were allowed to enter it only after a river bath (Govindraj 2014: 235). Women were barred also from the dyehouse for longer periods. Smritikumar Sarkar notes that in undivided Punjab, the presence of young women near the vat thus poses a risk to her fertility as well as that of the vat (Sarkar 2014: 119–20). The work of the women dyers remains an unwritten facet within indigo dyeing practice.

Conclusion

The concept of natural and traditional indigo dyeing is deeply important to Salimji, but not merely as a livelihood; his craft is a matter of respect. It is a distinguishing characteristic for him, as well as the art of dyeing, as his mastery of indigo is not a generational inheritance but a hard-won expertise. Skilled artisans like Salimji claim that the lived experience of acquiring the knowledge of dyeing skills is 'natural' or a 'cultivated tradition'. Thus, their dye practice reconstructs the 'natural' and 'traditional' with changing times.

Natural dyeing production at scale will ensure the survival of the industry, allied industries, and most importantly, the environment. '[E]fficiency and economy of production' that characterize synthetic dyeing result in, at best, a completely standardized product lacking originality and, at worst, in the distancing of producer communities from each other as well as the consumer (Coomaraswamy 1989: 55). The ideas of 'repairing', 'redeeming', 'regenerating' and 'reviving' natural indigo dyeing looks not only to the past but recognizes the unique opportunities presented by the intersection of non-natural practices. The language of the natural and traditional harkens to artisans, dyers, weavers, potters, as well as allied activities such as farmers, dhobis, masons and more, along with consumers in a sustainable chain of production and consumption.[30] But when married with artisanal narratives, the redemption of indigo natural dyeing must engage with the entangled histories of exoticization of labour, a deliberate obscuring of caste and gender barriers to the practise, issues of artisanal knowledge ownership, as well as the place of modern technology in artisanal practice. Taking these themes seriously enables us to design a sustainable methodology of production that prioritizes artisanal experiences and engages us meaningfully in the question: what is natural about natural dyeing?

Notes

1 Conversations about the relevance and future of indigo natural dyeing are still being debated, and methods of revival of cultivation, manufacture and dyeing of natural indigo are being vigorously propounded and shared. This demonstrates that natural indigo never fully recovered from its decline in the early twentieth century and the subsequent increased dependence on synthetic dyeing.

2 Mani Rao notes that the business of textile and apparel production is getting a reputation of being 'dirty and filthy' due to the water pollution associated with it and is compounded by the use of massive landfills that hold mountains of clothes that have nowhere else to go (Conversation with Mani Rao, December 2020).

3 The fieldwork was done from 2018 to 2020. Here, I take the opportunity to thank Mohammed Salim Pasha, Keshav Rao and

Jagada Rajappa for sharing their expertise; Uzramma for opening the doors for me into the world of indigo; Sita Reddy for inputs; Baishali Ghosh and Rajarshi Sengupta for their critical review.

4 Born in 1962, in Warangal, the son of a postmaster, Mohammed Salim Pasha (*Salimji*) worked as a power loom operator before moving to Hyderabad and taking up natural dyeing. He was trained under the natural dyeing stalwarts such as K. V. Chandramouli and Jagada Rajappa. His indigo guru was Kattubadi Yellappa, the master indigo dyer from Uravakonda, Andhra Pradesh.

5 Keshav Rao describes himself first and foremost as an artist and is a largely reluctant dyer. Along with his wife, Bina Rao, in 1995 he co-founded Creative Bee, a Hyderabad-based textile design studio prioritizing natural dyeing. He has learned natural dyeing and block printing from the artisans in Srikalahasti, Andhra Pradesh, and elsewhere, and supported his practice with the archival research. He widely collaborates with the artisans around the Hyderabad region. Creative Bee specializes in handwoven, natural dyed and printed fabrics.

6 Born and raised in Mumbai, Jagada Rajappa first encountered weaving at Kalakshetra, Chennai, in the early 1960s. In the 1980s, she enrolled herself in a weaving course at the World Trade Centre (WTC), Mumbai, and in 1986 participated in natural dyeing workshops in Gandhigram, Chennai. Since then, she has been actively pursuing her research in this field.

7 The process of converting the water-insoluble indigo into ready-to-dye *leuco*-indigo is called the fermentation process. The indigo vat is essentially an ovoid-shaped unglazed earthenware.

8 The time between indigo dyeing is set aside for allied activities, including dyeing the other colours such as red (with alizarin) and yellow (with pomegranate).

9 Particularly potent is the theme of exoticization of labour as inflicted by colonial interests on the colonized body – be it the indigo farmer or the indigo coolie. Also, see Dinabandhu Mitra (1861).

10 The Indian Industrial Commission Report 1916–18 identified the unsuitability of vegetable colouring matter due to the lengthy and

laborious processes involved, as opposed to synthetic/industrial dyeing (Government of India 1918: 195).

11 Mani Rao notes that with the influx of companies such as Swiggy, Zomato, Ola, Uber and Dunzo, skilled manpower in the craft sector is decreasing (Interview with Mani Rao, Hyderabad, November 2020).

12 According to Mani Rao, achieving reproducibility in natural dyeing on par with synthetic dyeing is a herculean task as it involves thorough control over the entire process (Interview with Mani Rao, Hyderabad, November 2020). Keshav Rao states, 'Trying to ape chemical standardisation may in fact result in an undesirable shade where the charm of the natural colour is lost' (Interview with Keshav Rao, Hyderabad, November 2020).

13 Rao elaborates: If indigo is adulterated with cow dung, the dyer requires larger quantities of the dye to fetch darker shades. When adulterated with synthetic indigo, major problems with colour fastness are observed (Interview with Keshav Rao, Hyderabad, November 2020).

14 The primary reason for burying the pots is insulation, which catalyses fermentation. Sheep or goat dung is used to pack the space between the vats suitable for maintaining a temperature of 30–5 degree Celsius (Interview with Jagada Rajappa, Hyderabad, March 2020).

15 At Creative Bee, the fermentation and dyeing process are separate functions. The fermentation vat yields a concentrate of indigo. This is portioned in different dyeing vats and mixed with a predetermined quantity of water to create the dyeing vat.

16 Mani Rao conveys that the successful marketing of natural dyed fabric rests on their impact on health: it is safer on the skin for children and adults. It is handwoven textiles that are harder to sell, as the craft of handweaving is perceived to have no direct health benefits and the urban-rural transportation is considered disadvantageous (Interview with Mani Rao, Hyderabad, November 2020).

17 Coomaraswamy noted that the aniline colours are 'almost always coarse and gaudy compared with the dyes they have replaced'.

He added that the colours are less permanent and, when they fade, become 'particularly ugly' (1912: 37–8).

18 The addition of sodium dithionite in the chemical dyeing process creates unfavourable by-products. This also leads to problems in a water treatment plant as 'the chemical can damage the activated sludge', causing environmental damage (Aino et al. 2018: 2).

19 One such story is that of Polu Pitchi Reddy. Reddy and his family were indigo farmers living in a village near Kadapa, Andhra Pradesh. Reddy converted his indigo farming land into real estate after receiving a large profit from selling his indigo crop to a foreign buyer. With the loss of this supplier, both Salimji and Rao are dependent on Tindivanam for their indigo supply. According to Keshav Rao, the Tindivanam indigo is inferior in quality to Reddy's indigo.

20 While Indigo cakes in Tindivanam cost about 2,800 INR/kg, transport and taxes hike up the final price to 3,000 INR/Kg. Indigo is further taxed at 18% GST. Interview with Salimji, Hyderabad, December 2019. Also, see Sry Balaje Indigo, 'Natural Indigo Dye Powder', https://www.indiamart.com/srybalajeindigo/textile-dyes.html (accessed 6 February 2021).

21 Kattubadi Yellappa was a third-generation natural indigo dyer based in Uravakonda, Andhra Pradesh. His work was key to Dastakar Andhra's efforts towards the revival of traditional natural indigo dyeing practices in the late 1990s.

22 By the time Dastakar Andhra (DA) had contacted him, his own practice had almost stopped. DA convinced the unwilling Yellappa to conduct workshops and invited him to set up an indigo vat at Chinnur in 2000. When the Chinnur weavers expressed disinterest, Yellappa refused to set up a vat anywhere else (Interview with Jagada Rajappa, Hyderabad, November 2019).

23 The World Crafts Council is an international non-profit NGO headquartered in Belgium. Kamaladevi Chattopadhyay, the grand patron of arts and crafts in India, was one of the co-founders in 1964. The association works to promote, assist and advise crafts persons across the world through craft-related programmes, exhibitions, workshops and more.

24 Designers such as 11.11 by CellDsgn and Maku have been using indigo in their collections steadily through the years. The prices of their indigo garments run upwards of 5,000 INR.

25 Jenny Balfour-Paul (1998: 141) notes that the complex issue of caste and religious attitudes towards textiles complicated the status of the Indian indigo dyer. C. A. Bayly elaborates that much like food, interactions with cloth can transform and transfer 'purity' and 'pollution'. Cloth in the hands of the weaver is seen as an act of 'creation' but in the hands of the tailor who cuts the cloth, it is seen as an act of 'destruction'. Merchants and traders who transact in cloth are 'higher' on the varna scale than artisans engaged in physical labour. Thus, he notes, each function in the production and commodification of textiles reflects the social hierarchy of the professional artisan (Bayly 1986: 294–6).

26 The *Garga Smriti* notes, 'a Brahmin should wear white, Kshatriya (warrior) red, a Vaishya (mercantile person or cultivator) yellow (a colour that implies easy, natural fecundity) and a Shudra (menial) 'dark and dirty clothes' (Bayly 1986: 291).

27 Fourteen dips in the indigo vat were needed to produce the deep blue-black of the *Chānḍrākāli* saree (Govindraj 2014: 228).

28 Jenny Balfour-Paul (1998: 126) implies that the indigo vat is considered women in many cultures due to the vat being characterized as 'temperamental', with the added connotations of birthing colour and therefore fertility. Annapurna Mamidipudi writes that Kattubadi Yellappa nurtured the living space of indigo through daily cleaning rituals, sweeping the floor, cleaning the rim of the vat, and veneration with *haldi-kumkum* and flowers as one would the space of a deity (Mamidipudi 2016: 143).

29 Leela Dube offers additional context: Men are increasingly shunning traditional occupations, which they think are beneath them. In such cases, it is often women who are left to carry on the traditional occupations (Dube 1996: 5).

30 'Livelihood enhancement' of the large number of human resources involved in the production of natural dyed, hand-spun, and handwoven textiles, is a key concern for organizations such as Malkha and Creative Bee.

References

Aino, Keiichi, Kikue Hirota, Takahiro Okamoto, Zhihao Tu, Hidetoshi Matsuyama and Isao Yumoto (2018), 'Microbial Communities Associated with Indigo Fermentation That Thrive in Anaerobic Alkaline Environments', *Frontiers in Microbiology*, 9 (2196). doi:10.3389/fmicb.2018.02196 (accessed 8 April 2020).

Balfour-Paul, Jenny (1998), *Indigo: Egyptian Mummies to Blue Jeans*, London: British Museum Press.

Bayly, C. A. (1986), 'The Origins of Swadeshi (home industry): Cloth and Indian society 1700–1930', in A. Appadurai (ed.), *The Social Life of Things: Commodities in Cultural Perspective*, 285–321, Cambridge: Cambridge University Press.

Buchanan, Francis (1907), *A Journey from Madras through the Countries of Mysore, Canara, and Malabar, Vol. 1*, London: T. Cadell and W. Davies.

Coomaraswamy, Ananda Kentish. (1912), *Art and Swadeshi*, Madras: Ganesh Publishers.

Coomaraswamy, Ananda Kentish (1989), *The Indian Craftsman*, New Delhi: Munshiram Manoharlal Publishers.

Dube, Leela (1996), 'Caste and Women', in M. N. Srinivas (ed.), *Caste: Its 20th Century Avatar*, 1–27, New Delhi: Penguin Books.

Government of India (1918), *Report of the India Industrial Commission, 1916–18*, Calcutta: Superintendent Government Printing.

Govindraj, Bharati (2014), 'Neelambari: The Mysticism of the Goddess of Blue', in Kapila Vatsyayan (ed.), *Culture of Indigo in Asia: Plant, Product, Power*, 226–35, New Delhi: Niyogi Books.

Hiltebeitel, Alf (1999), *Rethinking India's Oral and Classical Epics Draupadī among Rajputs, Muslims and Dalit*, London: University of Chicago Press.

Hodder, Ian (2012), *Entangled: An Archaeology of the Relationships between Humans and Things*, Malden MA: Wiley-Blackwell.

Mamidipudi, Annapurna (2016), 'Towards a Theory of Innovation in Handloom Weaving in India'. PhD diss. Maastricht: Maastricht University.

Mitra, Dinabandhu (1861), *Nil Darpan; or The Indigo Planting Mirror, A Drama*, translated from Bangla by Michael Madhusudan Dutt, Calcutta: C. H. Manuel, Calcutta Printing and Publishing Press.

Nadri, Ghulam Ahmed (1994), 'Indigo Production and its Organisation in Sarkhej During the Seventeenth Century', *Proceedings of the Indian History Congress*, 55: 336–44.

Sarkar, Smritikumar (2014), 'Indigo Dyers of India: An Ethno-Historical Study', in Kapila Vatsyayan (ed.), *Culture of Indigo in Asia: Plant, Product, Power*, 109–21, New Delhi: Niyogi Books.

Sry Balaje Indigo, 'Natural Indigo Dye Powder', https://www.indiamart.com/srybalajeindigo/textile-dyes.html (accessed 6 February 2021).

Taussig, Michael (2008), 'Redeeming Indigo', *Theory, Culture & Society*, 25 (3): 1–15.

Uzramma (2002), 'A Future Vision of Natural Dyeing', an unpublished paper for the National Biodiversity Strategy and action Plan.

About the Editors and Contributors

Editors

Baishali Ghosh teaches art history and visual studies at the University of Hyderabad. Her research explores migration theories and material culture, investigating the process, production and circulation of South Asian imageries. Her recent publications include '*Notes on Death Pictures on the Roads of Hyderabad*' (2022) and '*Thinking through the Residual Shrines on the Roads of SEZ Hyderabad*' (2023).

Rajarshi Sengupta is a practitioner and art historian, presently an assistant professor in Fine Arts, Department of Humanities and Social Sciences, Indian Institute of Technology (IIT) Kanpur (2021). Sengupta received his PhD in art history from the University of British Columbia, Vancouver (2019). His thesis reconstructed the undertheorized histories of the kalamkari textile makers of the Coromandel and Deccan. He received the IARTS Textiles of India Grant, Royal Ontario Museum, Toronto (2017–18), Indo-Canadian Shastri Travel Grant (2023–4) and has published on Deccani textile histories in the *Journal of Textile Design Research and Practice*, *Journal18* and *South Asian Studies*.

Contributors

Aparna Sinduri is an independent art professional. She graduated in art history and visual studies from the University of Hyderabad. She has worked at premier art and culture institutions, museums, and galleries, such as the National Museum, National Rail Museum, Sahapedia and DAG. She has also worked on international projects like the G20 Digital Museum: Culture Corridor. Her expertise includes research, building outreach programmes and capacity-building programmes in the heritage sector. She is an avid traveller, philatelist, deltiologist and regular Postcrosser. Her writing appears in *The Indian Express* and *The Statesman.*

Bijay Nath is an artist, writer, entrepreneur and founder-director of DISC, the Art (https://www.disctheart.org/) in Odisha. He graduated from the University of Hyderabad with a master's degree in Art History & Visual Studies. He is also a Hindustani classical music practitioner and curates international artist residency by collaborating with the rural artisan communities. Nath teaches at the College of Teacher Education, Rourkela. He does illustration and copyediting for books in the Odia language.

Keshawram is a photographer and first-generation graduate from an indigenous community in Chhattisgarh, India. He is a PhD scholar at Indira Kala Sangeet Vishwavidyalaya University. Keshawram holds a master's degree in Art History and Visual Studies from the University of Hyderabad. He is a recipient of the Bombay Art Society Award and the Junior Research Fellowship. His writing appeared in the *Kala Vaibhava* journal and *Sarvpriya Prakashan.*

Prajnna Vedavyas is an Odisha-based independent art writer and art educationist engaging in vernacular language. He holds a master's degree in Art History and Visual Studies from the University of Hyderabad. His primary engagement is creating visual literacy in the lives of ordinary people and children.

Shaista Anwar is a PhD scholar in Art History and Visual Studies at the University of Hyderabad. Her research interest engages with the lives of Urdu poetry, photographs, archives and architecture. She has worked with the Raza Foundation and the Amar Nath Sehgal Museum in Delhi. She has also taught the history of design and fashion at the National Institute of Fashion Technology, Delhi, from 2018 to 2022. Currently, she is working on her first Urdu poetry collection. Her recent publication is '*Eidgah: Multifunctional Open Architecture as a Shared Space for Memory and Emotion*' (2023).

Sayan Gupta is a doctoral candidate in the School of Arts and Aesthetics at Jawaharlal Nehru University. He is a recipient of the ICSSR Doctoral Fellowship and Sahapedia-UNESCO. His research interests are Vernacular and Bazaar Art, Museums and Memorials, and Sikh Visual Culture. His publications include '*Sikh Visual Culture in the Twentieth and Twenty-First Centuries: Suffering, Trauma and Martyrdom*' (2019). He teaches Art History and Aesthetics at Jamia Millia Islamia and the College of Art, New Delhi.

Somedutta Mallik is a curator pursuing a PhD at the Indian Institute of Technology Kanpur, India. She received her post-graduate degree in Art History and Visual Studies from the University of Hyderabad in 2017. Her research interest lies in the embodied knowledge of handloom weaving, the transmission of artisanal knowledge, and the role of sensory experiences and non-verbal communication in learning artisanal skills. Her curatorial work includes 'A Voice to a Voice', the seventh edition of the International Print Exchange Programme (IPEP) India. Her book chapter appeared as 'When Objects Write Back' (2023).

Tanaya Pashankar is a fashion and design consultant with experience in e-commerce, luxury retail and art history. She teaches at NIFT-Hyderabad. Her writing and research interests are Indian fashion history, industry and sustainability studies.

Index